An OPUS book

This Stage-Play World

Julia Briggs

This Stage-Play World

English Literature and its
Background 1580–1625

Oxford New York

OXFORD UNIVERSITY PRESS

Oxford University Press, Walton Street, Oxford OX2 6DP

Oxford New York Toronto
Delhi Bombay Calcutta Madras Karachi
Petaling Jaya Singapore Hong Kong Tokyo
Nairobi Dar es Salaam Cape Town
Melbourne Auckland

and associated companies in
Berlin Ibadan

Oxford is a trade mark of Oxford University Press

First published 1983 as an Oxford University Press
paperback, and simultaneously in a hardback edition
Paperback reprinted 1987, 1988, 1989, 1990, 1991

British Library Cataloguing in Publication Data
Briggs, Julia
This stage-play world.—(OPUS)
1. English literature—Early modern,
1500–1700—History and criticism
I. Title
820.9'003   PR421
ISBN 0-19-289134-0

Printed and bound in Great Britain by
Biddles Ltd, Guildford and King's Lynn

Preface

'Text rather than context, literature rather than criticism' – there would be everything to be said for such axioms, if all time were eternally present. As it is, literature, like the rest of experience, is constantly receding towards a horizon where, though still faintly shimmering, its contours are barely discernible. The purpose of this book is to bring them into sharper focus through a general survey of the landscape in which they feature. Attempts to characterize the English literary renaissance in terms of its setting are, of course, far from new, and my account necessarily owes a great deal to its authoritative predecessors, even where – perhaps especially where – it disagrees with them; it owes still more to those recent historians of the period whose fresh and stimulating analyses of early modern society and its attitudes go far towards justifying yet another attempt to bring the literature and the history of the age together.

Inevitably a degree of compromise must be present in any such undertaking, partly because it is impossible to be equally familiar with both disciplines, and partly because, as disciplines, they suffer from a certain lack of congruence in their main concerns. It has been said with some truth that historians are more interested in second-rank writing because it provides a more accurate, or at any rate a more typical reflection of an age's values and assumptions, while the peaks of literature are too exceptional, too idiosyncratic to afford reliable evidence; they tower over their times. Yet they are shaped and modelled by them too. I have no convenient theories as to how literature and history might most usefully be related, and offer only a number of tentative forays, based on different and perhaps inconsistent strategies, into this deeply fascinating and absorbing relationship. Nor does this book propose any single or readily definable thesis about the half-century it explores, which seems to me made up rather of actions, reactions and counter-actions, or as Grierson termed them, currents and cross-currents. If there is any overriding principle, it is that so persuasively formulated by Lionel Trilling in

The Liberal Imagination: 'The refinement of our historical sense chiefly means that we keep it properly complicated.'

My book is intended primarily for students and general readers, and so makes no apology to specialists for the obviousness or familiarity of much of its material, nor for a certain amount of simplification with regard to texts quoted and dates supplied: quotations have normally been modernized (titles, on the whole, have not) and dates given in the text are usually those of first publication except in the case of plays, where, since a time lapse commonly operated, the date of putative first performance is given instead, as supplied by Harbage's *Annals of English Drama 975–1700* (revised S. Schoenbaum, 1964). I have resisted the temptation to hedge these with 'circas' or question-marks, as at no point does my argument depend on a disputed dating; but it should be borne in mind that many, if not all, dates of first performance are, in the nature of things, uncertain. For similar reason, footnotes have been avoided, but among the suggestions for further reading are mentioned, chapter by chapter, the sources of several of the passages that remain unidentified in the text. This list has deliberately been kept short in the hope of tempting readers to try out for themselves some of the exciting new historical studies in the field. The epigraphs are taken from the work of Sir Thomas Browne who, though writing twenty years after my terminal date, perfectly formulated the characteristic dilemmas of the age.

As well as drawing heavily on the work of modern historians, I have also had a great deal of help from conversations with friends: Dr Toby Barnard has talked to me about Spenser and Ireland; Dr Paul Slack has answered various queries concerning chapter 2, and Dr Mordechai Feingold has modified my views on a number of issues, but especially on questions of science and the universities. It has been a source of constant reassurance as well as practical help that the general editor of this series, Keith Thomas, is also one of the greatest living experts on the period. Virginia Llewellyn Smith and David Attwooll of Oxford University Press have patiently unravelled numerous tangles, both of thought and expression. My husband, Robin Briggs, in addition to compiling the chronology, has given many hours of help and encouragement at every stage. The book is so much the outcome of his influence on my way of thinking that it seems almost more his than mine, in token of which it is dedicated to him.

JULIA BRIGGS

Contents

For Robin
ἔχω γὰρ ἄχω διὰ σὲ κοὐκ ἄλλον βροτῶν

Introduction:
Conservatism and Change

We have enough to do to make up ourselves from present and past times, and the whole stage of things scarce serveth for our instruction.

'O peerless poesy, where is then thy place?'

Pastoral poetry was not wholly new to the readers of 1579, but questions like this one, put by Piers to Cuddie in Spenser's October eclogue, clearly inaugurated a new phase in its seriousness. And, no less clearly, *The Shepheardes Calendar* as a whole marked the opening of a new phase in the development of English literature, a phase in which such questions would be eagerly debated. Spenser himself, in the argument prefaced to this eclogue, refers to his own discourse on English poetry, since lost. Sir Philip Sidney's *Defence*, probably composed at about this time, set out claims for poetry that had not been heard in this country before. Yet except for a nod towards Spenser as 'worthy the reading', such claims were inspired rather by hopes for a brighter future than by the negligible achievements of the recent past. For Sidney, the poet was a maker, as for Chaucer, Gower and Dunbar earlier. But Sidney attributed to that office a power akin to the divine, a power that, by presenting the world as it might or ought to be, could bring home to man the full degradation of his present state, while simultaneously instructing and delighting by means of an ideal vision:

give right honour to the heavenly Maker of that maker, who having made man in his own likeness, set him beyond and over all the works of that second nature: which in nothing he showeth so much as in poetry, when with the force of a divine breath, he bringeth things forth far surpassing her doings, with no small argument to the incredulous of that first accursed fall of Adam: since our erected wit maketh us know what perfection is, and yet our infected will keepeth us from reaching it.

Sidney's emphasis on man's fallen condition is traditionally Christian, but his high claims for the poet's function, like Spenser's serious and complex version of pastoral and his view of it (set out in the October eclogue) as a trial flight before soaring to the full height of the epic, are characteristic Renaissance themes. It had taken the best part of two centuries for that movement to reach England from Italy. (Its early exponents, Petrarch and Boccaccio, had been contemporaries of Chaucer.) The invention of the printing-press in the mid-fifteenth century speeded up the spread of new literature and learning. Later, at the court of Henry VIII, Sir Thomas Wyatt and the Earl of Surrey had set themselves to compose Petrarchan sonnets, but it was above all through the examples of Sidney and Spenser that Renaissance poetic practices and habits of mind were naturalized. These included the imitation of classical forms such as epic, pastoral and satire, a new artistic self-consciousness and self-analysis, and a view of love and poetry as essentially uplifting.

By arriving so late, this long-lived new wave coincided with a number of other forces bringing intellectual and cultural change, which were more effectively accommodated in the wider range of forms and modes now available. Yet the English have always maintained an attitude of suspicion towards European models, even in the act of borrowing from them, and the major achievements of the English Renaissance tend to look very different from their French or Italian prototypes: Spenser's *Faerie Queene* is the most idiosyncratic of epics, Shakespearian tragedy the most irregular, while comedy soon abandoned its traditional characters to take in the humours of Cheapside or Smithfield. English authors had grown up within the reformed church, under an emergent nationalism that was simultaneously religious and political; they had been encouraged to regard Catholic Europe with distrust, and Italy with something approaching paranoia. An instilled pride in church, state and monarch fostered a desire to equal or surpass the acknowledged masterpieces of pagan or papist nations. Such ambitions were brought closer to fulfilment by humanist educational reforms, themselves an offshoot of the Renaissance (see below, p. 97), which aimed at familiarizing English schoolboys with Latin literature. Thus Shakespeare, the son of a provincial glove-maker, was taught the comedies of Terence and Plautus, and so could set himself to excel them. Printing had played a crucial part in this, by making Latin textbooks available and cheap enough for the aspiring scholar, just as it had ensured the wide dissemination of the theological arguments that brought schism to the Western church, and was currently fuelling the scientific revolution with the drawings, diagrams, tables and figures that it needed.

The term 'renaissance', i.e. rebirth, was first used by the sixteenth-century Italian writer Giorgio Vasari, to express a conviction that men were awakening or reawakening to a new life, although the sense of emerging from a period of intellectual obscurantism had first been voiced two centuries earlier. Fourteenth-century Italian humanists had regarded the immediate past as barbaric, above all in its misreadings of classical authors, the correct comprehension of whose language, philosophies and way of life seemed to constitute an urgent priority. In its concentration on the classical world, the Renaissance was less forward-looking or intellectually optimistic than might be supposed. Men of the sixteenth century, like their predecessors, were inclined to rely upon the authority of the past, treating more recent innovations with a measure of distrust. Francis Bacon, whose enthusiasm for the new was exceptional, wrote in his *Novum Organum* of three inventions that changed the world – printing, gunpowder and the ship's compass; but his contemporaries did not share his confidence, and Milton in *Paradise Lost* was to present gunpowder as the work of Lucifer. The discoveries of new continents, new methods of communication and new facts about heavenly bodies more commonly induced anxiety than the optimism that greeted the American conquest of space in our own time. From the outset, missionaries to the New World were impressed and disturbed by its freedom from European greed and avarice, and the innate nobility of its inhabitants. In a comparable way the expanded universe could be seen as a threat to man's sense of his centrality within it, as Robert Burton, himself a leading teacher of such new scientific ideas at Oxford, pointed out:

But who shall dwell in these vast bodies, earths, worlds, 'if they be inhabited? rational creatures?' as Kepler demands, 'or have they souls to be saved? or do they inhabit a better part of the world than we do? Are we or they lords of the world? And how are all things made for man?'

(*The Anatomy of Melancholy*, part 2, section 2, member 3)

As for printing, it was something of a mixed blessing, being as liable to promote uncertainty, and even despondency and alarm, as intellectual excitement. The open clashes of principle perpetuated by the unresolved religious, political and legal debates of the day, now commonly accessible to those who could read them, under-mined that sense of shared assumptions previously enjoyed by educated Christendom, and forcefully expressed earlier by Erasmus and Thomas More. Gradually this was replaced by the painful recognition that some rifts were still widening, some conflicts permanently unresolvable, some truths irreconcilable or unattainable. The new ideas that printing had circulated were, as often as not, ultimately divisive, although intellectual leaders often believed that sufficient education and access to learning must lead to the adoption of their particular views.

Such an attitude presumed, of course, that a study of certain authoritative books would bring different men to the same conclusions, a view which persists even today, despite being repeatedly shown to be wrong. The greatest authority of all was vested in the Bible, the revelation of God's word. Some way after came the Church Fathers, and then the great classical authors. Contrary to modern assumptions, it was generally supposed that contemporary thinkers were inferior to the giant intellects of the past, and the best hopes for advancing knowledge therefore lay in the close study of their writings. Knowledge, like the world itself, was thought to be in a state of decay rather than active growth. Far from steadily increasing, it was always being spilled like water from a fountain; important secrets about the natural world, known to a group of ancient sages that included Moses and Zoroaster, had been lost, perhaps beyond recall. The authority of past thinkers still shaped and dominated contemporary intellectual procedures, and the Renaissance itself has sometimes been defined in terms of a shift in the relative attitudes to the greatest pagan philosophers, Plato and Aristotle.

From an early stage in its history, Christianity had absorbed some of the main elements of Plato's thought, and especially his notion of an ideal world of forms, of Being, to which all men, subject to the unstable world of Becoming, were drawn by an innate tendency to distinguish between beauty and ugliness, both physical and moral. But by emphasizing different elements within this scheme, contrasting conclusions might be reached. A concentration on the transcendent truths tended to result in a rejection of, or withdrawal from, the chaos and sin of worldly life, such as had been recommended by the church and enacted by some of the regular orders in the Middle Ages. The fifteenth-century school of Florentine Neoplatonists, on the other hand, were inclined to focus on the spiritual elements within man himself, to magnify human beauty, capacity and self-determining power. They might have exclaimed, with Hamlet, 'What a piece of work is a man, how noble in reason, how infinite in faculties', though the medieval counterweight, 'what is this quintessence of dust?' was seldom far off. Sir Walter Raleigh in his *History of the World* (1614) emphasized a comparable, if more traditional dichotomy between the divine potential of man as a reasoning animal, and the actuality of his frailty:

And though Nature, according to common understanding, have made us capable by the power of reason, and apt enough to receive this image of God's goodness ... yet were that aptitude naturally more inclinable to follow and embrace the false and dureless pleasures of this stage-play world, than to become the shadow of God by walking after Him, had not the exceeding workmanship of God's wisdom, and the liberality of His mercy, formed eyes to our souls, as to our bodies ...

(Book I, ch. ii, §2)

Man's simultaneous greatness and littleness, the dramatic antitheses contained within him and acted out upon 'this stage-play world' are a constant theme of the age's literature.

In addition to occasioning two such opposite views of the human condition, Plato was revered as the founder of political thought, who in his *Republic* had attempted to establish principles for the conduct of an ideal state, principles that were passionately debated in the sixteenth and seventeenth centuries, when centralized state power was a new and unwelcome reality. Aristotle also had contributed importantly to the study of politics, as he had to so many other major issues. Most influential at this period were his system of logic and his conception of the world as an elaborately interlocking mechanism, constituted from mixtures of the four elements, and classified in a series of neatly serried ranks, from inert stones to that complex wonder man. Aristotle's holistic account of the physical world was initially resisted, then enthusiastically embraced by medieval theologians. Thomas Aquinas had summarized all that was reconcilable with Christian dogma; similar syntheses by other schoolmen were prescribed for study at medieval universities, providing what answers there were to the question of how it all worked. By the sixteenth century a number of errors and inconsistencies were apparent, but the system as a whole withstood such piecemeal criticisms, for no one could advance an alternative of comparable scope, and though widely acknowledged wrong in matters of detail, the general framework survived well into the seventeenth century.

The authority of Aristotle, still largely promoted by the universities, risked discouraging or misdirecting new initiatives. Advocates of the new or more empirical approaches to knowledge, such as Francis Bacon, often recognized the need to loosen the stranglehold of the past, and devised various strategies for doing so, but the difficulties were considerable, and the advocates themselves seldom entirely escaped the influences they condemned. It remained customary to invoke the authority of the past for the acceptance and justification of the new. When Copernicus demonstrated in 1543 that the earth circled the sun, he began by citing in support of his thesis the authority of the Greek philosophers Pythagoras and Philolaus, Plato's teacher. Earlier, Machiavelli's subversive analysis of contemporary power politics had presented itself in the form of *Discourses* or commentaries on Livy's history of Rome. Practical politics, law and religion all tended to be conducted in terms of precedent, encouraging the assertion of unbroken tradition in these areas. The Lutheran Reformation derived its theology from close reading of biblical texts and the Church Fathers, in particular St Paul's Epistles and St Augustine's *City of God* (see p. 70). Later the Church of England was to claim that the disciple Joseph of Arimathea had anticipated Gregory the Great's Catholic mission to England, setting up a primitive church soon after the crucifixion itself. By this tactic the Anglican church could be seen to be restoring the original purity of the faith before it was tainted by Roman accretions (see p. 76).

Yet since the authority of the past could be reinterpreted to sanction the new, and opposing readings of the same texts could be advanced, old books themselves could not be regarded as single or definitive points of reference. More historical or scholarly approaches to texts might represent a step forward in one sense, but often risked conflict with the accepted view. The widening of horizons, both geographical and intellectual, and the shaking of older convictions, produced a complex blend of optimism and pessimism, credulity and doubt, as well as the beginning of that sense of the relative which is so characteristic a part of modern consciousness. Feelings of this kind were to find their fullest and most detailed expression in the writings of the French essayist Michel de Montaigne (1533–92). Montaigne's work as a whole, and in particular his comprehensive attack on man's presumptuous ignorance, remained unparalleled, yet in its general sensibility – its sense of searching rather than finding, its awareness of the instability of personality and of the relative, partial and transitory nature of opinion – his outlook closely resembles that of much late Elizabethan and Jacobean literature. In 'Of Repentance' he declared with disarming honesty, 'I do not portray being: I portray passing . . . My history needs to be adapted to the moment . . . I may indeed contradict myself now and then; but truth, as Demades said, I do not contradict.'

Bacon began his essay on Truth by posing the unanswerable question that so much troubled his age, and evading it as nimbly as did his own Pilate: 'What is truth? said jesting Pilate, and would not stay for an answer.' Beside those of Montaigne, Bacon's essays seem rigid, over-determined and exclusive, yet in their own way they too reflect the age's exploring impulse. No form, however, was so well adapted to express passionately conflicting convictions as the drama, where each character reveals his own bias, which is necessarily opposed to that of others in the interests of an action. Drama alone could avoid the direct expression of personal judgement altogether, and no dramatist has ever been more richly evasive than Shakespeare. But even within more direct or personal modes, a tendency towards doubt, argument or ambivalence is widely apparent: Sidney's sonnet sequence *Astrophil and Stella* enacts urgent debates between virtue and passion, poetic convention and individual feeling; Spenser's feelings about the court, celebrated in so much of his poetry, remain contradictory; Donne's poetry oscillates between momentary sensation and eternal aspiration.

Yet to concentrate too exclusively on the elements of doubt, inconsistency and the various uses of division in English Renaissance literature is to reflect our own tastes and interests as surely as our predecessors did when they found confidence, serenity and unity of purpose in the selfsame works. Different generations inevitably recognize what they are predisposed to understand; recent critics have correspondingly found hitherto unglimpsed complexities, ironies and ambiguities, a sense of personality as discontinuous, a sense of literature as an elaborate game governed by abstract rules of rhetoric or genre, rather than a way of directly articulating experience. Modern historians in their turn have been impressed by the economic and demographic causes of tension in society. They have seen the late sixteenth century as a period dominated by inflation, negligible by modern standards but severe in comparison to an earlier stability, a period of rapid urban development that combined with high unemployment to produce a restless, mobile society with a serious crime problem. Everywhere traditional values seemed under threat, and there was a fear that such a radical loosening of the bonds of community foretold the end of the world. In all such responses can be seen evident reflections of our own predicament; a degree of cultural determinism is inescapable, but need not lead inevitably to drastic oversimplifications.

By emphasizing the confusing plurality of truths available, as well as more immediate worries occasioned by violent, insanitary, or wretched living conditions, a grim, indeed horrifying, impression of the age can be evoked. Probably as much as half the population lived at subsistence level, while all were liable to sudden pain, incurable sickness and early death. Though there was little in the way of protective policing, the state reacted harshly to adverse criticism, fining or imprisoning religious leaders and torturing and executing outspoken opponents. Like so many other members of this society, writers often led miserable lives in penury and squalor, 'every hour hammering out one piece or other of this rusty iron age, since the gold and silver globes of the world are so locked up that a scholar can hardly be suffered to behold them', as Dekker wrote in the dedication of *Lanthorne and Candlelight* (1609). The pamphleteers certainly left unforgettable accounts of London as 'Nighttown', a surreal city in the grip of a crime wave or a visitation of the plague (see pp. 54, 59–60), or even both at once; but they were understandably eager to sensationalize their sufferings in order to make them saleable. While the miseries of the age are not in question, too dark an account of them can be as misleading as the eulogies of Merry England first voiced by Elizabeth's protégés, and later repeated in a variety of keys after her death. In Shakespeare's *Henry VIII*, performed in 1613, Cranmer prophesies over the new-born Princess Elizabeth,

> 'She shall be lov'd and fear'd: her own shall bless her;
> Her foes shake like a field of beaten corn,
> And hang their heads with sorrow. Good grows with her;
> In her days every man shall eat in safety
> Under his own vine what he plants, and sing
> The merry songs of peace to all his neighbours.
> God shall be truly known . . .'   (v. iv. 30–6)

Here, as for so many later writers, the age of Elizabeth is the golden age.

No doubt there are elements of truth in both these views – for some it was a golden age, for others an age of rusty iron. Though neither Elizabeth nor James took steps to relieve the hungry pamphleteers scribbling in their garrets, in different ways they extended patronage to Spenser, Shakespeare, Jonson and Donne. While the years from 1580 to 1625 brought plague, hunger and oppression to many, it was nevertheless a period of political and religious equilibrium, perhaps as necessary a precondition for literature to flourish as a certain amount of intellectual conflict. The 1580s, however, were tense with the expectation of a Spanish invasion, reflected in the savage persecution of Catholic missionaries and the ruthless campaigns to quell the Irish. The launching of the Armada in 1588 at once fulfilled a universal fear, and, with its decisive defeat, allayed it for good. Much of the literature of these years celebrates national virtues or explores heroic attitudes, from the undisguised chauvinism of Lyly's *Euphues and his England* in 1580 (see pp. 75, 136) to the cool analyses of Marlowe's *Tamburlaine* (1587), and including Sidney's *Arcadia* and at least parts of Spenser's *Faerie Queene*, though neither was published until the nineties. The example of *The Shepheardes Calendar* (1579) with its varied verse forms, and the even wider range employed by Sidney, as well as the Englishing of the first Italian madrigals, late in the eighties, combined with a native tradition of songs and carols to produce a stream of delightful lyrics in the next decade, the work of major, minor and sometimes entirely anonymous authors (see p. 125).

If the 1580s had ended on a note of triumph and renewed confidence for the English nation (whose implications are explored in Shakespeare's histories), the 1590s were probably the most difficult years of the whole reign, as a series of bad harvests and plague outbreaks brought widespread hardship, disruption and civil unrest. Crimes and riots increased, and the government reacted promptly to any potential threat. One nobleman, the Earl of Essex, was to express his personal dissatisfactions in a futile rising against Elizabeth in 1601. Disappointment, resentment and an often undirected bitterness are sharply reflected in the prose of the pamphleteers, Greene, Nashe and Dekker, whose precarious livelihood made them specially vulnerable to economic pressures; but disillusioned and cynical views were in any case becoming fashionable, perhaps against the idealism and patriotism of the older generation of writers. John Donne, John Marston (later a playwright) and Joseph Hall (later a bishop) wrote verse satire on topical themes, and although much lyric poetry remained strongly ideal in tone, the more avant-garde poets were twisting their Petrarchan models into all kinds of unexpected attitudes. Marlowe, before his early death in 1593, translated Ovid's *Amores*, descriptions of erotic encounters, and had begun a graphic narrative poem (technically an 'epyllion' or little epic) about the classical lovers Hero and Leander. These were widely imitated and in 1599 the ecclesiastical authorities officially banned a number of satiric and erotic poems, including Marlowe's (see p. 106). Since one outlet for it was now closed, the vein of satire, melancholy and social discontent was caught up by the dramatists, who learnt how to exploit it and make fun of it simultaneously, both in comedy and tragedy.

James's reign, from 1603 to 1625, was on the whole politically stable. He had, however, inherited debts from Elizabeth which he increased through his own extravagance, and thus found himself in conflict with the Commons over finance. But his over-optimistic attempts to balance alliances with both Catholic and protestant powers in Europe finally collapsed in 1624 when the negotiations for a Spanish marriage fell through (see p. 154) and the continued exile of the King's defeated son-in-law, the Elector Palatine, drew England back into further hostilities against Spain. A new and conspicuous form of extravagance developed under James was the court masque (see p. 150), highly popular with the royal family as a form of entertainment, even though it contributed substantially to their bills. The masque was Ben Jonson's speciality. Also at court, as well as in the public and private theatres, drama of all kinds was in demand, and attaining an unprecedented force and flexibility. Despite academic complaints of irregularity and lack of conformity to the classical rules, drama was among the most consciously structured of the age's literary forms and in this respect may be contrasted with prose, which still leaned towards a medieval expansiveness and comprehensiveness, when not compressed into the deliberately pithy format of essays or 'characters'. Seventeenth-century poetry is conventionally divided into classical versus metaphysical, the tribe of Ben (Jonson) versus the school of Donne, clarity and metrical smoothness versus 'strong lines', Horatian poise versus baroque extravagance, with its puns, paradoxes and surprising or far-fetched imagery. In fact Jonson admired and occasionally imitated Donne, while younger poets took what they wanted from either or both of them without settling too obviously into 'schools'. Both poets had written religious poetry (Donne rather more than Jonson), both had composed celebratory and occasional verse. Imitation of the latter soon took on a distinctly political colouring, while both kinds retained their popularity for much or most of the seventeenth century.

In the years from 1580 to 1625 English writers were open to new influences, from abroad and from the past, as never before. They discovered how to set about writing an epic or a pastoral romance, a satire, an ode or a sonnet, and even a correct comedy or tragedy, though in practice they preferred their traditionally mixed forms. Coridon and Thestylis, Orlando, Lesbia and Laura were naturalized, and might be discovered rubbing shoulders with English milkmaids and ballad-sellers, celebrating May games and gorging themselves on syllabubs and junkets, brown ale or strawberries swimming in cream. For what was taken over was consistently transformed, acquiring, if not 'a local habitation and a name', then at least a certain local colour. A wood near Athens, the forum at Rome, an Italian *palazzo*, a French court, were quickly assimilated to a familiar pattern and peopled with contemporary types engaged in topical debates. Larger libraries, many more translations, and wider horizons never eclipsed the sense of shared experience, of lived life, that Elizabethan and Jacobean writers brought to their creations. The new mass audiences, whether of readers or theatregoers, encouraged a vigour and simplicity, sometimes even crudity, in tastes that could otherwise have become over-fastidious. Spenser might have been surprised to discover that 'peerless poesy' was no longer confined to the court or great houses, but now found its place on the crowded stalls of Paul's churchyard and on the creaking planks of London's public playhouses.

1 Views of Nature

The world was made to be inhabited by beasts, but studied and contemplated by man: 'tis the debt of our reason we owe unto God, and the homage we pay for not being beasts.

The Elizabethans inherited from the Middle Ages, and particularly from Aquinas, the notion that the universe was made up of a complex but ultimately ordered and stable scale of existence, harmonious and benevolent to man, since it had been designed specifically for him; any shortcomings were therefore traceable to human, rather than to divine agency. Earlier in the century Sir Thomas Elyot had demonstrated God's tidiness in the first chapter of his *Boke named the Governour* (1531):

Behold ... the order that God hath put generally in all his creatures, beginning at the most inferior or base, and ascending upward ... every kind of trees, herbs, birds, beasts and fishes, beside their diversity of forms, have ... a peculiar disposition appropered unto them by God their creator; so that in every thing is order, and without order may be nothing stable or permanent.

(Book I, ch. i)

It is scarcely surprising that a highly hierarchical and structured society should have conceived the universe in its own image, nor that its formulation was subsequently used as an argument to bolster up that social structure, the elaborate ramifications being invoked as evidence that an arbitrary social system was in fact essential or inevitable.

This divinely ordained scheme was employed to sanction the claims of kingship, both in the *Homily of Obedience*, and later in Hooker's *Laws of Ecclesiastical Polity*, whose arguments buttressed the church settlement that had established Elizabeth as governor of the Anglican church. When E. M. W. Tillyard wanted to illustrate Shakespeare's subscription to this doctrine which, he asserted, 'everyone believed in Elizabeth's days', he cited Ulysses' magnificent speech on degree from *Troilus and Cressida*:

'The heavens themselves, the planets, and this centre
Observe degree, priority, and place,
Insisture, course, proportion, season, form,
Office, and custom, in all line of order . . .'   (I. iii. 85–8)

Yet within the context of the play, the audience responds to these words partly in terms of what they know of the speaker and his purpose. Traditionally Ulysses was regarded as the embodiment of wisdom and experience, but in Shakespeare's satirical reduction of the Trojan War he is presented as something of a political fixer, here attempting to persuade the aggressively individualistic Greeks to observe the basic rules of military discipline if they hope to make any headway in the siege of Troy. The force of his argument is thus modified by the sense that he is deliberately invoking notorious commonplaces for the purpose of persuasion, just as Elizabeth's government was inclined to do.

The serene optimism of such elaborate expositions of universal order was challenged not merely by their use or misuse as establishment propaganda, but by the evident chaos of nature itself and the harsh conditions of physical existence. A recent historian, Keith Thomas, has reminded us that

Tudor and Stuart Englishmen were, by our standards, exceedingly liable to sickness and premature death . . . those who survived could anticipate a lifetime of intermittent physical pain . . . There were periodic waves of influenza, typhus, dysentery and, in the seventeenth century, smallpox . . . most dreaded of all was the bubonic plague.

Paradoxically such grim and uncertain circumstances seem to have encouraged men to cling all the more tenaciously to a highly patterned and ordered view of life, rather than prompting them to question their traditional assumptions. Nevertheless, the age's more observant commentators tended to be realists, constantly measuring conventional or secondhand wisdom against their own experience. Montaigne in his essay 'To philosophize is to learn to die' gives his age as thirty-nine and says he hopes to live as long again, but he adds that he has already lived longer than most of his friends, and he considers that Jesus's age, thirty-three, more truly represents contemporary life-expectancy than Methuselah's. He was, of course, correct in this supposition. Robert Burton, never an optimist, includes a memorable subsection devoted to 'Discontents, Cares, Miseries etc.' in the first part of his *Anatomy of Melancholy* (1621). The discussion moves from a comprehensive account of the troubles that vex man to the dangers of the world he inhabits, and then proceeds to describe the difficulties of social life, the master's oppression of the servant, the parents' oppression of the child. He claims that 'for particular professions, I hold as of the rest, there's no content or security in any', concluding with the grim axiom here attributed to Silenus, 'Better never to have been born, and the best next of all, to die quickly.'

Many people did. Infant mortality rates were very high, and the imminence of death in an age when medicine could do little to relieve the patient, and often lowered his resistance by bleeding and purging, is attested at every turn. Death had been a favourite medieval theme for elaboration and continued to provide a frequent point of reference for sermons, often accompanying a warning to flee from the wrath to come. Although, unlike preachers, the essayists had no brief to instruct or edify, they often reverted to the topic, as Montaigne did in the essay referred to earlier, while Bacon gives a characteristically bracing account of it, dissipating the nightbirds of terror and superstition. Tragedy also had much to say about death, both about the spirit in which men encountered it, and also about the variety of means to achieve it. Resplendent in expression, if thoroughly traditional in content, is Walter Raleigh's apostrophe to all-conquering death that ends his *History of the World* (1614): 'O eloquent, just and mighty death! . . . thou hast drawn together all the far-stretched greatness, all the pride, cruelty and ambition of man, and covered it all over with these two narrow words, *Hic iacet.*' John Donne's great sonnet, though probably written earlier, sounds almost as if it was composed in reply to Raleigh's claims:

> Death be not proud, though some have called thee
> Mighty and dreadful, for, thou art not so . . .

In an earlier passage in his *History*, Raleigh finely restates another great commonplace when he contrasts the brevity of man's life with the undying, cyclical patterns of nature, quoting from a familiar lyric by the Roman poet Catullus to make his point, and translating thus:

The sun may set and rise,
But we contrariwise
Sleep after our short light
One everlasting night.   (Book I, ch. ii, §5)

The poem, 'Vivamus, mea Lesbia, atque amemus', was also translated by Jonson and Campion, and echoed by Marlowe, Marvell and
many others. Its theme, the transience of human life amidst the
changing but ever-renewed seasons, had occurred in medieval literature, but the hedonist ethic that was its corollary in the love poetry
of Catullus, Horace and Propertius for example, the instruction to
'Gather ye rosebuds while ye may', is more characteristic of Renaissance poetry. Elizabethan poets imitated these classical models
eagerly, but tended to bring to them subtle shifts of emphasis.
Horace celebrated spring and young love, mildly mythologizing
them as the return of Proserpina and the Graces, but the melting
snows, blossoming flowers and weeping fountains that he referred to
often acquired an emblematic force in the work of poets who had not
entirely outgrown the pervasive medieval habit of allegory:

The withered primrose by the mourning river,
The faded summer's sun from weeping fountains,
The light-blown bubble vanishèd for ever,
The molten snow upon the naked mountains,
Are emblems that the treasures we up-lay
Soon wither, vanish, fade and melt away.
                                         (Edmund Bolton: 'A Palinode')

Although London literary life was beginning to throw up pastoral
idealizations of the countryside, nature was more commonly invoked
to provide a context for human emotions than as a subject of interest
in its own right: the charms of solitary woods echoed the lover's
melancholy, the returning spring brought joy and hope, or alternatively misery, if he were the only lonely figure amidst the general
rejoicing. Autumn and winter were associated with old age and
death, and May was the month for love. Girls were flowers to be
plucked, roses and daffodillies, their beauty and sometimes their
lives as short as the flowers associated with them. The poet-suitors
urged them to submit to love, alternating blandishments and threats
– that they would regret it later if they missed the opportunity, or

that in refusing an earthly lover, they consigned themselves to the unlovely embrace of death. A hidden singer in Spenser's Bower of Bliss urges his listeners to

> Gather therefore the rose, whilst yet is prime,
> For soon comes age, that will her pride deflower;
> Gather the rose of love, whilst yet is time,
> Whilst loving thou may'st loved be with equal crime. (II. xii. 75)

A further unmentioned irony underlay the lover's pleas, for acquiescence might, in the harsh, everyday world, bring in its train childbirth and all the attendant dangers in an age that had no notion of antisepsis or other appropriate precautions. Such complications, however, have commonly been considered beyond the scope of love poets.

Arguments based on the transience of human beauty were sometimes countered by others based on the brevity of love itself. Marlowe's 'Come live with me and be my love' (the first line another Catullan echo) was answered by Raleigh in terms of the turning year, the fading spring and approaching autumn:

> But could youth last, and love still breed,
> Had joys no date, nor age no need,
> Then these delights my mind might move
> To live with thee and be thy love.

In a great many Elizabethan lyrics, man's life was telescoped so that its sequence of events was seen to parallel seasonal or diurnal change, but by contrast to renewing nature, sunset or winter was final for him. This merely natural existence constituted a closed system, the only appeal from whose transience was to a different and alien set of values, to the Christian revelation of resurrection. Indeed the really surprising feature of the Elizabethan lyric is its predominantly pagan character in a profoundly religious age; the classical emphasis on human transience evidently corresponded, in part at least, to men's experience of life.

To find the standard emblems of the love-lyric transmuted we must turn to a later religious poet, George Herbert, who in his poem 'Vertue' modulates them into the deliberately quotidian imagery of the sermon. Here the transience – and sickliness – of 'sweet day', 'sweet rose', or 'sweet spring' and falling cadences, are resolved into an energetically prosaic conclusion:

Only a sweet and virtuous soul,
Like season'd timber, never gives;
But though the whole world turn to coal,
    Then chiefly lives.

Milton, at the end of his elegy 'Lycidas', rearranged the Catullan image of the setting sun to show how Christian resurrection offers an equivalent to the sun also rising. Mutability had her realm on earth, but her powers were limited, according to a wider or more transcendent view of things. Spenser's *Faerie Queene* (1596) is a book chiefly concerned with the discovery of the permanent and eternal amidst the natural world of flux, change and accident. The last book is unfinished, but in its surviving cantos the titaness Mutability claims sovereignty over the whole world, only to be repudiated by Nature who argues that, since all things change according to a universal law, things may be said to rule over change, rather than change ruling over things. Change is thus a constant, and mutability can only truly change to become eternity at the final judgement. By just such a logic, man conquers in the very act of dying in Donne's great sonnet referred to earlier, as well as in Shakespeare's 'Poor soul, the centre of my sinful earth' (CXLVI).

Behind Spenser, and behind Shakespeare's sonnets too, lay the most influential of all accounts of mutability, Ovid's *Metamorphoses* or the Book of Changes. In Book 15, the sage Pythagoras discourses on the endlessly changing world of nature in which 'the generations of man have passed from the age of gold to that of iron'. Book 1 depicts man living in harmony with nature in a golden age in which labour and social distinctions have no place. Since then the world has degenerated through ages of silver and bronze to the present one of iron, characterized by its warlike savagery. The notion that man once existed in a better, happier and more peaceful state than the present one may be traced back to the early Greek poet Hesiod. Granted the 'wearisome condition of humanity', its manifest sickness, dangers, social inequalities, it was not difficult to suppose that man had undergone some kind of degenerative process from an earlier happiness. Nor was it difficult to assimilate Ovid's golden age to the Christian view that man had fallen from an ideal existence in the Garden of Eden – both provided convincing explanations of man's present wretchedness. Exactly how far man had fallen from God's grace was, of course, passionately debated and the question of whether men were capable of freely choosing good or evil, independent of God's predetermining influence, was, for the Reformation, a central one (see p. 72). But though there was disagreement as to the extent of the fall, both in man and the natural world, it was generally accepted (in accordance with Aristotle's view) that the earth was subject to change and decay and in this respect differed significantly from the heavens, which exhibited order and purpose, and were exempt from change. There God must reside, if indeed he could be supposed to reside anywhere.

The Middle Ages shared with the Elizabethans the assumption that only beyond the earth's sphere, governed by the changing moon, was permanence attainable; certain human activities – those of music and mathematics – were particularly associated with the unchanging movement of the heavens because of their constant proportions, a theme celebrated in Sir John Davies' poem *Orchestra* (see p. 125). Musical harmonies were recognized to relate to mathematical proportions – double a string, and the note it produces when plucked goes down an octave. Modern physics affords an explanation in terms of the number of vibrations per second, but Pythagoras, the notional founder of mathematical studies, was traditionally credited with the discovery. Pythagoras was also associated with the idea that mathematical harmonies governed the movement of the heavenly bodies, which in their courses produced an ethereal music, the music of the spheres; as Lorenzo explains to Jessica in the fifth act of *The Merchant of Venice*, however,

> 'Such harmony is in immortal souls,
> But whilst this muddy vesture of decay
> Doth grossly close it in, we cannot hear it.'   (v. i. 63–5)

Poetry in its own way aspired to the permanence of music and mathematics, and could be thought to include elements of both. While verse was often set to music and sung, it also created a verbal music of its own whose rhythms were traditionally measured, as both the sixteenth-century term 'numbers' and the modern equivalents, 'metre' or 'metrics', imply. Sir Philip Sidney, defending poetry and linking it with the sacred gift of prophecy, alluded to 'that same exquisite observing of number and measure in words' which 'did seem to have some divine force in it'. Poetry 'considers each word, not only ... by his forcible quality, but by his best measured quantity, carrying even in themselves a harmony – without [i.e.

unless], perchance, number, measure, order, proportion be in our time grown odious'. The musical and mathematical elements in poetry were connected with its central aspiration to aesthetic permanence, and Renaissance poets took an active interest in both these factors. The belief that the world had been created on mathematical principles and that numbers possessed a mystic force further promoted the conviction that lesser creative acts should be similarly based. There existed a tradition of numerological interpretation of the Bible with particular reference to the Book of Revelation (see pp. 75–6), as well as one of mystic mathematical thought supposedly descended through Pythagoras and Plato to his followers, the Neoplatonists, some of whom were fascinated by the mystic patterns that could be made from numbers. In their different ways, both these traditions encouraged poets to incorporate number patterns into their work in complex and often arcane ways, while precedent was supplied by certain medieval authors, notably Dante.

Formal numerological poetry makes significant patterns out of line, syllable or section numbers. The study of these patterns being comparatively recent, the full extent of their employment has yet to be explored, but it seems likely that Spenser and Milton were among its foremost exponents, and this may reflect their familiarity with Neoplatonism, as well as the seriousness of their poetic ambitions and their strong commitment to the protestant faith. Although protestants had no monopoly of numerological thought, a significant number of divines were engaged in reconstructing biblical chronology, and it is a well-attested feature of their belief. The Envoy that concludes Spenser's *Shepheardes Calendar* provides a straightforward example of such number patterning. Its theme is the poet's hope for lasting fame, and Spenser here makes use of the number twelve, associated with constancy. The verse consists of twelve lines, each made up of twelve syllables, a kind of square echoing the twelve-month cycle that constitutes the Calendar itself:

> Lo I have made a calendar for every year,
> That steel in strength, and time in durance shall outwear:
> And if I marked well the stars' revolution,
> I shall continue till the world's dissolution.

Far more complex is his *Epithalamion*, where the changing balances of the hours of day and night during both a whole year and a single particular day (midsummer-day, the day of his marriage) are involved. The numbers used in measuring time (hours of the day, days of the week, month and year) and those connected with the planets, as well as biblical associations (three as the Trinity, four the gospels, twelve the Apostles, etc.) could all be drawn upon, and as an organizing principle, the method was not restricted to poetry. Milton's *De Doctrina Christiana* has thirty-three chapters in its first book, corresponding to the years of Christ's life, and seventeen in the second, which emblematically unites the Old and New Testaments, being made up of ten (the number of the commandments) and seven (the gifts of the Holy Ghost). Milton was following the precedent of Augustine, whose *City of God* was composed of twenty-two chapters, corresponding to the letters of the Hebrew alphabet.

Although the permanence of the heavens was contrasted with the flux of life on earth, the two were elaborately related. The universe was seen as interconnected at every point with man, its focal point and purpose, and actions of the heavens produced reactions on earth as surely as the moon governed the waters, both in the body politic and in the body of the individual, itself regarded as a microcosm or miniature world. Man's destiny thus inevitably seemed to be influenced by the stars, or at any rate foretold by them. Although the church officially discouraged judicial astrology (predictions about an individual's future derived from the casting of horoscopes), it was widely practised, and occasionally even by the clergy themselves. Man's harmony or conflict in society was seen to parallel similar events within the psychology of the individual: reason ought to be king and rule the potentially rebellious passions; his overthrow portended disaster. Similarly the natural world, divided (according to a tradition going back to Aristotle and Plato) into four elements, earth, water, air and fire, resembled the human body, the operative constituents of which were four liquids or humours, black bile, phlegm, blood and choler (or yellow bile), in turn corresponding to the four elements of the macrocosm. Ideally these humours were in balance, but one would normally dominate, giving a person his particular temperament, thus 'humour' came to mean one type of personality: a predominance of black bile induced melancholy, phlegm made men phlegmatic, blood sanguine and choler choleric, or bad-tempered. More substantial imbalances were the source of illness and required medical intervention. Even more elaborate parallels between the world and the human body were sometimes developed. Raleigh in his *History of the World* suggests that flesh corresponds to earth and rock to bones, while

> blood, which disperseth itself by the branches of veins through all the body, may be resembled to those waters which are carried by brooks and rivers over all the earth: his breath to the air; his natural heat to the enclosed warmth, which the earth hath in itself.   (Book I, ch. ii, §5)

In addition to these correspondences, man was joined to the whole of creation by a continuous chain or ladder, reaching from God's throne, through the various orders of angels, to his own structured society, from king to peasant, and then down to animal and vegetable, carefully ranked, to the final insensate condition of stones (see pp. 5–6).

By the early seventeenth century, the scheme as a whole, as taught by schoolmen in the universities, had long been under attack, particularly from the humanists and Neoplatonists (see pp. 3–4), who criticized it as narrow, pedantic and deadening, or too materialistic. Yet though several of its central premises had been called in doubt by philosophers or pioneering scientists, so comprehensive was it that no single alternative system could replace it, and the overall framework survived into the eighteenth century, albeit punctured in several places. Pope's *Essay on Man* (1733) is still expounding the great chain of being as evidence of the purposive and benevolent character of creation.

One systematic weakness that was becoming increasingly apparent was the traditional dependence on observation and common sense to explain the workings of the universe, and the consequent failure to allow for those invisible physical forces such as magnetism or gravity whose effects were just beginning to be recognized. In 1651 Thomas Hobbes, who was familiar with Galileo's work on gravity, exposed the evasive circularity of traditional accounts of the subject:

> If you desire to know why some kind of bodies sink naturally downwards toward the earth, and others go naturally from it; the Schools will tell you out of Aristotle, that the bodies that sink downwards are *heavy*; and that this heaviness is it that causes them to descend. But if you ask what they mean by *heaviness*, they will define it to be an endeavour to go to the centre of the earth. So that the cause why things sink downward, is an endeavour to be below: which is as much as to say, that bodies descend, or ascend, because they do.   (*Leviathan*, part 4, ch. 46)

Comparable difficulties arose when the movements of projected bodies were examined. Since the military, then as now, took a professional interest in ballistics, there was widespread speculation on the subject until Galileo solved various difficulties by positing the theory of inertial movement, that an object naturally continues in movement unless positively interrupted. Here as elsewhere, Aristotle's commonsense view that all movement presupposes a mover was revealed as inadequate to account for more complex physical laws.

The most serious attack on the Aristotelian system, with its unchanging heavens and its earth-centred universe, came from advances in astronomy. Traditional confidence that the skies were exempt from change was undermined by the appearance of novas in 1572 and 1604, and comets, notably in 1577, 1607 and 1618. Doubts on this score were increased when Galileo viewed the moon and the planets through his telescope. Observation had suggested that the sun circled the earth, and it was a process of deduction that led Copernicus to conclude by 1543 that the reverse was true. Only when Galileo used a telescope to observe the phases of Venus in 1610 could ocular proof be supplied. The heliocentric view of the heavens was introduced to English readers by Thomas Digges in 1576 in a relatively popular book mainly concerned with astrology. Yet despite its adoption in some Jacobean almanacs, the Copernican system took many decades to arrive at general acceptance, even though alternative explanations of planetary movement as seen from the earth had inevitably been problematic. The standard account given was that the planets, like the rest of the sky, naturally moved from east to west, but were also inclined to retrograde motion at inexplicable, but predictable intervals. There were several rather technical ways of describing the latter movements. This double motion provides a dramatic analogy at the opening of Donne's poem 'Good Friday, 1613, Riding Westward', where the poet's personal inclination to face the east in prayer is contrasted to his imposed task, which carries him westward. Elsewhere, in the *Devotions* (1624), Donne shows his familiarity with newer views, as he gets up, feeling dizzy, from his bed of sickness: 'I am up, and I seem to stand, and I go round; and I am a new argument of the new philosophy, that the earth moves round' (XXI, Meditation). In his giddiness, the theory of a spinning earth seems to him amusingly plausible. When Marlowe's Faustus demands that he 'reason of divine astrology', Mephostophilis provides the standard explanation, much to Faustus's disgust:

'Hath Mephostophilis no greater skill?
Who knows not the double motion of the planets . . .
Tush, these are freshmen's suppositions.'   (II. ii. 50–1, 55)

Although Marlowe gives no hint of it, he may have known Copernicus's theories of a heliocentric universe from an acquaintance, the mathematician Thomas Harriot, who possessed exceptional technical knowledge in this area. Half a century later, another poet, Milton, was still hedging his bets on the issue in his epic *Paradise Lost*, despite having apparently visited Galileo and looked at the moon through his telescope.

Though the vast interstellar spaces had begun to occupy a few men's minds, the minutest forms of existence still eluded observation, and nothing was known of the micro-organisms that cause disease in men and animals, while little danger was apprehended from familiar insects such as the malaria-carrying mosquito, the house fly and the fleas that carried bubonic plague. There were effectively no theories of illness, beyond the recognition that it could be contagious and the conviction that it unbalanced the liquids or humours of the body whose equipoise constituted health. Medical treatment therefore consisted mainly of crude adjustments to these liquids by bleeding or administering an emetic or purgative (purging upward or downward). The more sudden the onset of an illness, the more magical it seemed, though slow wasting diseases might also be attributed to malignant witchcraft. Herbal remedies were widely used. These were usually safer than the drastic intervention of doctors and were helpful in easing certain chronic conditions, but quite ineffectual in cases of serious organic malfunction. Appendicitis must often have proved fatal.

Ignorance of the creatures that prey on us to our cost probably encouraged a predominantly benevolent conception of nature, though not everyone saw it in this light. Donne, who was unusually aware of the frailty of flesh, perceptively compares man's diseases and sicknesses to the 'serpents and vipers, malignant and venomous creatures, and worms, and caterpillars, that endeavour to devour that world which produces them'. He concludes triumphantly 'can the other world name so many venomous, so many consuming, so many monstrous creatures, as we can diseases, of all these kinds? O miserable abundance! O beggarly riches!' (*Devotions*, IV, Meditation). For a few extreme kinds of Platonist (see p. 4) all material existence was corrupt and corrupting, but more often nature was conceived as closer to an ideal state than man, who had fallen further. Nature at least obeyed God's laws unthinkingly – both Raleigh in his *History of the World* and Hooker in the first book of his *Laws of Ecclesiastical Polity* point out what straits man would be in if the rest of creation were as disobedient to God as he regularly was: in Hooker's view,

> if the moon should wander from her beaten way ... the winds breathe out their last gasp, the clouds yield no rain ... the fruits of the earth pine away as children at the withered breasts of their mother no longer able to yield them relief: what would become of man himself, whom these things now do all serve? (Book I, ch. iii)

According to such views, man perpetually misuses his reason, given him to distinguish him from the beasts and raise him above them, in order to disobey God and thus shows himself unworthy of nature, created for his use. Nature is scarcely ever seen as ruthless or destructive, 'red in tooth and claw'. Monsters of the deep might prey on one another but their savagery resulted from appetite untempered by reason. Man had no such excuse. More often the natural order was invoked to provide models of desirable behaviour: the social organization of bees, for example, might point to the need for discipline and obedience in the commonwealth, as it does in *Henry V*:

> 'so work the honey-bees,
> Creatures that by a rule in nature teach
> The act of order to a peopled kingdom.' (I. ii. 187–9)

Other animals had their own peculiar virtues, as is indicated by Machiavelli's notorious reference to the strength of the lion and the cunning of the fox. In nature, good order was considered the norm; it was only breaches of it that required explanation.

Man was conceived as the hub or focus of his world, the apex of earthly creation. The Florentine Neoplatonists (see p. 4) had particularly developed this theme, and its finest expression occurs in Pico della Mirandola's oration *On the Dignity of Man* (1486), a characteristically optimistic assertion of man's versatility and capacities, his protean ability to be whatever he wishes: 'O highest liberality ... greatest and most wonderful happiness of man, to whom is given whatever he chooses to have, to be what he will.' Pico's essentially aristocratic assumptions as to man's freedom were influenced by

Plato and the Hermetic dialogues, a group of mystic writings traditionally associated with the mythological figure Hermes Trismegistus, and (wrongly) supposed to be of great antiquity (see p.128).
These claimed a divine origin for man.

Pico studied these sources in association with the mystic Hebrew
writings of the Cabbalah, trying to work out from them a system of
'natural magic' whereby man might assume power over the natural
world. This kind of magic was far removed from the charms for
toothache or potency or the techniques for finding lost objects
associated with the unlettered wise men or conjurors of the countryside, the witch-doctors of their age. Instead it involved wide scholarship, a lifetime of study, holding out the hope of some great
discovery or power, perhaps even the philosopher's stone, that
recurrent will o' the wisp.

In England under Elizabeth, John Dee was the most notable practitioner of natural magic, and, not untypically, he was entirely taken
in by a fake medium, Edward Kelly, who fed him whatever he
wanted to hear. Together they visited the court of the Holy Roman
Emperor, Rudolf II, himself a great patron of all kinds of magic. It
was Rudolf's patronage which brought together the greatest practical
astronomer of the day, Tycho Brahe, and the greatest theoretician,
Johannes Kepler. The result of their meeting was to be Kepler's
discovery of the elliptical paths of the planets and the mathematical
formula that governs them. Rudolf, however, was employing them
as practising astrologers, to cast horoscopes for him. In this context,
the term 'magic' itself may prove a stumbling-block if it obscures the
essential continuity between older animistic ways of thinking about
the universe and what we term 'scientific' discoveries. The fact that
Kepler recognized important truths about the workings of the solar
system does not make him share our scepticism as to the influence of
the stars on human activity. His predecessor, Copernicus, sub-
scribed to mystic doctrines which acknowledged the sun as the life-
giving force in the universe. His mathematical calculations reinforced his personal convictions when he concluded that the sun
stood at the centre of the system: 'the sun sits as upon a royal throne
ruling his children the planets which circle round him.'

Alchemy was another of the old magics that helped to stimulate
later scientific investigation. Francis Bacon, with characteristic
perspicacity, found a vivid analogy for the process in his *Advancement of Learning* (1605). He begins by admitting that alchemy,

'both in the theories and in the practices' is 'full of error and vanity', but, he adds,

it may be compared to the husbandman whereof Aesop makes the fable; that, when he died, told his sons that he had left unto them gold buried under ground in his vineyard; and they digged over all the ground, and gold they found none; but by reason of their stirring and digging the mould about the roots of their vines, they had a great vintage the year following: so assuredly the search and stir to make gold hath brought to light a great number of good and fruitful inventions and experiments.

The metaphysical poet Abraham Cowley was to celebrate Bacon as a latter-day Moses, leading the new science into the Promised Land; but though the account of Salomon's House in *The New Atlantis* is sometimes regarded as a blueprint for the Royal Society, today Bacon's place as usher of the scientific revolution has been seriously challenged. His experiments were inconsequential, not governed by any informing theory, and worst of all, he took no interest in mathematics, which was even then beginning to emerge as the foundation of all other sciences. In this respect, the Neo-platonists and number mystics he disparaged were nearer the mark. Even if their obsession with number was too often uncritical, at least they recognized its importance in a way that he notably failed to do.

Nevertheless, while no great practitioner, Bacon was a great propagandist of the scientific revolution. One of his aims in this respect was to cut science loose from the religious restrictions that regarded it as a threat and a dangerous prying into forbidden mysteries – a view Marlowe had taken in *Faustus* and the Catholic church was to adopt, faced with the challenge of Galileo. In his *Novum Organum* (deliberately named after Aristotle's *Organon*, whose assumptions it set out to question) he proposed that while men should 'Render unto faith the things that are faith's', they 'should not build a system of natural philosophy on the first chapter of Genesis'. Bacon was following a tradition, derived from Aquinas, that the book of nature, far from being the devil's showcase, provided an alternative revelation of God's glory. The opening sections of *The Advancement of Learning* are similarly concerned to clear away possible objections to scientific investigation: 'let no man . . . think or maintain, that a man can search too far, or be too well studied in the book of God's word, or in the book of God's works, divinity and philosophy.' (Philosophy was the current term for scientific study.) He adds that it is only 'a little or superficial knowledge of philosophy' that inclines the mind of man to atheism. Undoubtedly the popular conception of an atheist was of a man who explained all mysteries exclusively in terms of natural causes and effects. D'Amville, the titular villain of Tourneur's *The Atheist's Tragedy*, is a figure of this sort, with an unhealthy disrespect for thunder. In his preface to *The History of the World*, Raleigh felt himself obliged to insist that nature could not possibly be regarded as the sole power of the universe. His need to do so suggests that a few thinkers already held radically sceptical views.

The conviction that men ought to observe, even investigate, the wonder of God's creation reflected an optimistic view both of the natural world and of man as a reasonable creature, such as found expression in Pico's oration *On the Dignity of Man* (see p. 24). The classical tag, 'Man is the measure of all things' was often quoted in support of this confident attitude, but the age's tendency to swing to extremes was to find in it a more critical implication. Man might consider himself the measure of all things, but what in nature justified such egotism? The kind of relativism that makes us question our right to interfere with existing balances in nature or despoil natural resources has its origin in the sixteenth century. Its great exponent was the philosopher Montaigne, who refused to take for granted man's supposed superiority to the rest of creation, insisting that 'Presumption is our natural and original malady'. His most extended examination of the subject occurs in the 'Apology for Raymond Sebond'. Montaigne, at the request of his father, had translated Sebond's *Natural Theology*, which argues along traditional lines that nature is the second book of God's creation, and that the elaborate correspondences of the cosmos attest His power. Montaigne gestures towards a defence of Sebond and then turns away to reveal far-reaching doubts about the book's underlying assumptions, and profound scepticism as to the possibility of attaining knowledge at all. Man's claims that the universe centres upon him, and the stars direct their influence toward him are dramatically exposed, while his aspirations to rationality are refuted in the light of his uncontrollable emotions:

We have indeed strangely overrated this precious reason we so much glory in, this faculty of knowing and judging, if we have bought it at the price of that infinite number of passions to which we are continually a prey.

Montaigne's vision of human folly and arrogance provides a sharp corrective to the age's soaring illusions of power, knowledge and reason, echoing in a different key the church's perennial assertions of man's sin, helplessness and wretchedness. His concluding question, 'Que sais-je?' echoes the earlier scepticism of Erasmus as to the possibility of knowing anything beyond how little we know, voiced in the mock-encomium *In Praise of Folly* (1511).

Though relativism found an eloquent advocate in Montaigne, the habit of judging and considering topics from standpoints other than those normally or traditionally adopted had been increasing since the fifteenth century. Machiavelli had considered political action from the point of view of effectiveness rather than morality, while Bacon's essay 'Of Custom and Education' reveals the extent to which an Elizabethan could regard the manners and *mores* of his time as relative rather than absolute:

We see ... the reign of tyranny or custom, what it is. The Indians ... lay themselves quietly upon a stack of wood, and so sacrifice themselves by fire. Nay, the wives strive to be burned with the corpses of their husbands.

The discovery in the Indies and the Americas of people living under entirely alien cultures and conditions, with unrecognizably different values, was in itself an obvious stimulus to relativism.Nevertheless, the stultifying influences of custom and education that Bacon had written of made it difficult for Europeans to assess these new societies in terms other than those of existing stereotypes. Indians were thought of as fallen, unredeemed, benighted pagans whom the gospel's literal good news had not yet reached. The Italian chronicler of Columbus's expedition, known in English as Peter Martyr, wrote in *De Novo Orbe* that the Indians 'should be the happiest in the world, if only they knew God', yet elsewhere he sees them in another light altogether, apparently considering that it is they, not we who are unfallen:

they seem to live in that golden world ... wherein men lived simply and innocently without enforcement of laws, without quarrelling, judges, and libels, content only to satisfy nature, without further vexation for knowledge of things to come.

The view that in some respects Indian society was superior to our own because more innocent and less corrupt was not an unusual one: it is forcefully presented by Montaigne in his essay 'Of Cannibals'.

This was inspired by a series of conversations with an Indian servant, whose descriptions of cannibal practices in his own society led the essayist to observe 'I am not sorry that we notice the barbarous horror of such acts, but I am heartily sorry that, judging their faults rightly, we should be so blind to our own.' He goes on to denounce the cruelties and tortures inflicted in his own time and country, 'not among ancient enemies, but among neighbours and fellow citizens, and what is worse, on the pretext of piety and religion'.

Even more forceful was Montaigne's denunciation of the conquests of Mexico and Peru in his essay 'Of Coaches', where he shows how the integrity and good faith of the Indians were met not merely with treachery and exploitation but with gratuitous cruelty and sadism on the part of the conquerors. Both essays are concerned chiefly with the light thrown on our own so-called civilization by these depressing episodes, and their implications are as pessimistic as they are objective. Both reveal Montaigne as deeply aware of the way in which the high ideals of Christianity might in practice lead to brutal hypocrisy. In 'Of Coaches' he enquires how the conquerors could not only bring themselves to admit their actions in the New World, 'but boast of them and preach them. Would it be as a testimonial to their justice or their zeal for religion?' The conviction that contemporary European society was degenerate, strongly held by sceptics such as Montaigne, underlay two much-used literary myths, those of pastoral and the golden age. These implied that increasing complexity in society was inevitably accompanied by greater moral corruption. When the Indians were not being regarded as primitive savages, conveniently in need of imposed rule and rulers, their way of life had been associated with a mythical long-lost golden age, and idealized for its unpossessiveness, social equality and harmony with nature. The loss of these virtues was one aspect of the high cost of civilization.

There were, of course, wild men or savages nearer home than the New World. The remoter corners of the North and of Ireland were inhabited by people often considered little better than savages – indeed rather worse since, far from being innocent pagans like the Indians, some of them were obdurate papists. The Tudor administration had no time for the independent faith and traditional social structures of the Irish which could not easily be integrated into English law: Irish chieftains were elected, an arrangement regarded as messy, potentially troublesome and obviously inferior to the English system of primogeniture, inheritance by the eldest son. Bureaucrats were eager to substitute for these and similar peculiarities the English traditions and legal system, in the interests of convenience and uniformity. Elizabeth spent much money and many lives in an attempt to impose English rule on the recalcitrant Irish. The poet Spenser, as a civil servant based at Dublin Castle, was deeply involved in these efforts, and in 1598 was driven from his estate in Munster by Tyrone's uprising, the last and greatest. He wrote a notably harsh proposal for dealing with the Irish, *A Vue of the Present State of Ireland*, but elsewhere he shows a genuine affection for the countryside, if not for its rightful inhabitants. Ireland is home in *Colin Clout's Come Home Againe*, and its topography pervades *The Faerie Queene*, culminating in the description of Arlo Hill in the Mutability Cantos. The landscape of his epic poem is wild, heavily forested, inhabited sporadically by 'salvages', descended from the alarming medieval wild men, green men or 'woodwoses', yet also perhaps reflecting Elizabethan attitudes to 'lesser breeds without the law'. Most of these savage men are either positively good or positively evil, and in this respect differ interestingly from Shakespeare's presentation of a wild man in *The Tempest*. Caliban's name is a variant of 'cannibal', itself connected with the name 'Caribbean'. He is both Indian and traditional wild man. Caliban is treated as a moral degenerate by Prospero, not unreasonably since he is the son of a witch and attempts to rape Miranda and murder his master; like a child, he must be disciplined with blows and pinches, rather than with reason. By the end he knows enough to seek for grace, which largely justifies Prospero's treatment; yet the audience's view of him is rather less straightforward. Despite his brutishness, Caliban is the true heir of the island, familiar with all its secrets, the sole witness of its transcendent visions. His wanting to rape Miranda is an animal drive, uninhibited by reason, that should be contrasted with Antonio and Sebastian's sophisticated and 'rational' scheme for killing Alonso. The play includes more than verbal echoes of Montaigne.

Spenser's savages tend to alternate between the stereotypes of the innocent and virtuous primitive and the totally depraved savage, unlike Caliban, who includes features of both. The forester who pursues the fleeing Florimell and the lustful cannibal ogre who imprisons Amoret are horrific figures, very different from the 'salvage nation' of fauns and satyrs who rescue and worship Una in Book I, canto vi, and, after she has tried to teach them the true faith, naïvely revert to worshipping the milk-white ass that has brought her to them. The most startling juxtaposition, however, occurs in Book VI, which is especially concerned with nature and natural behaviour, as opposed to the court and courtesy, whose virtues it nominally celebrates. A 'salvage man' who dwells shaggily and speechlessly in the depths of the forest rescues Calepine and nurses him and Serena back to health, feeding them and waiting on them like a faithful dog. But soon afterwards Serena falls into the hands of a very different 'salvage nation', who exist by stealing and carrying out border raids; they are on the point of killing and eating her when timely help arrives. Spenser's reaction to the Irish, among whom he had lived for so long, seems to have been ambivalent. Individually they made gentle, considerate and faithful servants, babbling incomprehensibly in their own barbaric tongue; on the other hand, half-starved uprooted tribes on a night raid, their knives and the whites of their eyes glittering in the moonlight, must have been a recurrent nightmare to English settlers. Spenser's habit of thought was in any case insistently dualistic – here personal experience may have endorsed his dualism.

Book VI's concern with nature makes it inevitable that it should include a pastoral interlude; it was a mode whose blend of realism and idealism particularly appealed to Spenser, as *The Shepheardes Calendar* and a number of other poems attest. The pastoral society here presented is strongly idealized: the shepherds have a wise homespun philosophy that makes them content to exist in a commune whose competitiveness is limited to song contests and games, and whose mutual happiness is expressed in dancing. But Spenser is enough of a realist to perceive how vulnerable such a peaceful and harmonious way of life would really be. It only requires brigands to smash the idyll to pieces. One day the hero Calidore returns from hunting to find the shepherds' huts empty and sheep and shepherds driven away.

Spenser and Sidney between them effectively introduced the classical pastoral convention into English verse and prose through Spenser's *Shepheardes Calendar*, his book of twelve verse eclogues, and Sidney's *Arcadia*, a prose romance whose sections were broken up by groups of poems. In verse, the form could be traced back through Renaissance Italian exponents to Vergil's Eclogues and the work of the Alexandrian Greek poet Theocritus and his disciples. In prose the earliest models were late Greek romances like *Daphnis and Chloë*. Pastoral was enthusiastically adopted by Elizabethan poet-asters who promptly followed the example of their masters in identi-fying themselves by bucolic names: Sidney had been Sidrophel or Philisides, Spenser more prosaically Colin Clout. In the 1590s a host of Coridons and Shepherd Tonys mushroomed overnight. It is amusing to read the anthology *England's Helicon* (1600), in which those poems not originally composed in the pastoral mode are thoughtfully disguised by a suitable title, such as 'The Shepherd's Solace' or 'A pastoral ode to an honourable friend'. It was only with a deliberate irony that George Herbert could write in 'Jordan I'

> Shepherds are honest people; let them sing.

Idealizing conventions familiar within educated circles might, however, be less apparent to the general public. John Fletcher was disconcerted when the audiences for his literary tragi-comedy *The Faithful Shepherdess* (1608) turned out to have expected

> a play of country hired shepherds in gray cloaks, with curtailed dogs in strings . . . and, missing Whitsun-ales, cream, wassail, and morris-dances, began to be angry.

He felt obliged to explain that a pastoral properly represented

> shepherds and shepherdesses . . . not to be adorned with any art, but such . . . as nature is said to bestow, as singing and poetry; or such as experience may teach them, . . . such as all the ancient poets have received them; that is, the owners of flocks and not hirelings.

Late Elizabethan taste was ripe for the development of pastoral as a major literary form. The growth of London as a substantial city, a mercantile and administrative centre increasingly independent of the countryside, created the right conditions for pastoral, an idealized account of the shepherd's life, which is also commonly an urban exercise in nostalgia. Theocritus, a citizen of Alexandria, wrote affectionately of the rural Sicilian society which he had left behind him. The more individualistic, competitive and capitalist sixteenth-century men became, under political, economic and demographic pressures, the more eagerly they dreamt of an alternative society based upon contemplation, passivity and communal values. The more complex grew the rules of society, the more attractive was the idea of a life governed by instinct, rather than one that demanded its suppression. The more native traditions were officially discouraged, the more they acquired the appeal of the forbidden. So the elaborate rituals of courtly behaviour, designed to occupy and cultivate the impulses of a privileged few, came, on occasion, to be rejected in favour of a prettified version of the life of the working man. The traditional antithesis of pastoral was the artifice and hypocrisy of court life, which, though it figures elsewhere in Spenser's work, in Book VI of *The Faerie Queene* is mainly conspicuous by its absence.

Sometimes the values of pastoral were asserted by showing a great man, weighed down by the burden of responsibility, envying the quiet and carefree life of the underling. This motif is poignantly expressed by Shakespeare's Henry VI on the battlefield at Towton:

'O God! methinks it were a happy life
To be no better than a homely swain, . . .
Gives not the hawthorn bush a sweeter shade
To shepherds, looking on their silly sheep,
Than doth a rich embroider'd canopy
To kings that fear their subjects' treachery?'

(*3 Henry VI*, II. v. 21–2, 42–5)

The corruption, pretence and necessity for diplomatic compromise at court were traditionally contrasted with the honesty, integrity and simplicity of the countryman and his way of life. *As You Like It* sets out such a contrast, but the traditional antithesis is treated ironically and with those unexpected twists so characteristic of Shakespeare's art. The play begins at the court of the bad duke, where the affected courtier Le Beau is introduced, but instead of behaving with the duplicity his manners suggest, he gives the hero a piece of kind, confidential advice to leave while he can. In the ideal world of the Forest of Arden, the harshness of nature is emphasized in the songs, and contrasted with the less tolerable harshness of man. There is even a plea such as Montaigne might have made for the rights of the deer who are being hunted and eaten, the true inhabitants of the forest. Shakespeare's pastoral tends to be 'hard', rather than 'soft', acknowledging the difficulties of existence in a natural environment, rather than glossing over them to paint an idealized picture of life in the wild. His shepherds have greasy hands which 'are often tarred over with the surgery of our sheep'.

If court life looked superfluous when set against the simple necessities of country life, courtly conduct in love affairs seemed gratuitously formal, artificial and long-drawn-out. Their natural impulses untrammelled by imposed rules, 'country copulatives' sported among the hay, while milkmaids were reputedly more 'coming on' than fine ladies, as well as cleaner and less made-up:

> I care not for these ladies that must be wooed and prayed;
> Give me kind Amaryllis, the wanton country maid.
> Nature Art disdaineth; her beauty is her own.
> Her when we court and kiss, she cries: forsooth, let go!
> But when we come where comfort is, she never will say no.
>
> (Thomas Campion's *Book of Ayres*, I.3)

The association of unrestricted sexual freedom both with shepherdesses and later with the primal innocence of the golden age were favourite themes of seventeenth-century poetry, but there is little reason to suppose that such erotic fantasies had much basis in everyday experience. Country girls normally married much later than court beauties. They probably no more resembled the shepherdesses of Restoration verse, so often portrayed as 'natureless, in ecstasies', than Shakespeare's Audrey did: she was content to be plain, so long as she might be honest (i.e. chaste). Elsewhere, Jane Smile with her chapped hands, greasy Joan keeling her pot and Marion whose nose was red and raw lend support to the assumption that Shakespeare's country girls were drawn from life.

Although many of his contemporaries wrote within far more stiffly conventional frameworks, few used the form as sentimentally or self-indulgently as the Restoration poets were to do. Earlier pastoral was nourished by the consciousness of a rapidly changing society, and its regret for the loss of older communal values, yet few writers at this time enjoyed an exclusively urban existence, with the result that the liveliest examples of the form are touched by irony or a sense of the reality lurking beneath the surface of the convention. Small towns like Stratford were closely in touch with the rural communities around them, as were those poets who grew up in them. Even Ben Jonson, a Londoner and the most urban (and urbane) poet of his age, walked, on one notable occasion, all the way to Scotland. Courtiers, whose way of life was the most artificial, nevertheless expected to spend half the year on their own, or other people's, estates. Sidney's *Arcadia* predictably does not anticipate Shakespeare's delightfully vivid sense of country life lived on a day-to-day basis, but it shares a comparable scepticism as to its ideal nature. He gives us one glimpse of Arcadia as it was traditionally envisaged, at the moment when his hero Mucedorus first sets eyes on it:

There were hills which garnished their proud heights with stately trees; humble valleys, whose base estate seemed comforted with refreshing of silver rivers; meadows enamelled with all sorts of eye-pleasing flowers; thickets, which being lined with most pleasant shade, were witnessed so to by the cheerful deposition of many well-tuned birds; each pasture stored with sheep feeding with sober security, while the pretty lambs with bleating oratory craved the dams' comfort; here a shepherd's boy piping as though he should never be old; there a young shepherdess knitting, and withal singing, and it seemed that her voice comforted her hands to work, and her hands kept time to her voice's music.

It is a moralized landscape: even if pastoral society is egalitarian, the very contours of the land bespeak elevation and baseness, a baseness content with its allotted position. All is order, rhythm and harmony, an image of musical co-ordination which takes in the well-tuned birds, the bleating lambs, the boy piping and the girl singing and working in time to her song. This is the stock Elizabethan world picture set out in topographical terms. It is what we and Mucedorus see when we first survey the scene. Nothing else in the book or in the reality of the age endorses this as anything but an ideal. Sidney reveals his Arcadians to be as prone to discontents in their wilderness as men are in civilization, as restless, as greedy, as subject to uncontrollable passions. Even love, aspiring to the highest selflessness, still drives men to seek the basest gratifications here. The higher a man's position in a community − and Mucedorus is a prince − the greater his responsibilities to his people, and the more serious his evasion of them. Even the good judge Euarchus must beg the Arcadians to 'remember I am a man − that is to say, a creature whose reason is often darkened with error.' Somewhere between the bright dreams of reason and the darkness of error most men lived out their lives, while literature carefully charted their hesitations.

2 Living in Society

Think not that mankind liveth but for a few, and that the rest are born but to serve those ambitions which make but flies of men, and wildernesses of whole nations.

The myth of the golden age, an imaginary past characterized by peace, plenty and social equality, when common wealth belonged to all in common, was both potent and potentially subversive. It challenged a belligerent, capitalist, hierarchic society to justify its values, and only hard-headed realists like Machiavelli or Hobbes were equipped to reply. In Book V of *The Faerie Queene*, where he is concerned with the chief threats to Elizabeth's realm, Spenser is obliged to explain that contemporary political necessity imposes attitudes very different from the ideals of the golden age that operate elsewhere in his epic. Simple truth may be 'of all admired' but it is no longer strictly relevant to modern *realpolitik*:

> For that which all men then did virtue call,
> Is now called vice; and that which vice was hight,
> Is now hight virtue, and so used of all;
> Right now is wrong, and wrong that was is right,
> As all things else in time are changed quite.   (v. i. 4)

This confusion of values is a measure of the world's degeneration, yet there can be no turning the clock back. Book V reveals with embarrassing candour the extent to which Spenser's government relied on coercion (here represented by the iron man, Talus) rather than reason to make its subjects share its standards and conform to its rules. The hero, Artegall, personifies the abstract quality of Justice, especially as represented by contemporary law, but also stands for a particular individual, Lord Arthur Grey, who in 1580 was appointed Lord Deputy of Ireland, with Spenser acting as his private secretary. Artegall rescues the maiden Eirena (Ireland) from the ogre Grantorto, who combines the savagery and Catholicism of the Irish. But on his return, the hags Envy and Detraction attack him, loosing on him the Blatant Beast (slander). In reality, Lord Arthur Grey had been summoned home in 1582 and rebuked for his harsh treatment of the Irish. Spenser considered this unjust, believing his tough, repressive policies more likely to succeed than Elizabeth's vacillating and inconsistent attempts to combine concession and coercion.

Spenser's opinion sprang not from any enthusiasm for brutality for its own sake, but from a profound horror of Catholicism and a desire for what he considered to be good order. His anxiety that the status quo be preserved, and his consequent rejection of attempts to restore the lost harmony of the golden age are explored in an earlier episode where Artegall and his iron servant Talus come upon a giant by the seashore. The giant holds a pair of scales, the displaced emblem of Justice (who has bequeathed Artegall her sword, but not her balance), and is preaching equality. Naturally he has assembled quite a crowd, even if mainly of 'fools, women and boys'. Echoing Spenser's own assertion that the world has degenerated from its former perfection, the giant concludes that the time is now ripe for all things to be restored to their former state. This will involve levelling out differences, since in the golden age all men were equal:

'Tyrants that make men subject to their law,
I will suppress, that they no more may reign;
And lordings curb, that commons over-awe;
And all the wealth of rich men to the poor will draw.   (v. ii. 38)

Artegall begins by arguing that the giant cannot restore things to their former state since he does not know how they were originally distributed. Interference will merely upset the existing status quo, since 'all change is perilous'. He then tries to persuade him to use his balance to weigh right and wrong, but the intemperate creature will only weigh extremities, so Talus simply pushes him off the cliff (his position is literally as well as metaphorically vulnerable), and chases away the assembled crowd who now form an armed rebellion. Artegall looks on. It is not for noblemen to stain their hands

'In the base blood of such a rascall crew.'

The episode is revealing. Spenser, an aspiring bourgeois, had thrown in his lot with the ruling classes and like them feared the 'cherles rebellynge', and the fanatic's dream of a commune where all property was shared. (Sir Thomas Elyot had actually avoided using the word 'commonwealth' as a translation of 'republic' because of its embarrassing implication that wealth should be held in common.) Yet Spenser strongly felt the appeal of the traditional golden age with its harmonious anarchy and its repudiation of the capitalist ethic that dominated so many Elizabethan policies. His is a characteristic liberal dilemma, even though, by our own standards, his political attitudes were so markedly illiberal.

Occasional demands for social justice were natural enough in a society where so few enjoyed so large a share of the total resources. They had preceded the Reformation, from which they acquired a particular colouring, and survived well into the seventeenth century, to be forcefully voiced by the Levellers and Diggers under the Commonwealth. The authority of the Bible might be invoked in support of the sense of social injustice. It was man, not God, who had created divisions of status and wealth:

> When Adam delved and Eve span
> Who was then the gentleman?

was a favourite medieval saying. It was difficult for committed Christians not to acknowledge that Christ had condemned wealth and worldly display, condoned Lazarus not Dives, instructed the rich to give away what they had to the poor and Himself been of humble birth and lived among humble people. The ardent Christian and humanist Sir Thomas More in 1516 published his *Utopia*, which posits an ideal society based on social equality, where all but the most learned share both labour and its fruits. Its force as a thesis is strengthened by a number of specific criticisms of contemporary English society made by Raphael Hythloday in the first part. He argues that men are being punished, even executed, for crimes to which they have been driven by hunger and need. One cause, he suggests, anticipating a recurrent grievance of the sixteenth century, is the practice of enclosing common land in order to farm sheep on it, thus depriving the working man of his traditional rights to graze his animals.

In the year after *Utopia* appeared Luther nailed up his theses, and in the chaos of theological conflict that followed seeds of social unrest that might otherwise have lain dormant began to develop. Radical, apocalyptic sects sprang up, dominated by charismatic leaders, and a group usually identified as Anabaptists achieved a startling, if short-term, success in the North German town of Münster, where in 1534 John of Leyden briefly organized a commune based on shared property and free love. Besieged by the forces of the German Princes, to whom the threat to property appeared peculiarly heinous, Münster fell, and John of Leyden was carted around Europe imprisoned in a wagon as a side-show for a year or two. The episode, which made a profound impression, is re-created by Nashe in his novel *The Unfortunate Traveller*. Extreme radical sects such as Anabaptists were thereafter widely feared and distrusted, even by more moderate nonconformists. The Amsterdam Brethren in Ben Jonson's *The Alchemist* are sarcastically dismissed as 'my brace of little John Leydens'. But though inspirational and egalitarian sects had been so decisively put down and were deeply feared by all European governments, Luther's Reformation was inextricably bound up with the issue of self-determination; freedom to determine how one approached God, through what rites and sacraments, and perhaps how ministers were to be chosen, were among its central demands. Many protestants remained convinced that God might speak directly to each man's heart, that church hierarchy was merely a historical accretion, and that the original church had been an altogether more democratic institution. The Elizabethan settlement had compromised, retaining church hierarchy, and locating the Queen as overall governor of the church, whereas in Scotland the more democratic Calvinist system of church government by elders had been adopted. In England, however, attacks on church hierarchy tended to be considered subversive, linked with threats to state hierarchy, which, like that of the church, culminated on earth in the Queen (see p. 80–1).

It was Hooker in his extended plea for the compromise of the Anglican Settlement, *Of the Laws of Ecclesiastical Polity* (1593), who presented the mutually supportive hierarchies of church and state as figuring on the human plane the hierarchy of all existence created by God; attacks on one part of the system could thus be equated with attacks on another. The defensive tag 'No bishop, no king' reveals this, as does the tendency to equate the authority of God, of the monarch, of bishops, magistrates and even heads of families, defending one by analogy and association with the others. In practice, society's hierarchies were experienced as obligations of one kind or another. Family, social status and state all made their own particular claims on an individual, and such obligations were increasingly liable to conflict as society grew more complex. The most overriding claims, those of God and king, had been particularly affected by the Reformation; men might find themselves torn between their loyalty to their faith and to their ruler, if these no longer coincided. The most passionate arguments of the age centre on the nature and extent of the power of God and king. History and political theory focused almost exclusively on these questions, and by the mid-seventeenth century in England (and earlier elsewhere) they ceased to be merely contentious issues and became a matter for swords and guns.

Drama was well suited to express the age's conflicting demands. Self-interest or self-determination, always an important element in the resolution of claims, was easily translated into theatrical terms, for the histrionic art is of its nature self-centred and egotistic; revenge was only one of several themes that confronted the protagonist with intensely opposing obligations such as Shakespeare's tragedies present. Timon, in a moment of agony, invites society to throw off all traditional constraints:

> 'Matrons, turn incontinent!
> Obedience, fail in children! Slaves and fools,
> Pluck the grave wrinkled Senate from the bench,
> And minister in their steads! . . . Bound servants, steal . . .
> Degrees, observances, customs, and laws,
> Decline to your confounding contraries;
> And yet confusion live!'   (IV. i. 3–6, 10, 19–21)

In an entirely different vein, Macbeth carefully iterates the various claims that forbid his murder of Duncan ('First as I am his kinsman and his subject . . . then as his host . . .'), while *Lear* seems to explore the entire range of social or familial obligation, setting child against parent, servant against master, brother against brother, subject against king. A series of extraordinarily conflicting demands tear individuals apart. Gloucester disobeys his 'great arch and patron', the Duke of Cornwall, to bring help to the King, who has not formally abdicated; an unnamed servant attacks and kills Cornwall, overcome with horror at his vicious revenge on Gloucester, and determined to prevent him from further sadism. Similarly it is to save Lear from himself that Kent attempts to stop him exiling Cordelia, while Edgar lies to and tricks his despairing father in order to save him from committing suicide. Love constantly intervenes, an insubordinate and even subversive force in the play. Albany is forced to choose between his obligation to defend the rightful king or protect England from invasion, between opposing or supporting the wife he knows to be wrong. Even the wretch on the lowest rung of fortune's ladder, Bedlam Tom, is driven by hunger and thirst, although he is free of the diverse obligations that fall so heavily upon the other characters: 'Thou ow'st the worm no silk, the beast no hide, the sheep no wool, the cat no perfume' (III. iv. 103–5).

'Honour thy father and thy mother', the fifth commandment, was treated with the utmost seriousness in this society. The ingratitude and lack of respect shown by Lear's daughters and Gloucester's bastard son would have seemed far more outrageous to Shakespeare's audience when upper-class society insisted on elaborate displays of deference to parents, sons doffing their hats and daughters kneeling or standing in their parents' presence. It was also customary for children to kneel each morning before their parents to ask their blessing, and to do the same, even when grown up, on arrival or departure from their parental home. These conventions made Lear's curses (instead of blessings) on his daughters seem even more unnatural, and added a further dimension to the fourth-act reunion where the old King kneels before his daughter Cordelia as if to ask her blessing. Both episodes deliberately and dramatically reverse familiar patterns of behaviour. Kneeling is a symbolic gesture of submission (parallels are to be found in animal behaviour), and children were expected to submit to parental authority at all times. If on occasion children might be thankless, parents might equally be repressive or even brutal. Burton, describing the general misery of the human condition in his *Anatomy of Melancholy*, wrote that 'children live in a perpetual slavery, still under that tyrannical government of masters.' Lady Jane Grey gave Roger Ascham (who included it in *The Schoolmaster*) a disturbing account of her parents' harshness, saying that she was 'so sharply taunted, so cruelly threatened ... sometimes with pinches, nips, and bobs, and other ways which I will not name for the honour I bear them, so without measure misordered that I think myself in hell.'

Despite the tensions of the parent–child relationship, the chief purpose of marriage was self-perpetuation, and, with mortality rates so high, for many it was a race against devouring time. The rich and great might leave acts and monuments behind them, artists their enduring works, but for most people children embodied their future, and despite the dreadful hazards of childbirth, those who married, unless miserably poor, normally expected and hoped for children and were bitterly disappointed if none came. The more men had to leave, the more urgently they desired a son to leave it to, since primogeniture was the system of property-holding in this society. Few frustrated fathers can have resorted to more desperate remedies than Henry VIII, who, when two successive wives failed to produce a male heir, divorced the first and beheaded the second. Daughters, on the other hand, were something of a liability, since fathers were expected to endow them at marriage. Nunneries had provided, as Milton crudely put it, 'convenient stowage' for expensive or unmarriageable daughters, but these had been abolished during the Reformation. Daughters could not inherit titles, nor hold property in their own right after marriage. Shakespeare had taken that crucial and characteristic step from being a respectable yeoman to becoming a gentleman, by applying for the valued title on behalf of his father. It must have been an intense disappointment that he had no heir on whom to confer it, his only son having died at the age of eleven. Shakespeare's property went to his two surviving daughters, but would legally have been at the disposal of their husbands. Married women had no property rights for another three hundred years. Within the family there existed as precise a hierarchy as in the state, women being subservient to men (strictly including all male children over seven years old) and children to parents. Deference, as we have seen, was exacted.

For the upper classes, an important aspect of parental authority lay in the choice of marriage partner for one's children. Marriages were normally arranged as long as there was any possibility of substantial property changing hands. Effectively this meant that only younger sons who would not inherit could expect to please themselves, and even younger sons were expected to listen to advice, as were orphans who, if propertied, would probably have an interested guardian, appointed by the Master of the Wards. As in Islamic countries today, privileged people generally accepted this as a sensible and practical arrangement; here as in so many other respects society seemed to require obedience, rather than confer personal freedom on its partici-pants. Fewer expected marriage to be the intensely absorbing relationship we consider it today, seeing it primarily as providing for mutual economic support and the rearing of children. Slightly lower expectations of personal fulfilment in marriage would certainly have enhanced its chances of success, but on occasion couples might be bitterly mismatched, and in such a circumstance they had little hope of redress. There was, also, a small but significant number of upper-class marriages made without parental authority, sometimes in the teeth of parental opposition: Desdemona deceives her father to elope with Othello, while Leantio in Middleton's *Women Beware Women* steals Bianca away from Venice to marry her. He is a factor, a poor clerk, whom Bianca's noble father would never have countenanced as a son-in-law. Such elopement might be seen as a kind of theft, and this seems to have been the view taken by Sir George More when faced with the secret marriage of his eighteen-year-old daughter Anne to the poet John Donne. Donne was imprisoned and Anne came under pressure to declare that the marriage had not yet been consummated, and thus made legally binding. When she refused to do so, Donne was released only to find he had lost his employment. The result was disastrous. In the years that followed, the rapidly increasing family lived in comparative poverty and frequent sickness at Mitcham. Donne referred to his marriage as the 'misfortune of my life' and seems to have believed that he had also ruined Anne's life, which was probably true. Some of the passionate love poems written for her may have been intended to make some small amends. Men's assumption of superior status carried with it the onus of superior responsibility, an important point to bear in mind when reading *Paradise Lost*.

Secret marriages were not impossibly difficult to effect, since marriage, to be legally binding, did not require formal civil or religious sanctions. In Catholic countries the sacrament was now required, but in England there were two other forms of marriage (admittedly rare in practice) in addition to those contracted before a minister. Marriage 'per verba de futuri' made a promise to marry or an engagement binding if followed by consummation, so Mariana in *Measure for Measure*, and perhaps Helena in *All's Well* are effectively married to Angelo and Bertram by the bed-tricks that consummate their promises, though both plays pose questions of action and intention that are legally and morally difficult, and *Measure for Measure* explores such questions on a wider front. Marriage 'per verba de presenti' involved an exchange of promises before witnesses, and it is for this purpose that the Duchess of Malfi conceals Cariola behind a screen so that she may witness her coming interview with Antonio, and thus guarantee that any vows he makes will be binding. Systems of this kind had developed within more stable and parochial conditions, and were becoming less and less appropriate to a more mobile society. Bigamy could be a serious problem. One pamphlet, *The Defence of Cony-Catching* (1592), relates how a confidence-trickster who had married sixteen times was finally castrated by his ex-wives in revenge.

Although upper-class marriages were normally arranged, the idea of marriage as a voluntary, mutually supportive relationship seems to have been widely accepted by the mass of the population. Here, where there was less at stake in terms of titles, property or personal prestige, young couples normally took the initiative themselves, with parents on occasion advising or perhaps exercising some sort of informal veto. It is tempting to suppose that Shakespeare's romantic view of love and marriage was derived as much from personal experience in the freer air further down the social scale as from literature. Love leading to marriage, often in the face of some kind of opposition, had always been a favourite theme of romance and romantic comedy, and was always waiting to be updated. In Middleton's *A Chaste Maid in Cheapside* the Yellowhammers' determination to marry off their daughter advantageously, and against her own inclination, should probably be regarded as further evidence of their absurd social pretensions, satirized throughout, even though the theme itself may be traced back to Roman New Comedy.

The concept of marriage for love is sometimes associated with the rise of protestantism, which had sanctioned a married clergy while abolishing those traditional enclaves of celibacy, monasteries and nunneries. Spenser's knight of chastity in *The Faerie Queene* is the warrior Britomart, a maiden associated with fertile (but unpromiscuous) wedded love, not the bright virgin, Belphoebe. Quite a different factor, town life, may also have tended to isolate couples from kin and community more than country life had done, thus requiring them to be more self-supporting. A more romantic view of marriage certainly demanded greater flexibility from parents, and a readier responsiveness to the child's needs and wishes. Thomas More in *Utopia* had amused his readers by insisting that prospective bridegrooms ought to see their brides naked before marriage. Such an attitude was based on the sensible recognition that sexual attraction was important if a marriage was to be successful.

Three unexpected characteristics of married life must be mentioned: the first is its relative lateness; second, the small size of families, and third its instability. Shakespeare's Juliet, a bride of fourteen, is a much-remembered but misleading example. It is true that where large amounts of property were at stake, marriages might be arranged earlier, sometimes for children in their early teens. Even then, the couple were not expected to spend more than one night together, as required by law. Thereafter the bridegroom would be sent abroad on the grand tour for a year or two, until he and his wife were ready to conceive children without undue risk to her health. The average age for upper-class marriages was, nevertheless, twenty rather than fifteen. Further down the social scale it was considerably higher, twenty-four for women, twenty-six or twenty-seven for men, and still rising. This late age for marriage, as much as ten years after the onset of puberty, was characteristic of Western European society as a whole, and can only be explained on prudential or economic grounds. Apprentices were indentured for seven years to their trade, and it might be even longer before they could practise independently. In the country, a labourer would need either to save or to inherit in order to marry. Interestingly, the life expectancy of a man of thirty was on average another twenty-five or thirty years, so a son might reasonably expect to inherit around the age of twenty-five or thirty. Late marriage had the important incidental effect of reducing the number of children in a family. As the average age of a woman at marriage rises by two years, so she is statistically likely to bear one child less.

Family size probably resembled that of today; parents would typically have two or three children living at home. Vast families on the Victorian scale would have been exceptional. Infant mortality was one crucial factor here – as many as one in every seven babies died within the first year of their lives, and thereafter mortality rates remained high – around a quarter had died by the age of ten. Another factor was that some time between the ages of seven and fourteen children would normally be sent away from home, to be apprenticed, go into service or, among the upper classes, join another nobleman's household or go to school or university. Obviously the size of individual families varied – perhaps four or five children might survive, of whom the two eldest might well have left home. Noblemen, with their advantages in terms of lifestyle and nourishment, probably had larger families than peasants, and their children were likely to survive in larger numbers.

Broken marriages were as much a feature of society then as they are today, but for a rather different reason: not divorce, which was effectively impossible, but death was the great home-breaker. Couples occasionally separated, but could not remarry. On average, marriages lasted twelve or fifteen years, so that remarriage was common, and many people married two or three times. Remarriage might be undertaken as much for the children's sake as for the bereaved parent, despite the innumerable traditional stories of the cruelty of step-parents. That formidable Elizabethan lady, Bess of Hardwick, was married exceptionally early, and made four marriages altogether. Spenser married twice: Elizabeth Boyle, for whom he wrote the *Amoretti* and the *Epithalamion*, being his second wife. Milton married three times.

It is impossible to generalize with any confidence about parental attitudes to children. Montaigne, who was not an unfeeling man, admits with alarming vagueness 'I have lost two or three children in infancy, not without regret, but without great sorrow.' High infant mortality may have discouraged strong emotional investment in those fragile little lives. Yet the frequency with which sermons and morality plays denounce over-indulgent parents who spared the rod and spoiled the child, tells another story, suggesting that warm parental affection survived in the face of official disapproval. Montaigne's assertion that he was unwilling to have his children nursed close to him (in 'Of the Affection of Fathers for their Children') can be set against More's Latin verse epistle to his children:

I never could endure to hear you cry. You know, for example, how often I kissed you, how seldom I whipped you . . . Brutal and unworthy to be called father is he who does not himself weep at the tears of his child.

Literature can provide many touching, not to say sentimental, moments of concern for children. The Duchess of Malfi's dying anxiety that her son should take some syrup for his cold, and the girl say her prayers, provides an obvious example. Throughout the play Webster seems anxious to present her as a devoted mother. Ben Jonson composed poignant epigrams on the death of his son Benjamin and his eldest daughter which, within a framework of classical wit, bespeak deep feeling; but one cannot generalize from particular examples. As some sections of society became more leisured, they probably spent more time with their children and came to find them more rewarding than they could otherwise have done. For families struggling at subsistence level, however, a new baby was just another mouth to feed, and a certain negligence might conveniently diminish its already thin chances of survival. Figures for infanticide, whether by deliberate murder or merely by neglect, are quite impossible to guess. Macbeth's witches throw in their cauldron

> 'Finger of birth-strangled babe
> Ditch-deliver'd by a drab'   (IV. i. 30–1)

It is to be feared that this was not a specially rare ingredient. At the opposite end of the social scale, parents put out their children to wet-nurses, and subsequently had them cared for and taught by servants of one kind or another. Shakespeare's Juliet is on much closer terms with her old nurse (who had been her wet-nurse, and reminisces about the lost baby who would now be the same age as Juliet) than with her mother. The nurse's uncontrollable grief at Juliet's death contrasts with her mother's more formal lament.

Juliet's old nurse provides a vivid reminder of the comparatively open attitude to sex, both among men and women; bawdy talk was not considered the sole prerogative of the former. Shakespeare's heroines Beatrice and Rosalind can joke easily about sexuality without incurring disapproval. People's lives were in most respects a good deal less private than they are today, and there was certainly less secrecy about this aspect, and none of the Victorian assumption that 'nice' women were 'above that sort of thing'. Virginity certainly had a marketable value, and brides were expected to be virgins, as is shown, in very different ways, by *Much Ado About Nothing* and *The Changeling*. Women were nevertheless expected to take at least as strong an interest in sex as men, and were proverbially vulnerable on this score: 'Frailty, thy name is woman.' Campion in his *Fourth Book of Ayres* has a charming lyric whose speaker is a young girl understandably anxious not to miss out on this experience:

> Fain would I wed a fair young man that day and night could please me,
> When my mind or body grieved that had the power to ease me.
> Maids are full of longing thoughts that breed a bloodless sickness,
> And that, oft I hear men say, is only cured by quickness.

(Quickness here means pregnancy.)

While the cold or marble-breasted mistress who will not requite her lover is a familiar figure in courtly love poetry and its derivatives, the best of Campion's lyrics achieve greater psychological realism than more conventional postures allow.

Granted the hierarchic arrangement of family life, it was important that one's possessions should behave as such, and not make one look a fool in public. Disobedient children were humiliating enough. A wayward wife was an even worse affliction, subverting the natural domination of husband over wife. The fact that any man's wife might make him a cuckold was a source of intense anxiety in this society, and, it follows, also one of laughter. Nothing was more surely guaranteed to raise a laugh than the mention of horns, the traditional invisible accompaniment of being cuckolded. That this anxiety could reach pathological proportions (as it can even today, in a society far less threatened by its implications) is attested by Jonson's portrait of the merchant Kitely in *Every Man in His Humour*, and the even more alarming figure of Corvino in *Volpone*, who seems to dread and desire his horns with equal violence. Its tragic implications are fully explored in *Othello*.

Being cuckolded was not merely painful in itself, exposing the husband to derision for failing to keep his possessions in good order; it also threatened society's assumptions about the subordinate role of women, as did overbearing, scolding or shrewish wives, wives who 'wore the trousers'. The countryside exercised traditional sanctions against them in the form of skimmity rides or ducking stools. The husband's adultery, on the other hand, was not considered either particularly comic, interesting or unusual. It was too commonplace to feature importantly in drama. Many men, including noblemen and kings, had illegitimate children whom they openly acknowledged and made provision for in their wills – Edmund's position in *Lear* may be regarded as invidious, but it can scarcely be thought of as exceptional. The double standard operated, insisting that women should be virgins at marriage, and subsequently chaste, while in practice no such expectations governed men's behaviour, although the church condemned all forms of sexual misbehaviour. Fathers were therefore expected to protect their daughters, husbands their wives. The ultimate humiliation was to have someone else's child palmed off on you, as Soranzo almost has in *'Tis Pity She's a Whore* and Leontes fears he has in *The Winter's Tale*.

Only one group of women might act with any degree of freedom, and these were widows of independent means or women left in charge of a substantial household, as Olivia has been in *Twelfth Night*. Friends would try to arrange suitable matches for them but they were free to choose for themselves, and sometimes caused scandal in this class-conscious society by marrying a social inferior, often a member of their own household. When Frances Brandon, Countess of Suffolk, married her good-looking secretary and groom of the chamber, sixteen years younger than herself, Queen Elizabeth demanded 'Has the woman so far forgotten herself as to marry a common groom?' Perhaps she slightly envied the Countess her self-indulgence. Such marriages were assumed to be motivated by women's proverbial lust. The grandest servants in a large household, particularly the steward, might well be gentlemen by birth, perhaps younger sons without portions. Such gentlemen servants (like De Flores in *The Changeling*) occupied curiously awkward positions in households, and might be sources of potential tension. *The Duchess of Malfi* is the story of a woman who marries her gentleman steward, and since the obvious assumption would have been that she did so from lust rather than from love, Webster is at considerable pains to show that the Duchess values Antonio for his moral qualities and makes a tender mother and devoted wife. Her brothers naturally assume the worst. Olivia's steward Malvolio, though probably no gentleman, indulges in fantasies of marrying her.

It would not have been so unreasonable for a lonely young woman to form a liaison with a household servant, even though society frowned upon it when it was not sniggering, since servants could come and go freely about the house, and in smaller establishments would have lived at close quarters with their employers. One-third of all households employed living-in servants and such employment extended well down the social scale. The great majority of young girls from poor families would have gone into service where their relationship with their employers might, in a small household, be very close, sometimes too close. Great households would have employed gentlewomen, as well as gentlemen, and the relationships between the Duchess of Malfi and Cariola, Desdemona and Emilia, Hero and her waiting ladies were close and confiding ones. Apprentices to a trade might also live in their master's house and Francis Beaumont's *The Knight of the Burning Pestle* reveals how fond a couple could grow of an amiable apprentice: the grocer's wife could scarcely be prouder or more delighted with Ralph's talents than if she were his own mother. Normally servants felt a strong involvement with the household whose livery they wore (if it was grand enough to have one) and tended to be touchily proud of it. Family feuds were often perpetrated by brawling servants whose actions their masters felt obliged to support, as happens in the opening scene of *Romeo and Juliet*. On the other hand, servants occasionally harboured deep resentments against an employer they thought had treated them unjustly. In 1628 the poet Fulke Greville, by then an old man, was stabbed to death by a servant who did not consider that he had made suitable provision for him in his will. And no one who has read it can forget the traditional ballad of Lamkin, the unpaid mason who joins the wet-nurse in cutting the throats of mother and baby while father is away.

Tudor and Stuart society worked largely through formal relationships that imposed mutual obligations – squire or landlord and tenants, master and servants, artisan and apprentices. Higher up, an elaborate system of patronage was in operation. In addition to the maintenance of a large, liveried household, a great nobleman would have a number of clients who paid court to him, threw in their lot with his, and in return hoped to receive some office or position from which they could continue to support his interests as well as their own. The conferring of mutual benefits commonly involved the exchange of money or gifts and might even take the form of bartering sexual favours for wealth or position. Jacobean tragedy seized on such arrangements and dramatized them with genuine horror, while comedy and satire concentrated on their potential absurdity. Both were inclined to associate corrupt 'new values' with court and city, regarding the countryside as the repository of traditional values and old-fashioned integrity, as pastoral had done. In reality, the rapid growth of city and court was as much a symptom of change as a cause of it, but contemporaries were in no position to discern this. To them it seemed that change was imposed by upstart urban profiteers on an unwilling countryside to the evident detriment of the older values and ways of life. The greed and rapacity of towns seemed to be flourishing at the expense of the land. *The Revenger's Tragedy* persistently returns to the theme, and in the following speech Vindice angrily denounces the permanent spoliation of the countryside to pay for the ephemeral fashions of the day:

'Who'd sit at home in a neglected room . . . when those
Poorer in face and fortune than herself

Walk with a hundred acres on their backs –
Fair meadows cut into green foreparts – oh,
It was the greatest blessing ever happened to women
When farmers' sons agreed, and met again,
To wash their hands and come up gentlemen;
The commonwealth has flourished ever since.
Lands that were mete by the rod – that labour's spared –
Tailors ride down and measure 'em by the yard.
Fair trees, these comely foretops of the field,
Are cut to maintain head-tires:'   (II. i. 209–20)

forepart] front portion of dress
foretop] front lock of hair
head-tire] head-dress

Changes in property-holding, a significant feature of the period, might well have tragic consequences for tenants if the land fell into the hands of tough businessmen, anxious to make a quick profit and feeling none of the traditional obligations of the older gentry towards their dependants. Poems like Ben Jonson's 'To Penshurst' that celebrate the hospitality and dignity of a great country house, often do so partly in terms of the absence of cruelty and oppression which had apparently become the norm elsewhere:

And though thy walls be of the country stone,
They are rear'd with no man's ruin, no man's groan,
There's none that dwell about them wish them down.   (45–7)

The enclosure of common land and the conversion of arable land to pasture (encouraged by the initial success of the cloth industry) were the worst of several ways in which city-sanctioned profit motives caused real distress in the countryside. Day-labourers, unable to graze their animals or find the casual seasonal labour required for ploughing, sowing and harvesting, were driven from the land, creating a class of unemployed who were thus forced, if they had any spirit at all, to take to a life of crime. In fact the government was not unresponsive to the dangers inherent in enclosure, if only because it feared the threats to order presented by the unemployed. Commissions of enquiry were set up to examine complaints about enclosure, and from 1536 the crown was empowered to prosecute individuals found carrying it out. This act was repealed in 1593, presumably because it had fallen into disuse, but a sequence of disastrous harvests and serious food shortages followed and a new act of 1597 required the rebuilding of decayed farms, and the conversion of pasture lands to arable farming. During the parliamentary debate on the issue, Bacon pointed out that

Enclosure of ground brings depopulation, which brings first idleness, secondly decay of tillage, thirdly subversion of houses and decay of charity, and charges to the poor, fourthly impoverishing of the state of the realm.

Enclosure seems to have provided an explanation of social distress and unrest whose simplicity appealed to contemporaries, but it was no new phenomenon: it had been going on long before the sixteenth century and in those parts of the country where the population had never really recovered from the ravages of the Black Death, it might even be considered a useful and constructive policy. Moreover it was not uncommonly achieved by mutual negotiation between tenant and landlord which in the long run benefited the tenant, establishing his rights on a firmer footing than before.

In fact the real source of distress in the countryside, of unemployed labourers, high prices, low wages, changing patterns of land-holding, and the concomitant growth in numbers and power of the towns was one that the Elizabethans could do nothing to control, even if they had identified it with greater certainty. The historian and Justice of the Peace William Lambarde commented on 'the dearth of all things', asserting 'that the number of our people is multiplied, it is both demonstrable to the eye and evident in reason'. The problem was demographic. The population, which had remained effectively at a standstill during the fifteenth century, began to increase steadily and substantially in the sixteenth, progressing from about two and a half million at the beginning to perhaps four million by the end. The most plausible explanation for this increase was a greater resistance to the bubonic plague, which first struck with devastating force in the mid-fourteenth century, cutting a rising population by as much as a quarter, perhaps even a third. Though it continued to return in waves, causing massive deaths in London in bad years, its virulence was certainly abating in overall terms, and after the outbreak of 1665, it effectively died out. Smallpox, on the other hand, the disease mainly responsible for preventing population growth in the seventeenth century, had not yet reached its peak. Although the sixteenth century's rapid rise in population was anomalous in terms of the preceding and following centuries, it was, of course, in line with a more general growth over the whole millennium.

As population grew, prices rose and food became an increasingly sought-after commodity, but there was no parallel rise in wages since the market was saturated with people looking for work. The day labourers who constituted the general run of the populace could not always find the casual labour they needed to survive, and the cloth-making industry, which provided a substantial number of jobs in particular areas, failed to sustain its initial rate of growth. The gap between haves and have-nots increased, between those with a surplus to sell at the new higher prices and those who could not even sell their own labour. The poor grew poorer, their landlessness finally driving them to seek work in towns, which were in any case growing rapidly through increases in trade and other transactions promoted by the new wealth. The steady influx of migrants from the country-side maintained, indeed increased town populations, despite inade-quate sanitation and prevalent disease. London grew fastest, from around 50,000 at the beginning of the sixteenth century to four times that size by the end. Norwich and Bristol were its largest rivals.

Historians have debated what effect all this had on the gentry, who can be shown to be rising or declining according to the examples selected. Landowners should have benefited from higher food prices (which doubled over the period 1560–1620), but sometimes tenants with fixed rents under long leases might be the gainers, while the real value of rents fell with inflation. At the same time the gentry were under pressure to increase expenditure in order to maintain their status. The more successful were embarking on spending sprees, lavishing money on houses, clothes, furniture and, less obviously, dowries and education. Paying for such conspicuous consumption required good management, especially as costs were not spread evenly. Even the prudent found it necessary to borrow at times, while careless or extravagant gallants might fall hopelessly into debt, mortgaging off their land until the money-lenders finally foreclosed on their forfeited property. Reckless prodigals and grasping usurers were to become the stock-in-trade of Jacobean comedy.

The full stress created by demographic pressures was felt most acutely in the mid-1590s, when two very serious outbreaks of the plague in London (1593, 1597) combined with a sequence of disas-trous harvests to create a sense of panic, and fears of a more general breakdown in law and order. Although in terms of total numbers, the plague's impact had abated somewhat, its effect on a large tightly packed city such as London was indeed nightmarish, as contemporary accounts convey. Nashe's Unfortunate Traveller experiences a visitation of the plague at Rome in 1522, but Nashe may well have been thinking of that in London in 1592-3: heavy clouds hang over the city, and as many of the inhabitants die or flee, the professional criminals move in, raping and pillaging. Both Nashe and Dekker (in his pamphlet on the 1603 attack, *The Wonderful Year*) emphasize the suddenness of death and the unwillingness of others to console or help the stricken for fear of infection:

How often hath the amazed husband waking, found the comfort of his bed lying breathless by his side! his children at the same instant gasping for life! and his servants, mortally wounded at the heart by sickness! The distracted creature beats at death's doors, exclaims at windows, his cries are sharp enough to pierce heaven, but on earth no ear is opened to receive them.

Plague victims died in the streets, the fields and outside the houses of the terrified countrymen who barricaded themselves in and would not even give them water. The outbreak of 1625 was perhaps the worst of all in this period; more than 40,000 died in London, one in eight of the whole population.

The bad harvests of 1593-7 meant that the majority of workers who normally managed to maintain themselves by cultivating their own tiny plots (often no more than an acre on which to grow vegetables) and hiring themselves out, fell below subsistence level, and some were forced to take to the roads in search of work. In 1598 the clergyman Thomas Bastard addressed an epigram to the Queen alerting her to their miserable plight:

The forlorn father hanging down his head,
His outcast company drawn up and down,
The pining labourer doth beg his bread,
The plowswain seeks his dinner from the town.

Food riots were the usual consequence of bad times. The opening scene of *Coriolanus* gives a slightly unsympathetic, though not necessarily inaccurate picture of the rioters' logic. The first citizen, obviously the ringleader, proposes that they kill Caius Martius whom he describes as 'chief enemy to the people', concluding that then 'we'll have corn at our own price'. He seems to equate a real grievance (the food shortage) with an imaginary one against an unpopular senator. The citizens' claims

> 'For corn at their own rates, whereof they say
> The city is well stor'd'   (I. i. 189–90)

merely repeat the standard demand of food rioters in Shakespeare's lifetime. The government did what it could to avert these, by holding a watching brief over grain exports, and encouraging imports in times of shortage; by trying to ensure that corn was not hoarded but reached the markets and was sold at fair prices, and by shifting grain to areas of dearth from areas of plenty. In periods of crisis, like the 1590s, special powers were conferred on local Justices of the Peace to buy up corn and redistribute it, but inevitably such instructions were only as effective as the officers entrusted to perform them. Many JPs shared the sense, common among the gentry, of responsibility for the smaller people. This, coupled with a distrust of merchants and middlemen, probably encouraged their active interference in the grain market, and with it the prosecution of entrepreneurs, or badgers as they were called, where necessary. It was after all in everyone's interests to alleviate the worst deprivations if only to avoid the fearful alternative of riots. At the same time many JPs were also substantial landlords with a vested interest in the maintenance of high food prices, and so some, no doubt, carried out government instructions in times of famine with rather more alacrity than others.

The government could not close its eyes to the problems of the hungry indefinitely, for desperate men were dangerous, and landless peasants taking to the roads in large numbers provided the nucleus for a riot or a criminal gang. Since the Reformation there had been little in the way of institutional relief of the poor; charity had largely depended on the voluntary and informal mutual support that had traditionally been a feature of village life, but was obviously more difficult to maintain in times of shortages. The foundations of Elizabethan poor relief had been laid in 1576, but these were reinforced and elaborated by the statute of 1597, evolved to deal with the current crisis. This based responsibility for poor relief within the parish, where JPs were to assess the level of financial support required and levy the money as rates on parishioners. Funds were to be available for widows and orphans, helpless dependants who presented a permanent problem, and to buy raw materials (wool, flax, hemp or iron) on which the able-bodied unemployed might be set to work. Then as now, this class was regarded with some suspicion, even seen as skivers who positively preferred to be idle. In fact the hardest hit were forced to take to the roads from necessity, searching for work elsewhere, and thus became inextricably confused with a third, and probably much smaller class of homeless, the genuinely idle vagabonds who had traditionally been treated with great harshness, exiled, hung or put in the galleys. After 1597 they were punished by being whipped and placed in a house of correction along the lines of Bridewell in London. As the parish was the operative unit, the poor were encouraged to stay within their own; it was supposed to provide for them, but officers were only too anxious to whip vagabonds outside parish boundaries, since a sudden influx placed further strain on already depleted funds. In this way the poor law might be seen as reinforcing existing prejudices against strangers. The government tried to insist on all travelling professionals – tinkers, pedlars and the like – being licensed, and was always eager to discourage travel, though records suggest that despite strong local ties and official deterrents, the population as a whole was unexpectedly mobile.

The bands of wandering vagabonds who were one target of the Elizabethan poor law aroused both fear and curiosity in respectable householders; surprisingly early there developed an underworld literature, and not solely in response to a prudential interest in self-protection. Two pioneering accounts of criminal activity were written in the 1560s, John Awdeley's *Fraternity of Vagabonds* (1561) and Thomas Harman's *Caveat for Common Cursetors* (1567). The latter, a Kentish Justice of the Peace, was obviously fascinated by this world within a world, and lost no opportunity to find out more about it from the types he met both in Kent and London – part of his book takes the form of his reported conversations with a 'doxy' and a 'counterfeit crank'. Both Harman and Awdeley describe in some detail the activities of the vagabonds, sturdy beggars or tramps who apparently wandered the country eking out an existence by peddling, begging or stealing. Both divided these up into various categories, not necessarily mutually exclusive, which they saw as constituting a secret fraternity, with its own hierarchy and initiation ceremony, thus mirroring the guild structure. This was quite a common assumption to make about mysterious or subversive group behaviour, and a comparison can be made with witchcraft. Harman and Awdeley agree that there is a master of the order, who can call the others to account and have any of the women he desires, though Awdeley refers to him as the 'upright man', Harman as the 'ruffler'. In addition to tinkers and pedlars like Autolycus (swigmen, or bawdy baskets if they were female), a vagabond might beg for alms pretending to be an old soldier (ruffler), afflicted with sores (palliard), epileptic (counterfeit crank) or a madman (the Abram man or Tom a Bedlam, Edgar's chosen disguise in *Lear*). As petty criminals they worked as prostitutes (doxies), thieves (prigmen) or horse-thieves (priggers of prancers). Awdeley, in addition to his nineteen different types of rogue, includes, for good measure, 'a quartern of knaves for Cocklorel': these are not vagabonds at all but ne'er-do-well servingmen, divided into twenty-five types according to their various unpleasant personal habits. Harman, on the other hand, is more interested in their private language, known variously as 'canting' or 'pedlar's French'. This contributed substantially to the impression that its users belonged to a secret society. Underworld languages of this kind have been recorded in several European countries from the late fourteenth century and were partly made up by adapting familiar terms: night and day were 'darkmans' and 'lightmans', horses were 'prancers', while 'cheat' (thing, from 'escheat') was compounded with various participial adjectives to make 'smelling cheat' (nose), 'grunting cheat' (pig), 'quacking cheat' (duck), etc. Some words were taken from foreign languages: the kinchin cove (or mort) was a young boy (or girl) from 'Kindchen', German for a little child, 'bene' (good) came from Latin, 'vyle' (town) from French. A few — 'booze' for drink, 'cove' for a person (probably from Dutch and Romany respectively), have survived as slang till the present.

Whether there really was a class of professional vagabonds, and if so how many existed at any one time is difficult to judge. Harman lists 214 by name and type, but only 18 of those he names have been found in records of the period — these are, however, very incomplete. In any case it must always have been difficult to separate 'professionals' from the far larger group of vagrants driven to wandering by sheer necessity, whose ranks swelled as the century wore on and its economic pressures bit harder. Discharged soldiers and servingmen, evicted tenants and unemployed labourers thronged the roads. By the 1590s they may have numbered as many as 12,000.

Associated with professional rogues and vagabonds but ethnically distinct were Romanies or gypsies, so called since they were believed to have come from Egypt. Legends of their romantic way of life,

roaming the countryside and making their living by smuggling and
fortune-telling, peddling and petty crime, certainly caught the
popular imagination, but their distinctive names seldom appear in
records and do not figure in Harman's list. From the outset they
were associated with second-sight, palmistry and magic. Othello's
fatal handkerchief had been given to his mother by an Egyptian:

> 'She was a charmer, and could almost read
> The thoughts of people.'　　　　　　　　　　　　　(III. iv. 57–8)

Fortune-telling provides the central device of Jonson's masque *The
Gypsies Metamorphosed*, composed for Buckingham and his family.
Juggling and sleight-of-hand were their skills, and particularly the
trick known as 'fast-and-loose' in which a scarf or rope that appeared
o be tightly knotted ('fast') came untied ('loose') with a flick of the
wrist. Antony in Shakespeare's play exclaims against Cleopatra,
Egypt's Queen,

> 'Betray'd I am.
> O this false soul of Egypt! this grave charm, . . .
> Like a right gypsy, hath at fast and loose
> Beguil'd me to the very heart of loss.'　　　　　(IV. xii. 24–5, 28–9)

Although Harman and Awdeley refer to Bridewell, Bedlam and St
Paul's (a favourite haunt of villains), the vagabond fraternity they
describe seem to be on the move and are as likely to be encountered
in a Kentish lane as in a London street. Later underworld pamphlets
are much more exclusively concerned with urban crime, and its
obvious victims, the gulls who thronged to the city and as innocent
country rabbits (or conies) were skinned by the various pickpockets,
card-sharpers and footpads, the cony-catchers. The bewildering
variety of their confidence tricks, as well as those of the crossbiters
(or blackmailers) were eagerly exposed in the pamphlets of Dekker
and Greene. London was an urban jungle. In the Middle Ages,
robber bands had often operated from forest hideouts. Now, as the
great forests disappeared, London became the setting both of
organized and unorganized crime. It was to the cities that the dis-
possessed and wretched trekked, looking for work, huddling in
attics, cellars, tenements and even, in times of dearth or plague,
dying in the streets. The concentration of large numbers and the lack
of sanitation made towns dirty, smelly, crowded and unhealthy, their
populations maintained by the steady influx of migrants, not by

any process of natural renewal. Many of those who found work in towns wisely left their families behind them in the country, as commuters and migrant workers do today – Shakespeare chose to do so. The less fortunate had no homes in which to leave them.

It was not only waste disposal that failed to keep pace with the rapid increase in town populations. Current provision for crime had evolved in response to small town and village life, and these had been largely self-regulating. Everyone took care to know each other's business, and while there were endless denunciations for petty theft and sexual peccadilloes, there was comparatively little serious crime that remained undiscovered. Strangers were disliked, distrusted and generally regarded with suspicion. Such mutual supervision, possible in a small and intimate community, could not be achieved in a large, impersonal city, where a combination of poverty, stress, anonymity and inadequate means of law-enforcement acted as incentives to crime. Elizabethan society was in any case, by our standards, violent: quarrels and resentments were settled by blows, and sometimes fights to the death. Ben Jonson killed an actor in a fight; the poet Thomas Watson died in another, while Marlowe, who was involved in Watson's death in 1592, was himself killed a year later, also apparently in a brawl. Bad times like the 1590s exacerbated already difficult conditions. Provosts to enforce martial law were appointed in London and the adjoining counties when the city and the roads leading out of it had become alarmingly unsafe.

Policing, such as it was, was normally carried out by petty constables, unpaid volunteers whose local knowledge was more likely to prove effective in country districts than in the metropolis. Shakespeare has left an amusing picture of the constables Dogberry and Verges organizing their little posse of men, the watch:

DOGBERRY. This is your charge: you shall comprehend all vagrom men; you are to bid any man stand, in the prince's name.
2 WATCH. How if a' will not stand?
DOGBERRY. Why then take no note of him, but let him go; and presently call the rest of the watch together, and thank God you are rid of a knave. . . .
2 WATCH. We will rather sleep than talk, we know what belongs to a watch. (*Much Ado*, III. iii. 24–38)

Elbow, the constable in *Measure for Measure*, though far braver and more officious than Dogberry, is equally verbally confused and confusing. Escalus examines his indictment of Pompey Bum, the tapster and bawd, and then tries to relieve Elbow of his office without hurting his feelings. It turns out that Elbow had agreed to act as constable when others had been nominated; in a violent city the position of constable was not an enviable one.

While allowing for comic exaggeration, it is difficult to suppose that such representatives of law and order, even if considerably more intelligent than Dogberry or Elbow, would have been able to stem the increase in crime that accompanied the cities' increase in numbers. Certain areas lying outside the city walls, notably Clerken-well, were notorious for the number of brothels they contained. Nashe denounced them in *Christ's Tears Over Jerusalem* (1593): 'London, what are thy suburbs but licensed stews? Can it be so many brothel-houses of salary sensuality and six-penny whoredom (the next door to the magistrates) should be set up and maintained, if bribes did not bestir them?' With brothels come bribery, pimps and protection rackets. There is ample literary evidence of an energetic criminal underworld, and though one should be wary of relying on evidence drawn from literature that includes a strong titillating element, it is hard to believe that the detailed and consistent accounts of criminal activity to be found in pamphlets, satires and plays did not have some basis in fact, granted current economic conditions. It is noticeable that the business of conciliar courts, earlier dominated by riots and crimes of violence, had shifted, by the early seventeenth century, towards conspiracy, forgery and fraud.

The first pamphlets to concern themselves almost exclusively with the London underworld were the five cony-catching pamphlets of that versatile literary hack Robert Greene, composed between 1591 and 1592 (the year of his death). These relate stories of different types of confidence tricks, frauds and thefts practised on the unwary (the conies), and judging from his attitudinizing deathbed *Repentance of Robert Greene*, the author considered their composition an act of public benefaction. *The Defence of Cony-Catching* (1592) by one Cuthbert Cony-Catcher (conceivably Greene himself) ironically blames R. G. for having spoilt 'so noble a science' by giving away trade secrets. Later Cuthbert comes across some farmers playing cards in a remote corner of Devon, one of whom attempts to cheat the others, but is firmly put down with 'What, neighbour, will you play the cony-catcher with us? No, no, we have read the book as well as you', at which discouraging news the writer makes himself scarce. Greene's purpose was, on the face of it, the wholly admirable one of preventing the innocent from being robbed or cheated, but he was shrewd enough to see that edification could be combined with sensationalism. As well as providing supposedly useful information, his pamphlets pander to vulgar curiosity about criminal life, particularly its erotic aspects. Unlike Thomas Harman, who was animated by an intense, almost scientific curiosity about the alien world whose inhabitants appeared before his judicial bench, Greene belonged to the underworld he wrote about. According to his own account he frequented whores, drank too much and kept bad company, notably that of playwrights and players, although he adopts a primly moral tone when writing of the criminal classes.

A more radical note is struck in *The Defence of Cony-Catching*, where Greene himself is criticized for straining at gnats, and letting the real villains of society pass uncensored, 'those caterpillers that undo the poor, ruin whole lordships, infect the commonwealth, and delight in nothing but in wrongful extorting and purloining of pelf [money], when as such be the greatest cony-catchers of all.' An attack on usurers follows, and a justification is offered for fraud along Robin Hood lines, if its victim is 'a miserable miser, that either racks his tenants' rents, or sells his grain in the market at an unreasonable rate'. Beneath this somewhat transparent piece of special pleading may lie a genuine sense of social injustice. Jacobean city comedy, which catches up many of the kinds of trickery exposed in the pamphlets, often reveals the apparently worthy and respectable burgesses to be as ruthlessly and immorally self-seeking within the social system as the excluded tricksters and cony-catchers were outside it. The fact that the bourgeoisie do not run the same risks or accept such a view of themselves only shows them to be less honest and more hypocritical. Increasing capitalism, bringing with it thriving middlemen and moneylenders, could still shock the conservative, who regarded these activities as little better than cony-catching and cross-biting. The medieval condemnation of usury (lending money at interest) survived despite its legalization as a practice; yet usury was becoming increasingly common in a society beginning to move away from commodity exchanges, at a time of price inflation and shortage of coin. Those who were lucky enough to have money to spare were frequently approached for loans, and inflation, as well as demand, justified them in asking for rates of interest. The unease created by the whole issue is reflected in Shakespeare's *Merchant of Venice* which inevitably links it with trade, and the merchant's precarious dependence on the success of his ventures. The Royal Exchange had been built to facilitate English trade but there were still critics who did not consider that mercantile speculation constituted an honest day's work. So prosperous tradesmen, merchants or lawyers might from one point of view be regarded as worthy citizens of substance and standing, from another as grasping usurers, exploiting their clients or tenants, caterpillars battening on the commonwealth. Jacobean comedy was quite sophisticated enough to present this increasingly important social group both as they saw themselves and as others sometimes saw them.

Although Robert Greene had written comedies, these were essentially romantic in tone, lacking the quality of sordid energy that distinguishes his pamphlets. By the turn of the century a new comedy was developing, whose subject was the London citizens that provided its audience, and whose attitudes were derived from the cony-catching pamphlets and verse satires of the 1590s. Dekker's *The Shoemaker's Holiday* of 1599 creates in Simon Eyre the shoemaker a characteristic hero, but is uncharacteristic of later developments in that it tends to accept him at his own valuation. Marston's *The Dutch Courtezan* (1604) provides a much more typical example. It opposes the rogue Cockledemoy, whose elaborate ruses, confidence tricks and disguises are very much in the cony-catching tradition, to the apparently virtuous Mulligrub, rising in wealth and social status at the expense of other people's indulgence in alcohol. Cockledemoy speaks in a highly idiosyncratic and obscene slang which, while it owes little or nothing to the canting terms recorded by Harman, establishes him as an individualist operating outside the norms of linguistic exchange, just as his social malpractices function outside the norms of social exchange. The play's climax involves a comic reversal of expectation since it is Mulligrub, not Cockledemoy, who is arrested and nearly hanged for theft. Marston's underlying point here is that the London rogue differs in status rather than kind from the man of substance – tradesman or merchant – who resembles the rogue in making a living out of other men's weaknesses.

Thomas Middleton (*c.*1580–1627) was the dramatist most closely associated with the city, and he gave some of the most convincing accounts of citizen life and values. The city authorities commissioned pageants and entertainments from him and in 1620 appointed him City Chronologer, their official recorder of important events and transactions. Middleton's comedies often employ elaborately fantastic plots, yet their central concerns – tension between gentry and bourgeoisie or country and city ('They're busy 'bout our wives, we 'bout their lands'), profitable business deals, advantageous marriage bargains, inheriting a relative's wealth or alternatively being done down in such ventures – are those of the society he was portraying; they are in turn reflected in contemporary trends in litigation. Middleton is less concerned with rogues, and more with the wheeling and dealing of the middle classes whose hopes, dreams, self-deception and illusions he viewed with a complex mixture of sympathy, humour and disapproval. Quomodo, the shifty woollen-draper of *Michaelmas Term* (1606), whose deceits are based on those of a real merchant, Howe, prosecuted a few years earlier, indulges in a self-congratulating fantasy about a piece of land he hopes to gain as the forfeited security for an unpaid loan. Its present owner is, naturally, a spendthrift gallant:

'Now come my golden days in. – Whither is the worshipful Master Quomodo and his fair bedfellow rid forth? – To his land in Essex! – Whence comes those goodly load of logs? – From his land in Essex! – Where grows this pleasant fruit? says one citizen's wife in the Row – At Master Quomodo's orchard in Essex – Oh, oh, does it so? I thank you for that good news, i' faith.'   (III. iv. 12–18)

Ben Jonson (1572–1637) was substantially less interested than Middleton in the average citizen. If Middleton dressed up familiar anxieties in extravagant plotting, Jonson was more interested in the extravagant for its own sake, and his imagination was consistently drawn to the extreme, the eccentric, the odd. Brilliant as his depictions of contemporary society are, with every character defined by an appropriate slang or jargon, his classical training inclined him to look through the veneer of topicality at the substructure of essential human folly. It is not the characteristic aspirations of a particular class that concern him, as they do Middleton, but the permanent fantasies of humanity itself. Greed may appear to be the driving force of society, but beneath it lies the urge to power, to self-assertion and self-aggrandizement. So Volpone hazards his wealth in order to gratify his desire to laugh at his clients and see them disappointed – a typically self-destructive act of homage to ego. Jonson's great confidence-tricksters, Brainworm, Mosca and Face, drawn strongly in the cony-catching tradition, find important satisfactions in the manipulation and deception of others, while Volpone admits that pulling the wool over the eyes of the whole Venetian court was more thrilling than the enjoyment of the beautiful Celia would have been:

'The pleasure of all womankind's not like it.' (v. ii. 11)

Surly, in *The Alchemist*, turns down the prospect of a wealthy match in the hope of unmasking the criminals instead. Jonson's suggestion that we reject real, available gain in favour of fantasies of self-assertion is more inward and subtle than the more normal and commonplace drives presented elsewhere.

Bartholomew Fair (1614) develops this theme in a subversive direction. Here the fair provides opportunities for a variety of vendors and rogues (each brilliantly realized through a particular speech pattern) to deceive the customers, a relationship which may echo that of actor and audience – indeed, one of the tricksters is a puppet-master. But Jonson is less interested in the petty criminals and their victims than the quasi-authoritarian figures who attempt to organize or control the world about them, the officious servant Wasp, the zealous puritan Zeal-of-the-Land Busy, but above all Adam Overdo, the local JP obsessed with an ambition to expose the various petty crimes of the fair. Instead he himself is beaten, set in the stocks and his drunken wife almost put 'on the game'. The play shows just how far from conventional attitudes the great Jacobean dramatists could travel in their explorations of human behaviour. Here authority itself is seen as sharing the fantasies of power in which all indulge and which lay all men open to the dream-pedlars, and their get-rich-quick schemes. Jonson elsewhere satirizes the free-booting activities of the projectors, aspiring citizens, rogues and whores alongside those of the busybodies who set out to control or expose their fellow-men. Nowhere does he leave room for complacency. His writing is more concerned to analyse the permanent patterns of self-delusion than too insistent an emphasis on his vivid rendering of contemporary life can convey. At the same time such an emphasis is difficult to avoid since his record of London life remains unequalled in its range and ebullience.

The best of Jacobean comedy challenges conventional attitudes, sharply questioning the virtues of wealth and respectability, but by the 1620s complex and abrasive exploration had relaxed into more schematic accounts in which stock types of prodigal gentry and sinister usurers figured with decreasing subtlety. Massinger's *A New*

Way to Pay Old Debts (1621) seems almost an exercise in nostalgia. Set in the country rather than the city, it matches old breeding against new men, as caricatured in the monstrous and implausibly villainous Sir Giles Overreach. Based on the contemporary figure of Sir Giles Mompesson, whom he resembles in significant details, Overreach's aspirations to make his daughter a lady, his methods of evicting tenants by harassment and of accumulating land by foreclosing on mortgages were commonplaces of the genre. At the same time Massinger blandly assumed that the prodigal gentry, as they lapsed increasingly into debt, retained a basic decency entitling them to their position as the rightful inheritors of England, that breeding always tells and that the daughter of an upstart, however wealthy, could consider herself lucky to marry a gentleman's impoverished younger son. Such assumptions verge on the sentimental. New money has, after all, always tended to prop up old names, and the related interests of court, city and gentry could not be reduced convincingly to such simplistic terms. In the 1630s, those interests were to polarize around the issues of religion and constitutional power into fresh patterns that no dramatist was sufficiently skilled to define. Even Massinger's comedy, with its almost pastoral values of old decencies and fine breeding, seems to look back nostalgically to an earlier time, a time before that depicted by Jonson and Middleton. By the next decade the lost golden age was no longer located in a remote past; it was being more and more closely identified with the age of Elizabeth; thus the (apparent) social unity, militant protestantism and community spirit of her reign were warmly remembered, long after more discordant or disquieting elements had sunk into oblivion.

3 Religion

Let me be nothing if within the compass of myself I do not find the battle of Lepanto – passion against reason, reason against faith, faith against the Devil, and my conscience against all.

If there was a single issue that preoccupied men above all others in the half century from 1580, it was religion; yet, with the important exception of the Authorized Version itself, a substantial amount of the literature most widely read today does not directly reflect this preoccupation. This is partly the result of the selections made: the sermons and pamphlets that poured from the press are seldom reread or reprinted, and commonly have to be consulted in the great Victorian editions. Drama, on the other hand, controlled by the censorship of the Revels Office, was not supposed to concern itself with contentious questions or indeed, to name God in the singular at all. It is nevertheless evident that the dramatists, as much as any other group of educated men, were deeply concerned with religion in one way or another: Marlowe, at the time of his death, was comprehensively accused of atheism; Jonson, when in prison, became a Catholic convert, and remained so for a number of years – according to one view, he was personally involved in the Gunpowder Plot; Marston retired from the stage to take orders and an Anglican living; Middleton was particularly associated with city protestantism and is the probable author of *The Marriage of the Old and New Testament*, a pamphlet concerned with the fulfilment of biblical prophecies. Yet by and large their religious concerns were seldom reflected directly in their plays, and a comparable secularism is apparent in much Elizabethan poetry, which tends to be classical in tenor. The church settlement of 1559 had provided one of the conditions of stability necessary for a literary renaissance, but religious issues may have been felt to be too serious for expression in the lighter lyric forms. Significant exceptions must, of course, be made for particular well-established (and protestant) traditions, such as metrical translations of the psalms, for 'our sage and serious poet Spenser', as well as for the fine Catholic poet Robert Southwell. Towards the end of the sixteenth century poetry grew more intro-spective, and so turned more frequently to spiritual occasions. Shakespeare's Sonnet CXLVI, 'Poor soul, the centre of my sinful earth' is deeply religious without being in the least sectarian. The seventeenth century was, however, to be one of the great ages of religious poetry in Britain.

In order to consider the issues involved, some account of the English Reformation must be given, however inadequate. It is diffi-cult to do justice to the full variety of reactions it provoked, but one interesting response was recorded by quite an ordinary individual, a man who was neither especially imaginative nor, initially, even literate: a certain William Malden vividly recalled the setting forth of the English Scriptures to be read in churches in 1538:

Immediately after, divers poor men in the town of Chelmsford in the county of Essex, where my father dwelled and I [was] born and with him brought up, the said poor men brought the New Testament of Jesus Christ, and on Sundays did sit reading in the lower end of the church, and many would flock about them to hear their reading.

Malden's father, distressed at finding his son in the group, called him away and made him say his Latin prayers.

Then I saw I could not be in rest. Then, thought I, I will learn to read English, and then I will have the New Testament and read thereon myself; and then had I learned of an English prymer as far as *Patris sapientia*, and then on Sundays I plied my English prymer. The May-tide following, I and my father's prentice Thomas Jeffrey laid our money together and bought the New Testament in English, and hid it in our bed straw and so exercised it at convenient times.

From here Malden apparently progressed to reading Frith's book on the sacrament, which questioned the physical presence of Christ in the communion bread and wine. When he criticized his mother for worshipping the crucifix, his distraught father beat and almost strangled him.

Malden's account of his reaction has a twofold significance: the excitement and importance of reading no longer lay merely in its worldly usefulness – it had become an essential qualification for godliness. The Reformation shifted the emphasis away from a passive participation in a Latin mass to the active reading of the Bible as the vital and central Christian experience, and while this clearly changed the nature of faith from within, it also had secular implications – the spread of literacy and the ideas it made accessible were obviously accelerated. Its second significance, perhaps less tangible, was in some respects even more crucial. Malden, in discovering the Bible for himself, had gained access to an intellectual, even spiritual independence, a freedom which society, as represented by his father, recognized as dangerous, yet ultimately could not deny him. Traditional views had emphasized the individual's subordination to his community, both socially and spiritually, and the necessity for intercession by clergy and saints if one was to be saved. Protestantism appeared to place the key to salvation in the hands of the individual, to invite him to discover his own calling and find God within the circumstances of his own life, while conferring a special dignity on him in the process of making that discovery. He appeared to minister to his own spiritual needs; ironically it was only a matter of appearance. Luther differed essentially from the humanist reformers in believing that the individual had forfeited his free will through the fall of Adam, that his salvation was not a matter of personal choice, but depended entirely on God's grace. Calvin took this approach a stage further, believing that the recipients of grace, God's elect, had already been chosen before time began. Despite this theological paradox at the heart of protestantism, men often experienced within it a new sense of self, of independence and self-determination; yet the cost was high. Those who felt that the old values, truths and stabilities had been thrown aside for a thousand private and conflicting schisms might have pointed to the appalling civil and religious wars that racked Europe in the century following the Reformation. The assumption that reading the Bible would lead all men to the recognition of a single protestant truth was over and over again shown to be disastrously wrong. The reformed church that had urged its own spiritual, as opposed to temporal, existence and had argued for universal priesthood and liberty of conscience soon found itself demanding that state machinery support its cause, that its clergy actively preach its word, and that papists and sectarians be forcibly deterred from their heresies. The religion of a zealous minority operates very differently when it becomes the established church.

The necessity for some kind of ecclesiastical reform had been widely acknowledged by the end of the fifteenth century. Indeed John Wyclif and the Lollards had been arguing in the fourteenth century for a preaching clergy and a vernacular Bible, to which end they themselves produced translations (begun around 1382). Their contemporaries Chaucer and Langland left their own testimony to the degeneracy of some of the lower clergy, and the worldliness of some of the celibate orders. More than a century later, Erasmus (*c.*1469–1536), who had himself been in orders, made similar charges against the regular clergy in his *Praise of Folly* (published 1511 and translated into English in 1549); he complained that 'Most of them are a long way removed from religion ... they can't even read.' Here and elsewhere he attacked superstition; his 'Colloquy on the Eating of Fish' made fun of the worship of particular saints for particular kinds of protection, of the buying of pardons and saying of prayers to offset punishments incurred for sins, the giving of chantry endowments so that masses might be recited for the soul, and other naïve forms of fire-insurance. At every level the church seemed to have fallen into disrepute. With profound horror Erasmus described Pope Julius II's ruthless campaigns in northern Italy: in his eyes war was the greatest crime against God. Through Latin, the universal language of European intellectuals, and the more effective reproduction techniques of the printing press, Erasmus's opinions reached a wide audience, adding force to the demands for change, which rapidly passed beyond anything their author had intended. He had envisaged Christendom as indissolubly united and capable of reforming itself from within, but the world about him was changing too and the schism that followed was more fundamental and permanent than any that had yet occurred in the Western church.

Relics, pardons and the use of signs and prayers as if they were charms to ward off evil all helped to reduce faith to little more than superstition, at least in the eyes of the reformers. At the simplest level, men recognized that virtue was rewarded (though this might be as much a prudential as a spiritual conviction) and were inclined to subscribe unconsciously to the Manichaean heresy, seeing the world as an endless struggle between the powers of good and evil, a view that underpinned witchcraft accusations, the notion of good and evil ('dismal') days and other ideas of good or bad luck. Between such simplistic tenets and the elaborate webs of theological disputation lay an enormous gap, a gap that the parish priest was increasingly expected to close, but only too often he was scarcely in a greater state of enlightenment than his parishioners. The zealous Bishop Hooper's visitation to his Gloucester diocese in 1551 revealed that, of 311 clergymen examined, 168 could not repeat the ten commandments, thirty-nine did not know where the Lord's prayer was to be found in the Bible, thirty-four did not know its author and ten could not even recite it. The education of the clergy was one area in which both Reformation and Counter-Reformation made significant advances, but it was a more limited and manageable goal than the education of the laity. The reformers were constantly to be disappointed by the effects of their message on unregenerate, ignorant humanity. A man of sixty who had attended Anglican sermons all his life, both during the week and twice on Sundays, was catechized on his deathbed:

Being demanded what he thought of God, he answers that he was a good old man; and what of Christ, that he was a towardly young youth; and of his soul, that it was a great bone in his body; and what should become of his soul after he was dead, that if he had done well he should be put into a pleasant green meadow.

The old man's need to visualize and his inability to think in terms of concepts suggests that for the simplest a religion strong on icons and demanding an established pattern of works and observances might really have been more suitable than the spiritual introspection that the reformers hoped to impose; but the instigators of change, both protestant and Catholic, were all intellectuals and it was difficult for either side to recognize the magnitude, perhaps the impossibility, of the educative tasks before them.

In the *Encheiridion* of 1503 ('The Handbook of the Soldier of Christ'), Erasmus had reminded his readers of St Paul's condemnation of the automatic and soulless adherence to Judaic laws:

St Paul was incessant in his attempt to remove the Jews from their faith in external works. I feel that the vast majority of Christians have sunk once again into this unhealthy situation.

It was a new reading of Pauline doctrine that enabled another monk, Martin Luther, to divert attention from the temporal church, its thrones and powers, priests, prayers and acts (as recommended in the crucial Epistle of St James) to the church spiritual, and the inner life of the believer. The conclusion of Paul's Epistle to the Romans 3:28, that 'a man is justified by faith without the deeds of the law', was to provide one cornerstone of protestantism, yet Luther, anxious to avoid the unremitting tensions associated with a religion of works and free will, insisted that faith was achieved only through grace, and not through the exertion of will, an assertion which a humanist like Erasmus, and indeed the Catholic church as a whole, could not accept. For Luther, faith consisted in a reassuring trust and confidence in God's goodness, just as for Calvin, subsequently, the apparently harsh doctrine of predestination could be seen as 'full of sweet, pleasant and unspeakable comfort', as the Thirty-nine Articles of the English church expressed it.

But the relaxation of one form of religious anxiety soon provided the occasion for others. If man was helpless to influence God's decision to grant grace to the sinner (decisions – according to the Calvinist system – made long ago), he might also be helplessly reprobate. It was a nightmare that remained to haunt the protestant imagination, a peculiarly inescapable theological blind-alley. The majority of believers, however, saw themselves as sheep rather than goats, the elect rather than the damned, finding in the misery or misbehaviour around them unmistakable signs of their own superiority. Although works were not valued for themselves, their status as evidences of grace exerted indirect pressure to perform them. As a view of life, Calvin's doctrine of election may be glimpsed behind unswerving heroines and unregenerate villains, for the predetermined character of a literary work has a certain natural affinity with the conception of a predetermined universe. In the first scene of his tragedy, Marlowe's Faustus makes much allusive and scholarly play with biblical texts in the process of proving that man is unavoidably damned and that theology is yet another waste of time. His account omits any reference to God's grace or redemption, but nevertheless suggests a parody both of the casuistry of the medieval schoolmen and of the potentially circular Calvinist system in which men cannot help themselves by any act of will:

'The reward of sin is death. That's hard. . . .
If we say that we have no sin we deceive ourselves, and there is no truth in us. Why then, belike we must sin, and so consequently die.
    Ay, we must die an everlasting death.
    What doctrine call you this? *Che sera, sera.*
    What will be, shall be. Divinity, adieu!'

                                            (I. i. 40–6)

Ironically, in view of Faustus's dismissal of such a passive status, the whole play could be read as a Calvinist thesis within which the reprobate scholar cannot humble his heart to repent. Yet in practice each of the moments where he is urged to do so is tense with the possibility that he might still save himself by that action, and without such a possibility the play would be almost entirely lacking in suspense. Calvinists probably responded to particular moral decisions as being important, while recognizing God's inescapable omniscience as a total scheme, rather as the play can be felt to combine a completed pattern with moments of individual decision.

The theology of the Elizabethan church, manned as it was by clergymen who had spent the five years of Mary's reign in Geneva, Zurich or Strasbourg, was basically Calvinist and predestinarian. Today this system seems so obviously unjust that we can only suppose it to have been reached by the relentless and absurd pursuit of a single-minded logic. This is partly the result of an optimistic assumption that God's goodness must be comprehensible to us. Men of the sixteenth century, constantly subject to inexplicable and irresistible natural disasters such as sickness, plague or fire, were less confident of understanding God's purposes as manifested on earth. Indoctrinated in the myths of equal opportunity and the freedom of free enterprise, we are reluctant to acknowledge the extent to which our lives are determined by birth and endowments, both physical and mental. Determining factors of this kind had a far more paralysing effect in Elizabethan society, with its publicly voiced disapproval of social mobility. It may also be that predestination provided a rationale for that inner conviction that each of us is living out a story that moves with continuity and meaning towards some significant end, finding that story's most attentive auditor in God. For whatever reason, the harsh doctrines of election and reprobation were widely accepted by devout Elizabethans and passionately held by many Jacobean protestants in the face of a widespread revival of the belief in free will advocated by the Dutch theologian Arminius (1560–1609). By the end of the 1620s, however, Arminian doctrine had attracted considerable support within the Anglican church, and was beginning to provoke bitter controversy, especially once it began to be associated with William Laud's attack on Calvinist beliefs (see p. 81).

One of the several crucial demands resulting from Luther's emphasis on the spiritual city of God, as opposed to the temporal, was that the church's secular power be abandoned. The church's wealth and lands had too often resulted in greed among the clergy themselves and envy or hatred from those who resented its powers and activities as a landowner. Luther proposed, as an alternative to the church's worldly rule, government by a godly prince who would administer the law justly, leaving the church to its proper spiritual concerns. Such a proposal afforded considerable opportunities to a grasping and needy prince like Henry VIII, who found himself thereby provided with an idealistic charter to dismantle and appropriate the church's wealth, a programme he proceeded to initiate. It was prosecuted even more eagerly by the two Lord Protectors acting during the minority of Edward VI. Although their commitment to the protestant cause was never entirely cynical, the church under this series of depredations was systematically reduced from a position of power, wealth and authority to one of financial weakness from which it was never wholly to recover. In 1553 Mary Tudor came to the throne and for five years reversed the previous protestant policies in favour of Catholicism. Whatever might have happened had she lived longer, the country to which Elizabeth succeeded had not had time to grow accustomed to these changes, and had been shocked at the burnings of protestants at Smithfield, while those that had escaped abroad returned filled with a passionate Calvinist ardour.

The question of how far the country that Elizabeth inherited was genuinely protestant is at once absorbing and unanswerable. One might further ask, as the historian Penry Williams has done, whether the population as a whole was 'in more than a nominal sense, Christian? How many adults understood the basic tenets of their Church? How many attended divine service regularly?' Different social groups and different regions had responded to protestantism in significantly different ways. The most remote areas were naturally least accessible to the reformers and so tended to retain their Catholicism longest, as the Highlands of Scotland did while the Lowlands were eagerly following John Knox to a radical and Calvinist form of protestantism. In England, Lancashire remained the great Catholic stronghold, while London and the south-east, the Thames valley, Kent and East Anglia, traditionally highly populated and exactly those areas where Wycliffite and Lollard dissent had been strongest, were most actively protestant. Over the rest of the countryside, much depended on the inclinations of each particular parish priest: Margaret Spufford, in her study of Fenland villages, has shown how a popular reforming minister might lead his flock towards active involvement in the cause. Generally it was at the middle levels of society that the new beliefs made their strongest impact. William Malden, the Chelmsford shopkeeper quoted earlier, was typical of the yeomen, small-time business men, industrial workers and artisans who made up the ranks of their staunchest supporters. Urban conditions were favourable, since in towns contacts with new ideas were made more rapidly and sustained more easily. Catholicism, on the other hand, increasingly centred upon the old once-feudal household, often physically isolated, with a tradition of independence and internal loyalty. A substantial number of English converts were made among the families, servants and tenants of Catholic squires, whose households operated as Catholic cells where masses could be said and protection provided for the Catholic missionary priests who began to operate in England from the 1580s onwards.

Perhaps the widest range of religious beliefs was to be found among the upper classes, who had the easiest access to learning and the greatest opportunities for thought and study, doubtless combined with the greatest temptations to worldliness and sensual indulgence. Their ranks included men like Sir Philip Sidney and the Earl of Leicester, who were committed to supporting the protestant cause in Europe and promoting more radical and zealous ministers at home, as were the third and fourth Earls of Pembroke in the seventeenth century. At the opposite end of the spectrum were a number of great and influential aristocratic families like the Howards and the Petres who kept to the old faith; and with them many lesser gentry prepared to endure the severe financial penalties and loss of opportunity that this entailed. Although the court remained immensely varied and idiosyncratic in its beliefs, the fashionable protestantism of Elizabeth's reign gradually gave place to a fashionable Catholicism under the Stuarts which, in Charles's reign (1625–49), centred upon his wife Henrietta Maria and her French entourage, and contributed substantially to his increasing unpopularity.

The exiles back from the Continent to endorse Elizabeth's church settlement of 1559 returned with more than a commitment to Calvin's theories of predestination and an admiration for his well-ordered city on Lake Geneva. They brought two books with which to establish the new faith – the Calvinistic Geneva Bible (1560), the translation most widely used by Shakespeare and his contemporaries, and the Latin prototype of England's first martyrology, subsequently to be known as John Foxe's *Acts and Monuments*, or simply Foxe's Book of Martyrs (1563). Apart from the Bible itself, this was the book most likely to be found in homes that had books right up to the nineteenth century. Foxe's compilation, which expanded greatly in later editions, did not merely set out to remind its readers of the sufferings of those persecuted for the protestant faith under Henry VIII and his daughter Mary. It fitted them into a wider eschatology which expected the Second Coming and regarded zealous protestants as God's chosen people, with a vital role to play in the establishment of the reign of the blessed on earth. It was a short step from here to that crudely chauvinistic pride in the Anglican church voiced by Lyly in *Euphues and his England* (1580): 'Oh blessed peace, oh happy prince, oh fortunate people: the living God is only the English God.' Much of Foxe's scheme derived from current protestant interpretations of St John's Book of Revelation, which was read as a symbolic account of Christian history culminating in a prophecy of the end of the world, with the conversion of the Jews, the thousand-year reign of the saints on earth (the millennium), even the Second Coming of Christ Himself. The symbolic gestures witnessed by St John – the sounding of the seven trumpets, the breaking of the seven seals and the rest – were explained as particular historical or contemporary incidents in the continuing struggle with Rome, commonly identified with St John's Scarlet Woman of Babylon on her Great Beast, its seven heads associated with the city's seven hills, or simply with Antichrist. While there was no agreed timetable for this sequence of events, many committed protestants between 1550 and 1650 felt themselves to be participating in the beginning of the end of the world, and it lent a special urgency to their demands. Spenser, the great poet of the protestant imagination, naturally gives this vision priority of place in his epic *The Faerie Queene*. The first book presents the historical, theological and psychological struggles of the English nation, as represented by St George the Redcross Knight, against the wiles of Rome, figured as Archimago and Duessa, the Scarlet Woman. With the help of Una, the true faith, St John's woman clothed with the sun, he finally overcomes the dragon and is granted a glimpse of the New Jerusalem, reminiscent of that in the Apocalypse. Not everyone was convinced by such identifications. Richard Hooker criticized the tendency to identify all older rituals as 'borrowed from the shop of Antichrist' and commented wryly of the reformers, 'Nothing more clear unto their seeming, than that a New Jerusalem being often spoken of in Scripture, they undoubtedly were themselves that New Jerusalem'. Ben Jonson reduced such pretensions to a moment of wonderful comic bathos when, in *The Alchemist*, his puritan deacon Ananias denounces Surly who has unluckily disguised himself in Spanish costume – his Spanish 'slops' or trousers become

> 'profane,
> Lewd, superstitious, and idolatrous breeches! . . .
> Thou look'st like *Antichrist*, in that lewd hat.'   (IV. ii. 48–9, 55)

The interpretation of the struggle with Rome in terms of the Apocalypse did not merely look forward to a glorious future; it also involved the establishment of an ersatz pedigree for the English protestant church, in part as an answer to those who asked, in Hooker's phrase, 'where our church did lurk, in what cave of the earth it slept for so many hundreds of years together before the birth of Martin Luther?' Although King Lucius was traditionally credited with bringing Christianity to Britain, Foxe dates this further back, to Joseph of Arimathea. Spenser, referring to Lucius in *The Faerie Queene*, follows Foxe:

> 'Yet true it is that long before that day
> Hither came Joseph of Arimathy,
> Who brought with him the Holy Grail, (they say)
> And preached the truth, but since it greatly did decay.'   (II. x. 53)

Joseph and the disciples of the Apostle Philip were credited with the establishment of a true church here long before the Roman missionaries, who merely muddied the waters of this earlier and purer faith. After Gregory the Great, the church sadly declined and when the millennium after Christ's birth ended, in accordance with the supposed numerology of Revelation, Antichrist was once more released on the world, taking Peter's throne at Rome as his own, and true faith was driven into the wilderness. Certain English kings had stood out against him, notably Henry II and John, who rather implausibly became an early protestant martyr. Foxe includes a dramatic strip-cartoon of John being poisoned by the evil monk, Simon of Swinstead. More recently the battle had been fought out by Tyndale, Frith and the protestant martyrs, Ridley, Latimer, Cranmer and others who had died at Mary's hands, witnesses to the truth of the English protestant cause.

In Foxe's view history did not merely exemplify the mystic truths of Revelation. It also manifested God's providence in the form of active intervention on behalf of His elect who, like the Israelites of old, could expect to succeed as long as they adhered to the true faith. Protestant confidence in adversity depended on the conviction that no enemy could prevail over them if God was with them. For some at least, clear evidence of God's divine purpose for the Anglican church was provided by the defeat of the Armada in 1588 and the timely discovery of the Gunpowder Plot to blow up King and parliament in 1605. These were commonly interpreted as providential, since important events embodying Catholic threats to security were involved; but God's hand might further be detected wherever one looked, in the patterns of individual lives. Books of judgements became popular, one of the most widely read being that of Thomas Beard, later tutor to the young Oliver Cromwell. His *Theatre of God's Judgements* (1597) gives a characteristic account of the death of that naughty play-maker and supposed atheist, Christopher Marlowe.

But see what a hook the Lord put in the nostrils of this barking dog: it so fell out, that as he purposed to stab one whom he owed a grudge unto with his dagger, the other party perceiving, so avoided the stroke, that withal catching hold of his wrist, he stabbed his own dagger into his own head, in such sort, that notwithstanding all the means of surgery that could be wrought, he shortly after died thereof: the manner of his death being so terrible (for he even cursed and blasphemed to his last gasp, and together with his breath an oath flew out of his mouth) that it was not only a manifest sign of God's Judgement, but also an horrible and fearful terror to all that beheld him.

Despite Beard's disapproval of play-makers and poets of scurrility, he here shows himself influenced by (and, in his turn, influencing) dramatic writing. The use of the word 'theatre' in his title is in no way accidental, for this view of life makes God the supreme dramatist, fitting the punishment to the crime so that the atheist and blasphemer dies appropriately gasping out curses with his last breath. Thirty years earlier, the tragic interlude of *King Cambises* had presented the angry tyrant impaled on his own sword in the final tableau, so that he appeared as a living – or rather, dying – emblem of the deadly sin of wrath, traditionally pierced with his own weapon. Marlowe's *Jew of Malta* has the Jew finally fall in his own cauldron of boiling oil, thus anticipating the standard punishment for usurers in hell; while in 1609 Tourneur showed men the hand of

God exemplified in the death of the atheist D'Amville who, like Marlowe and Cambises, dies on his own weapon, splitting his head open with the axe with which he is attempting to execute the patient hero. Another popular book of judgements, *The Triumphs of God's Revenge Against The Crying and Execrable Sin of . . . Murder*, written by a puritan merchant of Exeter, John Reynolds, supplied Middleton with the plot of *The Changeling*.

One significance of Foxe's providential history was that it created a sort of instant ancestry and tradition for the English church. The age's excessive respect for the authority of the past demanded precedents for everything, and this was all the more important where the church was concerned, since its claims to direct men's lives partly depended on the recognition of its continuity with the missions instituted by Christ's disciples. The English church consisted of an anomalous mixture of Calvinist theology and largely Catholic hierarchy and liturgy, though the latter had been translated into the vernacular and adjusted to suit the new tenets – salvation by faith alone, the denial of free will (but see p. 72) and an emphasis on the Bible rather than the priesthood as the foremost purveyor of religious truths. The use of modified forms of the old service as perpetuated by the Book of Common Prayer (1549, 1552, the latter edition being substantially that used under Elizabeth) as well as the system of church government through bishops and archbishops (as opposed to that of lay elders proposed by Calvin) occasioned much resentment among ardent reformers, who saw these as idolatrous or popish relics. By far the most powerful and comprehensive defence of this characteristically English compromise was composed by Richard Hooker, whose book *Of the Laws of Ecclesiastical Polity* (1593) constructs a magnificent edifice based on the concept of universal and natural order, and controlled at every level by appeals to moderation and common sense. For Hooker, as for many later Anglican apologists, the church's strength lay in its being a *via media*, a middle way that could take advantage of the best elements in both the old religion and the new. Though Hooker was exceptionally tolerant and humane for his age, much of his discourse inevitably condemns the extremes of papists and reformers in favour of a third way, as in his consideration of scriptural authority:

Two opinions therefore there are concerning sufficiency of Holy Scripture, each extremely opposite unto the other, and both repugnant unto truth.

By the seventeenth century this account was so well established that George Herbert in his poem 'The British Church' could characterize the overdressed wanton church of Rome, and the shy naked reformed church, dismissing them both in favour of a third alternative:

> But, dearest Mother, what those miss,
> The mean, thy praise and glory is,
>   And long may be.
> Blessed be God, whose love it was
> To double-moat thee with His grace,
>   And none but thee.

Of the seven original sacraments of the Roman church, Luther had acknowledged only two, baptism and communion. While the former was generally accepted within the English church, the latter occasioned unending arguments as to its exact significance, though it was increasingly regarded in a symbolic light, to be taken in remembrance of the crucifixion rather than the literal eating and drinking of God's flesh and blood. Communion was normally administered at a table placed at the crossways of the church, and there was further argument as to whether the communicant should kneel or whether he might not stand or even walk about, a habit that shocked traditionalists. Only later was Laud (see p. 81) to replace the communion table with an altar at the east end, a change that has survived to the present but which aroused the deepest resentment at the time. Behind the arguments over kneeling communicants lay the whole question of the role of priests as administrants. Anxious to avoid any suggestion of magical powers in that office, the protestant church allowed them to marry like everyone else, referred to them as pastors or ministers instead of priests, and considered that their function was to bring men to God by persuasion, rather than transformation, to act as evangelists opening men's hearts to His Word; the good clergyman was thus required to be a preaching clergyman. The endowment of preachers and lecturers and the encouragement of religious discussions in the forms of conferences and prophesyings were causes dear to the reformers' hearts. The prophesyings were the occasion of a serious quarrel between Elizabeth and her newly appointed Archbishop of Canterbury, Edmund Grindal, in 1576. These seem to have begun as teaching sessions for the clergy, at which a sermon was preached and a text expounded, with the participants later asking questions and raising particular points. Increasingly, lay audiences wished to join in, coming with their Bibles and later on their wives and servants to something that on occasion resembled a great open-air teach-in (see p. 102). In Elizabeth's eyes such large meetings were undesirable, and she was unhappy about the doctrines taught and the disputatious tendencies thus encouraged. To her insistence that they be banned, however, her Primate found as high-handed a response:

Remember, Madam, that you are a mortal creature. 'Look not only . . . upon the purple and princely array, wherewith ye are apparelled, but consider withal what is that that is covered therewith. Is it not flesh and blood? Is it not dust and ashes? Is it not a corruptible body, which must return to his earth again, God knoweth how soon?' . . . And although ye are a mighty prince, yet remember that He which dwelleth in heaven is mightier.

Elizabeth was not accustomed to such frankness, one consequence of appointing men of intellect and integrity to high office. Grindal was suspended from his office, though not actually deprived of it, and never exercised his functions again. Spenser, an admirer of Grindal, introduced him and his downfall into *The Shepheardes Calendar* (1579) in May and July, thinly disguised as 'Algrin'. Thomalin describes how an eagle (presumably the Queen) dropped a shellfish on his head, thinking its baldness was chalk –

> So now astonied with the stroke,
> He lies in ling'ring pain.

To which Morrell optimistically (if flatly) replies

> Ah good Algrin, his hap was ill,
> But shall be better in time.

Spenser's curious allegory carefully avoids putting the blame on the Queen, whose patronage he hoped for, but it cannot quite ignore this disturbing episode altogether.

Disapproval of church vestments (effectively the surplice only, for the rest were no longer used) was another expression of the desire to reduce the clergyman to the same level as his flock in all external aspects. Calvinist church government, adopted by the presbyterian Church of Scotland, did away with bishops altogether; the laity itself, or rather a committee of elders amongst them, selected the minister. In England this was felt to be a particularly dangerous demand, for though the conferring of such responsibility on laymen obviously promoted active involvement in the church, at the same time it provided a model of self-determination far more democratic than the state afforded, and the attack on bishops tended to be thought of as an attack on hierarchy on a wider front. Yet despite strong impulses to reform church government from within, especially in the 1570s (which Hooker's *Laws of Ecclesiastical Polity* set out to counteract), bishops like Hooper, Latimer, Ridley and Cranmer had been enrolled in the list of Marian martyrs, while a committed protestant Primate like Edmund Grindal tended to reinforce traditional respect for the office. Elizabeth and James (who unlike his predecessor was a Calvinist) had both governed a protestant church in which those eager for reform, while pressing for changes, still envisaged the possibility that these might be achieved under the auspices of the established church. There had been bishops like Bancroft, who disliked and distrusted the reformers and preached against them, but he had failed to dislodge them on any significant scale. It took a man of very different tastes and temperament to discredit the Archbishopric of Canterbury in the eyes of militant protestants: William Laud, Bishop of London from 1628 and Primate from 1633, by reversing previous policies on church ritual and attacking Calvinist predestinarian theology, was to alienate their sympathies entirely.

There was, however, a significant group of radical sectarians who had never participated in Elizabeth's Anglican church. Known as separatists or nonconformists, these included Anabaptists, who insisted on adult baptism and had been associated with the notorious Münster episode (see p. 39); Familists, who belonged to the Family of Love, founded by a Dutchman, Henry Niclaes; as well as a group of English exiles who had sought greater religious freedom in the Netherlands, and were usually known as the Amsterdam Brethren. The eccentric practices of these sects were a favourite target for jokes both by the right and left wings of the church, the former simply finding them antipathetic, the latter seeing their fanaticism as liable to bring their own reforming enthusiasms into disrepute by association – rather as socialists fear to be labelled communists today. Jonson pilloried the Amsterdam Brethren as 'the exiled saints' in *The Alchemist*, where their deacon Ananias and pastor Tribulation Wholesome are presented as shameless crooks and hypocrites. Entrusted with the goods of the widows and orphans, they embezzle them in the deluded hope that Subtle can convert them not merely into gold but into Dutch dollars with which to perpetuate the religious wars in the Netherlands – a topical aspiration, since a truce had been concluded between Spain and the Netherlands in 1609, and the play was staged in the following year. John Marston, in his play *The Dutch Courtezan*, makes another hypocrite, Mrs Mulligrub the vintner's wife, a Familist – not implausibly since that sect seems to have flourished among city merchants; while Thomas Middleton (who might reasonably be characterized as strongly protestant in outlook) wrote a play entitled *The Family of Love*, which presents the prayer meetings of that sect as a cover for sexual orgies – by then a well-worn jest. Spenser's contempt for the Anabaptist giant in Book V of *The Faerie Queene* (see p. 37) provides a comparable dismissal.

A very different view of the persecutions that drove them to cross the Atlantic in search of religious freedom is, however, provided by the early American settlers themselves. William Bradford in his *History of Plymouth Plantation* (written *c.*1630–50) described how 'some were taken and clapped up in prison, others had their houses beset and watched night and day'. On one particularly harrowing occasion a barge full of women and children who were going to meet their husbands to escape to the Netherlands ran aground, so that they were forced to look on helplessly as a party of soldiers arrived by land and frightened off the ship with their husbands on board, which turned and set sail for the Netherlands without them. They were thus stranded without money or clothes:

what weeping and crying on every side, some for their husbands that were carried away ... others not knowing what should become of them and their little ones; others again melted in tears seeing their poor little ones hanging about them, crying for fear and quaking with cold.

Closer inspection reveals the plight of the separatists to have been far from comic.

If various forms of protestantism and nonconformism spread among ordinary people rather like a virus in the bloodstream, the once established religion of Catholicism at first found it hard to adapt to its outlawed position, and it took a while before the missionary priests learnt to fight protestantism with its own weapons. Until then, Catholicism flourished largely under the protection of certain members of the gentry whose households were big enough to maintain an independent status and religious services according to the old forms, perhaps with their own chaplain to administer them. Elizabeth's formal excommunication by the Pope in 1570 occasioned a sharp increase in the measures taken against the old faith, since this act implied that the forces of international Catholicism refused to recognize her right to govern. It made England a potential target for internal sedition and foreign (effectively Spanish) invasion. Fines for failing to attend church (i.e. recusancy) were stepped up sharply and these were incurred in addition to other penalties that debarred Catholics from taking university degrees or holding state offices. A significant number of gentry preferred to attend services rather than pay crippling fines, believing external conformity to be unimportant or seeing in it a gesture of loyalty to the state, while maintaining their spiritual independence by receiving the old sacraments at home with their household. John Earle in *Microcosmographie* (1628) provides a satirical portrait of 'A Church-Papist' who, when he kneels with the congregation, 'asks God forgiveness for coming thither. If he be forced to stay out a sermon, he pulls his hat over his eyes, and frowns out the hour; and when he comes home, thinks to make amends for this fault by abusing the preacher.' Though Earle leaves his caricature 'hatching plots against the state', the Catholic gentry as a whole remained remarkably loyal to Elizabeth, despite the discrimination against them, and at the end of her reign a group of secular priests made a joint protestation of allegiance to her. Loyalty, or perhaps the fear of a stronger anti-papist backlash, induced a certain quietism, so that when missionaries began to visit England from the late 1570s, eager to spread the word and inspire a less compromising zeal in the faithful, though many welcomed and protected them, some feared that their activities would destabilize what up till then had at least been a tolerable situation. Though life was far from easy for the Catholics, government policy was mainly one of deterrence, except in Ireland and where the emigrant missionary priests were concerned.

At Elizabeth's accession a number of prominent Catholic clergymen had fled abroad. Among them had been William Allen, later Cardinal, who in 1568 founded a seminary at Douai to train Englishmen as priests so that the old religion might be maintained and even advanced in this country. It was gradually recognized that these priests would have to practise the active infiltrating and proselytizing techniques that up till then had been the exclusive territory of protestantism. The seminary priests who soon began to arrive in England to spread their mission exploited these new methods to powerful effect, preaching, writing and disseminating their beliefs wherever they went, as Greene's glancing reference to Father Person's 'book of *Resolution*' in the pamphlet describing his own repentance suggests. Catholic devotional literature seems to have been widely read and conversions were undoubtedly made, and not merely among those who had long lived abroad, like the poet Henry Constable or the composer John Dowland. Ben Jonson was converted by a priest in a London prison, and the protestant clergyman and poet William Alabaster became a Catholic, although after some difficult years in Rome he reverted to his original faith and ended his days in a country parsonage: such changes of heart were not always permanent.

The effective spiritual activities of the missionary priests gave the government one cause for concern, but their possible political activities were even more worrying. They were suspected, not always without justification, of acting as foreign agents for Spain and the Pope, and encouraging treasons, plotting the overthrow of Elizabeth and her replacement by a Catholic ruler – either Mary, Queen of Scots or some other claimant. Certainly the missionary colleges such as Douai or the Jesuit English College at Rome shared with international Catholicism the aim of reclaiming England for the church by whatever means were available. Jesuits were particularly suspect because of the Order's Spanish origins and the myth that they were actively engaged in promoting a world-wide Catholic conspiracy. The government reacted with a series of vicious persecutions, encouraging agents to pursue, entrap and torture the unfortunate missionary priests, who were liable to be publicly disembowelled and hanged, while those who afforded them shelter were imprisoned: John Donne's younger brother died while thus confined. Nothing can extenuate the brutality of such policies, which typified the intense religious intolerance of the age.

Fears of Catholic treason were obviously increased by Spanish aggression abroad, and at home by incidents such as the Babington Plot (1586), which attempted to set Mary Stuart on the throne, or the Gunpowder Plot of 1605. The years immediately preceding 1588, when Philip II launched his Armada in a misguided attempt to invade England, were particularly tense as his plans were known to

include a massive Catholic uprising, which in the event came to
nothing. The previous year at Deventer in the Netherlands Sir
William Stanley, an officer in Leicester's army fighting the Spanish,
had declared his loyalty to the old faith by handing over the town he
had taken and his own troops (who were mainly Irish) to the
Spaniards. Such an action aroused great uneasiness, and Cardinal
Allen's defence of Stanley on the grounds that there was no Catholic
obligation to keep faith with a heretic and excommunicate like
Elizabeth scarcely retrieved the situation. The dangerous implications of this argument, which might be advanced to persuade
Catholics to break their Oath of Supremacy to the Queen, clearly
interested Marlowe, who promptly incorporated them into his next
play, *Tamburlaine Part II*. Baldwin, Lord of Bohemia, here persuades the Catholic King Sigismund of Hungary to break the truce
he has sworn with the pagan Orcanes, King of Natolia on the
grounds that

> 'In whom no faith nor true religion rests,
> We are not bound to these accomplishments
> The holy laws of Christendom enjoin.'
> (II. ii. 34–6)

The Jew of Malta, extensively concerned with breaking oaths, bonds
and obligations in the cause of self-interest, gives the Jew an absurd
echo of Cardinal Allen's position when he argues with his daughter
Abigail

> 'It's no sin to deceive a Christian;
> For they themselves hold it a principle,
> Faith is not to be held with heretics:
> But all are heretics that are not Jews.
> This follows well, and therefore, daughter, fear not.'
> (II. iii. 307–11)

The Reformation had involved an extensive rejection of the rich
iconographical traditions of Catholicism, bringing to an end the
mystery plays and church pageants which had been such an enjoy-
able and enlivening feature of town life. It was chiefly Catholic
poets, with their direct access to the cancelled past, who would
perpetuate the great tradition of English religious poetry in the age
of Elizabeth. There was no obvious alternative to the moving
imagery of Catholicism, which was only gradually reassimilated into
poetry in the seventeenth century, although the language and

imagery of the church were preserved, to a considerable extent, in the Book of Common Prayer and the various translations of the Bible. Here, if anywhere, the protestant creative impulse is most clearly exemplified, in the tradition beginning with Tyndale (whose New Testament was published abroad in 1525), and passing through Coverdale's continuation and the Geneva Bible (see p. 74) to culminate in the King James Bible or Authorized Version of 1611. The balanced clauses of the latter and its graceful, if already somewhat archaic forms (reflecting an extensive dependence on earlier translations), contributed enormously and enduringly to English prose. Its language conferred dignity on religious and secular ceremonial, and helped to impart a new power, elegance and formality to English as a whole. At the same time, the vernacular Bible possessed an idiomatic vitality and immediacy that the fossilized Latin tongue could never have achieved. Any biblical translation, simply by being couched in the familiar language of everyday life, could push its message home far more directly than the unknown or uncurrent language of the Vulgate (St Jerome's Latin Bible). By the choice of individual words or phrases, a particular translation could, of course, move nearer or further from its readers' everyday experiences, and thus acts as a criticism or endorsement of contemporary theology. Tyndale's version remained the most radical: his translation of the Greek 'ecclesia' as congregation, rather than church, of 'presbyter' as senior or elder, rather than priest, meant that a reader would find little correspondence between the religious observances with which he was familiar, and the actual words of his Bible.

Translation was not to remain a protestant monopoly, however: the English College at Douai, temporarily housed at Rheims, printed their own English translation of the New Testament in 1582, under the direction of Cardinal Allen; it drew on the Geneva Bible and in turn made its contribution to the final wording of the Authorized Version. In this, as in several other Catholic initiatives occurring in response to demands for reform, there was some tendency to recapitulate protestant moves, though inevitably in quite a different way. The Counter-Reformation was also to lay stress on the importance of the individual's relation to God. In the following century the Jansenists were to recall Calvinist doctrine in minimizing the operation of free will, just as Arminian protestantism began to reassert it.

In one respect the tradition of translation fed back into Elizabethan poetry: protestants had replaced Catholic hymns with psalm singing, to some extent, so that making metrical versions of the psalms could be regarded as a pious undertaking when a sonnet on the crucifixion might seem a more dubious exercise. Sir Thomas Wyatt, at the court of Henry VIII, had composed metrical psalms, and Henry Howard, Earl of Surrey, followed his example, praising Wyatt's versions enthusiastically in another sonnet. Sir Philip Sidney also versified psalms, and John Donne wrote in praise of them. But poems on the great traditional Christian themes, the incidents of the life of Christ, Peter's remorse and Magdalen's tears, the Virgin and the Saints, tended, under Elizabeth, to be the hallmark of a Catholic imagination and are best exemplified in the movingly simple, deliberately old-fashioned poems of the Jesuit priest Robert Southwell, who was executed in 1596, and may have written them in prison. The sonnets of Henry Constable and William Alabaster, composed after their conversions, possibly partly as religious exercises, make use of similar themes. So does the poetry of John Donne, the age's most notable convert to the established church, although his imagination remained fundamentally Catholic and Counter-Reformation in its graphic realization of central Christian events and experiences.

Donne's family were ardent Catholics. His mother was Anne Heywood, daughter of John Heywood the playwright and friend of Thomas More, the memory of whose martyrdom remained as an inspiration to religious fervour within the family. It is not known exactly when Donne conformed to the Anglican church though it was presumably fairly early in his career; in his pamphlet *Pseudo-Martyr* (1610) he explains 'I used no inordinate haste nor precipitation in binding my conscience to any local religion.' His third Satire, perhaps the most passionate and moving poem on the choice of religion ever written, is nevertheless strongly opposed to the acceptance of 'any local religion' merely because it is imposed by the state. God has not

> Signed kings blank-charters to kill whom they hate,
> Nor are they vicars, but hangmen to Fate.
> Fool and wretch, wilt thou let thy soul be tied
> To man's laws, by which she shall not be tried
> At the last day? (91–5)

The poem is filled with bitterness and contempt for religious hatred and wars – they seem merely to provide opportunities for aggression that conveniently divert men's attention from their true spiritual state. Such intolerance resembles the absurd behaviour of gallants:

> must every he
> Which cries not, 'Goddess!' to thy mistress, draw,
> Or eat thy poisonous words?   (26–8)

Both here, and in his Holy Sonnet XVIII ('Show me dear Christ, thy spouse, so bright and clear'), the different churches are characterized as different kinds of women, flaunting or concealing their attractions. A distaste for religious persecution also seems to underlie Donne's early theological writings in which he attacks the Jesuits for what he sees as their trouble-making and provocation (*Ignatius his Conclave*, 1611) and urges Catholics to take the Oath of Supremacy rather than make martyrs of themselves (*Pseudo-Martyr*, 1610).

The enduring lessons of his Catholic upbringing enabled Donne, more than any other poet of his time, to draw back into the mainstream of English religious verse the kinds of image and analogy that had largely been in abeyance in the sixteenth century. Some of his allusions in 'The Canonization', 'The Relic' and perhaps 'The Ecstasy', references to pilgrimages and priests, saints and candles, are lighthearted enough, the discarded remnants of a discredited church. Yet the habit of mingling amatory and religious imagery has a long history in English poetry and might be easier to dismiss if it did not overflow into Donne's deeply felt religious sonnets, as in XIII, 'What if this present were the world's last night?', with its analogy between Christ's mercy and that imputed to his 'profane mistresses'. The subject matter of the sonnet group *La Corona* (the main events of Christ's life) and the stanzas on the Trinity, the Virgin, angels, apostles etc. that make up *A Litany* are profoundly traditional. Donne's protestant disciples were once more to move freely and without restriction among such images. Moreover the sense of drama and conflict that was so much a part of his poetic temperament was well suited to the increasingly dynamic quality of spiritual life as men now began to experience it, and to which the developing art of autobiography in the seventeenth century bears witness. Donne's religious poetry moves tormentedly between the blackness of his sins and his hopes for their forgiveness, while George Herbert, strongly influenced by Donne's example, both in life and art, describes the poems that make up *The Temple* (1633) as giving 'a picture of the many spiritual conflicts that have passed betwixt God and my soul, before I could subject mine to the will of Jesus my master'. A modern reader may find greater tranquillity than Herbert's phrase suggests, partly because the courteous and graceful manner in which the poet dresses his discontents can be deceptive.

Both Herbert and Donne were, in the latter part of their lives, engaged in preaching sermons as well as composing religious poetry. Donne, once he had finally accepted the necessity of taking orders (and he did so with apparent reluctance), quickly rose in the church through his riveting eloquence in the pulpit, ending as Dean of St Paul's. His sermons, much enjoyed by King James, show a responsiveness to the relationships between words and the ideas implicit in them which is also in evidence in his poetry: for example in the punning, in English and Latin, on the phrase *'per fretum febris'* (meaning through the stresses of fever or through tropical straits) in his 'Hymn to God my God, in my Sickness', or on his own name in 'A Hymn to God the Father':

> When thou hast done, thou hast not done,
> For, I have more.

At this period, puns were not regarded as the accidental or trivial resemblances that they are today but rather seen as the outer indication of some inner affinity or meaning that was not necessarily either comic or to be unthinkingly dismissed. A mystery might be expounded from them, as Lancelot Andrewes, another great Anglican preacher, was to do with the notion of Christ's infancy, the Word made flesh, itself 'in-fans', that is, not yet able to speak.

What, *Verbum infans*, the Word of an infant? The Word, and not be able to speak a word? How evil agreeth this! This He put up.

The habit of glossing a text, which all clerics were trained to do, and of explaining and enlarging upon its meaning is apparent in the movement backwards and forwards from Latin phrases which is so much a part of Donne's preaching technique as well. Here he describes birth as an escape from the threat of stillbirth:

But then this *exitus a morte*, is but *introitus in mortem*, this *issue*, this deliverance *from* that *death*, the death of the *womb*, is an *entrance*, a delivering over to *another death*, the manifold deaths of this *world*. We have a winding sheet in our mother's womb, which grows with us from our conception, and we come into the world, wound up in that *winding sheet*, for we come to *seek a grave*.   ('Death's Duel', 1630)

The precise attention given to the use and meaning of particular words to be found in the sermons of Donne and Lancelot Andrewes parallels the contemporary vogue for metaphysical poetry, although they were not composed in any frivolous or trivial spirit. They were nevertheless markedly different from the homely outspoken sermons of Latimer that had inaugurated the protestant preaching tradition, and the reformers consequently disapproved of them, feeling that they pandered to a taste for elegant entertainment instead of expounding God's word plainly for the plain man to understand. Yet the many reformers who criticized these elaborate displays of verbal fireworks were often, in their own way, just as concerned to achieve a forceful rhetoric, even in the very act of denouncing that of their rivals:

The gold upon the pill may please the eye; but it profits not the patient. The paint upon the glass may feed the fancy, but the room is the darker for it. The sword of God's spirit can never wound so deep, as when it's plucked out of these gaudy scabbards. Nakedness . . . is the best garnishing and ornament the truth can have.

wrote Valentine Marshall. The fact that the Anglican minister George Herbert made much the same point in both his 'Jordan' poems and *A Priest to the Temple* should warn us that we are not dealing with a simple antithesis of 'Anglicans' and 'Puritans', in whatever sense these awkward terms are taken. Herbert here asserts that

The parson's method in handling of a text consists of two parts: first, a plain and evident declaration of the meaning of the text; and secondly, some choice observations drawn out of the whole text, as it lies entire and unbroken in the scripture itself. . . . Whereas the other way of crumbling a text into small parts . . . hath neither in it sweetness, nor gravity, nor variety, since the words apart are not scripture, but a dictionary.

The significant difference between the practice of Donne and Herbert can be explained in terms of the difference between Donne's smart London congregation, expecting something witty, and the remote parish near Salisbury where the courtly and highly sophisticated Herbert passed the last years of his life as a country parson. But plainness might be adopted anywhere. William Laud, in every respect opposed to the reformers, was an unexpected exponent of the plain style of preaching.

Donne recognized, perhaps more clearly than any other man of his age, that while choice of religion was the single most vital question in life, every organization from the family unit to the state itself competed to pre-empt that choice and pressurize the individual into a reassuring conformity with its own position. Refusal to acquiesce might in itself be considered threatening, since it implied that a particular belief could actually be wrong; yet on that belief might depend a limitless future existence. The energy and fervour with which religious disputes were conducted might convert a man to the opposite viewpoint from which he himself had started out: the well-known brothers William and John Reynolds, Anthony Wood recorded, began as Calvinist and Catholic respectively, and each argued himself into the other's position.

A different reaction might be to feel that there was some virtue in most forms of Christianity. Sir Thomas Browne, a physician of strong religious convictions, could write of Catholicism in his account of his faith, *Religio Medici* (1642),

We have reformed from them, not against them . . . there is between us one common name and appellation, one faith and necessary body of principles common to us both; and therefore I am not scrupulous to converse and live with them, to enter their churches in defect of ours, and either pray with them, or for them.

This more relaxed attitude is anticipated in some Jacobean drama. For Marlowe, Faustus cheeking the Pope and hiding his dinner is good for a laugh, while the dragonish Mephostophilis is bidden to

> 'Go, and return an old Franciscan friar,
> That holy shape becomes a devil best.'   (I. iii. 25–6)

Yet Shakespeare's Friar Lawrence in *Romeo and Juliet* is kind and well-meaning, even if rather inefficient, and Vincentio's monkish disguise in *Measure for Measure* confers on him an appropriate spiritual authority. A decade or two later, Friar Bonaventura in Ford's *'Tis Pity She's a Whore* is a generous and sympathetic figure, although the Cardinal and Papal Nuncio here misuse their status to lend their protection to an acknowledged murderer, Grimaldi.

Webster seems to voice a similar disapproval of the upper echelons of the Catholic priesthood in *The Duchess of Malfi*, with its stereotypically cunning and lecherous Cardinal; the dumbshow in which the Cardinal is installed in the armour of a soldier, and then proceeds to exile his sister, may distantly echo Erasmus's strictures against military popes. Yet the play's attitude to Catholicism as a whole is less clear-cut. The Duchess wishes to disguise her flight as a pilgrimage to Loreto, but her maid Cariola begs her to think of another, more secular destination,

> for, if you will believe me,
> I do not like this jesting with religion,
> This feigned pilgrimage.
> DUCHESS. Thou art a superstitious fool:
> Prepare us instantly for our departure.   (III. ii. 315–19)

While the Duchess gives the proper protestant comeback, there is nevertheless an uneasy feeling that this breezy dismissal is somehow slightly hubristic, as is her earlier claim, after her secular betrothal:

> 'What can the Church force more? . . .
> How can the Church build faster?'   (I. ii. 404, 407)

Although a church marriage would necessarily reach the ears of her evil brothers, the unsanctified union seems slightly squalid, and is clearly ill-fated even in a society in which the corruption of the clergy is so graphically revealed.

The alternative to feeling that there might be some truth in several forms of faith was to feel that there was none in any, and the rancorous theological disputes of the age obviously induced in a few hardy individuals a deep scepticism, perhaps even a thoroughgoing atheism. Shortly before Marlowe's death in 1593 his former companion and rival Richard Baines denounced him to the Privy Council for heresy and atheism. Some sentences from his list of Marlowe's supposed opinions may be discounted as the sort of thing that an anti-Catholic spy might be obliged to say in order to elicit his interlocutor's opinions, yet there remain a number of prurient suggestions as to the meaning of certain New Testament events that cannot so readily be dismissed:

That Christ was a bastard and his mother dishonest.

That the woman of Samaria and her sister were whores and that Christ knew them dishonestly.

That St John the Evangelist was bedfellow to Christ and leaned always in his bosom, that he used him as the sinners of Sodom.

There were also a number of early rationalist views that sort oddly with the theological conservatism of *Faustus*:

That the Indians and many authors of antiquity have assuredly written of above 16 thousand years agone whereas Adam is proved to have lived within 6 thousand years.
He affirmeth that Moyses was but a juggler and that one Heriots, being Sir W. Raleigh's man can do more than he.

and further, a cynicism traditionally attributed to Machiavelli,
That the first beginning of religion was only to keep men in awe.

Even if Marlowe believed such things (and it is not at all clear what he *did* believe), they were certainly not the sort of opinions that it was wise to express. Raleigh at his examination was accused, among other things, of scepticism as to whether there was an after-life and suggesting that the standard arguments for God's existence were circular. Though far less outrageous and subversive than Marlowe's views, according to Baines's deposition, such lines of thought were still considered dangerous.

With an increasingly wide range of religious outlooks now existing, men naturally tended to associate with those whose views they shared, but inevitably they met, mingled with and sometimes married those who held very different convictions, and one man's convictions might change startlingly in the course of a lifetime. It is always difficult to guess exactly which elements in his belief a person holds of first importance, and particular individuals do not always conform to a predictable pattern. For an Elizabethan, royalism and reforming zeal might go hand in hand, as they did for Sidney or Spenser. Sixty years later royalists faced reformers on the brink of civil war. A puritan propagandist like John Milton might accept many aspects of Calvinist teaching, yet as regards the freedom of the will he followed the doctrine of Arminius (see p. 72), a doctrine whose insensitive imposition had been partly responsible for splitting the reformers from the main body of the established church. Between the Elizabethan poets and Milton lay a not untroubled period in which the Anglican church, for all its anomalous compromises, began to find an identity and justification for itself in terms of a commonsensical middle way that avoided the stark alternatives of Roman Catholicism and German protestantism. Elizabeth may have seen herself as consciously steering her church between extremes, while James congratulated himself on his role as peacemaker and conciliator. 'To stand in the gap between puritanism and popery, the Scylla and Charybdis of ancient piety' has always been a valid Anglican ideal. Perhaps for a short time in the early seventeenth century such a compromise seemed tolerable, even workable. By 1625 the young King Charles had married a Catholic, that intransigent cleric William Laud was already a bishop, and in eight years' time would be Primate of England. The old church settlement was firmly set on a runaway course that would soon shake it to pieces.

4 Education

Most men of ages present so superstitiously do look on ages past, that the
authorities of the one exceed the reasons of the other.

To turn from a consideration of religion to one of education is to
realize how far the latter was intended to reinforce the former at
every level: the child's very first reading matter was his hornbook, a
wooden tablet on which a parchment sheet, mounted and covered
with a transparent layer of horn, provided an alphabet and the
Lord's Prayer; at the other end of the scale, after seven years at
university and two degrees, the scholar was ready to embark on the
crown of his labours, the Doctorate of Divinity, often a matter of a
further fourteen years' study. At every stage of the educational
process, religion was a pervasive influence. That this influence
extended beyond the mere content of education to the motivation to
obtain it has already been indicated: demands for the education of
both clergy and laity were central to the protestant church, and
became so for the Catholic church, with the launching of the
Counter-Reformation in the 1560s. The pious hope that all men
should be able to read their Bibles and understand what they found
there obviously helped to promote literacy, while one sector of
society at least was sufficiently educated to appreciate the literary
achievements of the 1580s and after, many of which were written in
popular forms, intended for wide audiences. Lawrence Stone has
described the expansion of education at this time as 'a quantitative
change of such magnitude that it can only be described as a revolution. . . . It may well be that seventeenth-century England was at all
levels the most literate society the world had ever known.' Yet such
an assertion may reflect the continuing impact of that age's
educational propaganda as much as its actual effects. Another
historian, David Cressy, is more sceptical, while conceding that

the bulk of the evidence, strengthened by literacy figures, points to the first two decades of Elizabeth's reign as a period of unusual educational excitement and achievement. It may be no coincidence that Shakespeare and his talented literary contemporaries were of school age at this time and that part of his audience was uniquely well educated.

John Shakespeare, the playwright's father, left no evidence that he could sign his own name, and, more disturbingly, nor did his grand-daughter Judith. William, on the other hand, while wearing his learning lightly, was impressively well-educated, and the range and scope of his knowledge is in part a tribute to the effectiveness of an Elizabethan grammar-school education. Jonson's gibe at Shakespeare's small Latin and less Greek can only be understood comparatively. Despite his lack of Greek, Shakespeare knew considerably more Latin than most of his modern readers, and probably read French and Italian as well, although he also made substantial use of certain translations, notably North's Plutarch. Increasingly the finest products of classical and modern culture were becoming available in English, intended primarily for comparatively uneducated readers, as the translators often indicated: Philemon Holland in his introduction to Pliny's *Natural History* (1601) explained that he had framed his pen 'to a mean and popular style', while Florio prefaced his translations from Montaigne (1603) by declaring that 'Learning cannot be too common, and the commoner the better.'

Today it is natural to assume that education works as a democratic force in society. Such an assumption was less widely held when the most privileged had the easiest access to it. It may even be that the expansion of education among the middle classes was connected with the growing differential between those who bettered, or at the least maintained, their positions, and those who failed to do so, falling back to the poverty line. Education was more and more considered a desirable attainment, and not merely among the God-fearing, but by the middle and upper classes more generally. Both Elizabeth and James were, in their different ways, ostentatiously learned; both helped to set a fashion for cultural pursuits at court which may have influenced upper-class attitudes to education decisively, encouraging the gentry to send their children to schools and universities in far greater numbers than before. Yet, despite a degree of missionary zeal, little or nothing of the educational revolution reached the very poor who made up the larger part of the population and who could not have spared the child labour nor afforded the various incidental

expenses involved. Though schooling, at any rate grammar schooling, was theoretically free, the costs of entering, and subsequently of
books, paper and other necessaries such as firewood or candles, were
normally borne by parents. For the silent and unrecorded majority
eking out an existence at subsistence level, schooling would have
seemed irrelevant to the day-to-day struggle to eat and keep warm, a
luxury as impossible and unthinkable as a regular diet of meat.

It is tempting, but also misleading, to identify the demand for
education too exclusively with the reformers' programme. The
Middle Ages had seen a gradual, sometimes perceptible movement
towards secularization in which hopes that education might refine
both society and the individual figured with increasing importance;
such hopes were to fuel the Reformation as much as they fed on it.
Despite the unstable political conditions created by the Wars of the
Roses, the fifteenth century saw an expansion in English secular
education, measured in terms of the number of schools founded;
these were often paid for by guilds, as was the Stratford-upon-Avon
grammar school, established in the 1480s. By the early sixteenth
century, Sir Thomas More estimated that 60 per cent of the population was literate. Though this must be an exaggeration (even
allowing for the usual superiority, in this respect, of a London
sample) it is a useful reminder that the reformers consistently tended
to underestimate what the society they hoped to alter had already
achieved. In fact, the immediate result of the Reformation was to
throw the educational system − like so much else − into confusion.
But in its wake came a strong conviction that education was a high
priority, in part expressed by an increase in educational endowments. By 1577 William Harrison could write in his *Description of
England*

there are not many corporate towns now under the Queen's dominion that
hath not one grammar school at the least with a sufficient living for a master
and usher appointed to the same.

Shakespeare's generation, the first to be born and grow up in the
comparative stability of Elizabeth's reign, were its first obvious
beneficiaries. Although many of his literary contemporaries were,
like Shakespeare himself, the sons of artisans, their cultivated tastes
and attitudes reflect the virtues of a sound humanist education.

It was the fifteenth-century Catholic humanists, rather than the
protestant reformers, who laid the foundations for the kind of

education provided in Elizabethan schools. For the humanists, a central feature of the Italian Renaissance had been the reappraisal of classical literature and the rediscovery of a number of previously lost texts, chiefly in Greek, most notably those of Plato. Greek scholars and manuscripts were eagerly sought after in Florence, and intensive study led to a more critical and historical approach to antique literature at every level. One consequence of this was the recognition that Latin had changed considerably, even degenerated, since that model stylist Cicero had used it. The writing of correct (i.e. Ciceronian) Latin soon became one of the new educational goals, while Cicero himself was increasingly held up for admiration not merely as an example of good style but also of good morals (some purists were inclined to equate the two). Like Seneca, he had attempted to lead a life of integrity and moral rectitude within a corrupt society, and the humanists tended to see in this an equivalent to their own predicament. Roman and Greek authors began to be cited as moral authorities with fewer reservations as to their pagan status, while both their style and their moral content became the subjects of extensive imitation.

The close attention this involved inevitably conferred a more thorough and detailed understanding of the classical past than before, though from our incomparably greater historical perspective the real advances of the fifteenth and sixteenth century in this respect still tend to look naïve. Renaissance translations of the classics often blur what we would regard as significant distinctions between their own society and that of the ancients: pagan priests appear as bishops, *eques* or cavalry as knights. The one surviving drawing of a production of Shakespeare's *Titus Andronicus* shows that Roman dress on the Elizabethan stage included doublet, trunk hose, and farthingale, as well as the classical helmet and breastplate. Yet in its way this represented a considerable advance on those medieval manuscripts which portrayed Ovid's lovers dressed entirely in contemporary fashions, bewimpled and liripiped. Italian paintings and sculpture, like Elizabethan book illustrations, reveal a substantial knowledge of Roman life and costume. To judge one society's familiarity with another in terms of the accuracy with which it can reproduce its external features is necessarily superficial, particularly when the Renaissance artists' concentration on classical models has been taken into account; yet Shakespeare's Roman plays reveal a grasp of classical culture and values unparalleled in earlier writing. Their extraordinarily convincing account of Roman attitudes and policies could spring only from a powerfully well-informed act of historical imagination. So compelling is this vision that it is often difficult to conceive the episodes Shakespeare dramatized in any other terms.

Closer reading of classical authors, together with a greater knowledge of Roman society and its workings, perhaps helped as much as did the discoveries of the New World to create a sense of the relative; of the difference between one society and another, providing inner horizons against which one's own narrow conditions might be measured. It was no accident that the great sixteenth-century relativists revealed themselves to be deeply absorbed in classical culture, as Shakespeare did in his Roman plays, and as Rabelais and Montaigne had also done in their different ways. The latter had Latin and Greek quotations inscribed on the beams of the tower to which he retired, and his essays everywhere bespeak an easy familiarity with the great classical authors, their judgements being set beside his own and treated as the opinions of old and valued friends. Such intimacy with the classics is especially characteristic of the Renaissance, which was completed so late in England that this feature is still apparent in Jonson, Robert Burton or Sir Thomas Browne. In northern Europe its greatest exponent had been Erasmus, who moved among the classical authors as a man might pass among the members of his club. Following Petrarch's example, he had laid particular stress on the moral and ethical qualities to be found in them: it was primarily on these grounds that he advocated and justified their study. In Erasmus's opinion the great pagan authors had much to teach as to how everyday life might be conducted with virtue and integrity. He suggested that perhaps their hearts were moved by some divine power, and in his colloquy *Convivium Religiosum*, 1522 (The Godly Feast) Eusebius describes how reading Cicero sometimes prompted him to 'kiss the book and bless that pure heart, divinely inspired as it was', while another speaker, Nephalius, referring to Socrates' heroic death, admits 'When I read such things of such men, I can hardly help exclaiming, "Saint Socrates, pray for us!"' For Erasmus, Socrates was a secular saint, a man who had willingly surrendered his life in defence of his own fine principles.

The much-quoted phrase 'Saint Socrates' was probably intended to tease those narrow-minded clerics for whom the unbaptized

Socrates was eternally condemned. Erasmus though it no worse than some of the superstitious prayers to obscure saints whom he considered scarcely better than pagan deities. No one was more sharply critical of ignorance nor more convinced of the need for a renewed faith and education based on genuine understanding, rather than pattering automatically through rote-learned prayers or grammar rules. Mechanical repetition all too easily deprived religious services or educational experience of the necessary stimuli to thought or involvement. Criticisms of existing teaching methods had, of course, been made before Erasmus but never with such wit and incisiveness, nor did they have the printing press to disseminate them. Erasmus supervised the passage of his works through the press, working closely first with the great Venetian printer Aldus Manutius, and later with Froben at Basle. Educational reform was in the air, and the presses were to play a vital role in spreading the views of educationalists and providing the texts required for their new programmes, with an efficiency immeasurably superior to the laborious process of manuscript copying and circulation that had preceded them. A comparison between Chaucer's Clerk of Oxenford, with his twenty expensive volumes of Aristotle, and his sixteenth-century equivalent, with a library of a hundred or more books, ranging from large folios to pocket Testaments, all bought comparatively cheaply, reveals the new technology's contribution to scholarship as well as to education more generally.

For the first time in history, perhaps, self-education became a practical possibility. Its arrival in England was heralded by the publication of Edmund Coote's *The Schoolmaster* in 1596, from which the industrious student might teach himself to read and write, with the aid of a series of graded exercises. Its popularity is indicated by the appearance of twenty-five editions within the next thirty years. Although Latin remained the language of formal education, English grammars and dictionaries were also beginning to appear at this time, works such as William Bullokar's *Bref Grammar of English* (1586) or Alexander Gill's more ambitious *Logonomia Anglica* (1619), whose illustrations were drawn from contemporary poetry, especially Spenser. Early dictionaries such as Robert Cawdrey's *Table Alphabeticall* (1604) were, however, little more than lists of difficult words, as the title of John Bullokar's *English Expositor, teaching the interpretation of the hardest words in our language* (1616) indicates.

The printing press made classical and modern texts available on a scale hitherto inconceivable, to an audience rapidly acquiring a critical awareness of the text itself. The scholarly attention to changing Latin forms, a particular aspect of the general development of the historical sense, had resulted in more accurate dating of manuscripts, and increasing sensitivity to textual error, a problem endemic to manuscript transmission as a whole. Slips of the pen and misreadings naturally abounded in such a system, as do typographical errors in the printing-house, but they were even more difficult to correct, or control. The shortage of manuscripts and the extent of their unreliability, the accretion of errors from one copied manuscript to the next and the impossibility of appeal to long-deceased authors made the original reading hard to restore, as each manuscript posed individual problems and inherited one particular set of errors. Newly discovered manuscripts, sometimes Greek originals of works only previously known in a perhaps inaccurate Latin version, further encouraged more critical reading, and accuracy and correctness began to be valued for their own sakes. The first steps were taken towards establishing reliable texts of the most important classical authorities.

It was not long before similar scrutiny began to be applied to the Bible with rather more disturbing implications. Having learnt from Italian scholars that the great Vulgate Bible of St Jerome was manifestly corrupt in places, Erasmus set himself the task of retranslating the New Testament from the original Greek, a language he specially learnt for the purpose. This project created consternation among the conservative who rightly foresaw that a new version must create incessant and unresolvable arguments about the meaning of particular passages, while encouraging lay scepticism on the grounds that the clergy themselves could not agree as to what was meant by the Scriptures. Erasmus was, of course, translating from Greek into Latin, and thus writing primarily for an audience of European scholars. With subsequent translations into the vernacular (see p. 86), the interpretation of the Bible began to move out of the hands of the clergy into those of the laity, a process the former partly brought upon themselves by their widespread ignorance. In the long run, clergy and laity alike probably benefited from the demand that both should be able to read the Bible and understand the main theological issues in dispute, but aspirations of this kind inevitably involved some erosion of clerical power and control, such as occurred in protestant countries. Reading and discussing the meaning of particular passages was one aspect of the hoped-for 'priesthood of all believers', an essential part of religious life in the opinion of the reformers, who were sometimes inclined to forget that 'many . . . shall with God's grace, though they never read word of scripture, come as well to heaven', as More had put it. Families read the Bible together and women and servants (normally highly illiterate social groups) were often encouraged to participate. At prophesyings and conferences public discussions of particular biblical texts took place. A striking account of one such occasion is provided by the Catholic priest William Weston, who, while imprisoned in Wisbech Castle in 1588, witnessed a puritan gathering of this kind:

Each of them had his own Bible, and sedulously turned the pages and looked up the texts cited by the preachers, discussing the passages among themselves to see whether they had quoted them to the point, and accurately, and in harmony with their tenets. Also they would start arguing among themselves about the meaning of passages from the Scriptures – men, women, boys, girls, rustics, labourers and idiots . . .

Though such conferences were intended to promote uniformity of belief, they were also liable to open up endless possibilities for sectarianism, possibilities that came to fruition during the years of the Civil War. The aims of educators were always liable to go astray: a degree of intellectual independence might be conferred that could not be directed towards the desired end. Instead of making men more reasonably conformative and instilling a respect for basic religious and social structures, education sometimes produced the reverse effect. Nor was literacy itself any guarantee that the reader would wish for edification in the mastered medium. John Bunyan, who grew up in the first half of the seventeenth century, recalled the tastes of his youth:

The Scriptures, thought I, what are they? a dead letter, a little ink and paper, of 3 or 4 shillings price. Alas, what is the Scripture, give me a ballad, a news-book, *George* on horseback or *Bevis of Southampton*; give me some book that teaches curious arts, that tells of old fables; but for the holy Scriptures I cared not.   (*A Few Sighs from Hell*)

Many contemporaries must have shared his view. There is no reason to doubt the truth of Philip Stubbes's complaint, a familiar one at all

times, that 'books and pamphlets of scurrility and bawdry are better
esteemed and more vendible than the sagest books that be'.

The critical and textual approach to biblical studies, instituted by
the humanists and Erasmus, spread under the aegis of protestantism
with a rapidity that could not have been anticipated. In its early
phases, protestantism showed remarkable confidence in its own
powers of persuasion, and the appeal of its arguments to the well-
informed. There was a general conviction that if only learned clergy
preached, and the literate laity read their Bibles, society would come
to rest in a comfortably united protestant faith. This was not to be
the case, any more than the moral uplift the humanists expected to
gain from reading good classical authors was to be the sole outcome
of a sound humanist education. Just as putting the Bible in men's
hands encouraged them to take differing views of its message, so a
classical education might introduce men to pagan notions of religion,
philosophy and politics, as well as to a literature that, unlike that of
the Christian era, had suffered no consistent pressure to edify its
readers. Whether rightly or wrongly, one contemporary commen-
tator at least associated the radical demands of the mid-seventeenth
century with the impact of a classical education. Thomas Hobbes,
considering the causes of the Civil War in *Behemoth*, blamed the
universities, not only for the spread of radical presbyterianism, but
also for the potentially dangerous lessons they taught:

There were an exceeding great number of men of the better sort, that had
been so educated as that in their youth having read the books written by
famous men of the ancient Grecian and Roman commonwealths concerning
their polity and great actions, in which books the *popular* government was
extolled by the glorious name of liberty and monarchy disgraced by the name
of tyranny, they became thereby in love with their forms of government.
And out of these men were chosen the greatest part of the House of
Commons; or, if they were not the greatest part, yet, by advantage of their
eloquence, they were always able to sway the rest.

Certainly Machiavelli, early in the previous century, had based his
empirical approach to political science as expounded in the
Discourses (composed by 1519, published 1531) on readings from
Livy's Roman histories. He had played a leading role in the ill-fated
Florentine republic and had strongly republican sympathies, rever-
ing Brutus and condemning Caesar and the later emperors (another
reason for his black reputation in a monarchy like England). While
it seems unlikely that any seventeenth-century House of Commons

was animated by the kind of idealistic republicanism which Hobbes attributed to it (and which Machiavelli had actually felt – but he was an exceptional figure), the classical bias of education certainly introduced its beneficiaries to the possibility of alternative political systems, and may thus have encouraged them to ask searching questions about their own. The existence of such an educated élite does not, of course, make political disruption inevitable, but it does provide a fertile ground for the war of ideas and ideologies that so often precedes the resort to arms. Education encouraged men to explore topical issues through their reading, discover different views, and arrive at independent opinions. Just as with the wider dissemination of the Bible there was a point where control passed from the educator to the educated, so with the reading of the classics – a knowledge of Latin plus the availability of printed texts made accessible a much greater variety of material, some of it inevitably considered either immoral, or politically or theologically subversive. Far from being regarded as outdated and irrelevant wisdom written in a dead language, Latin opened for its readers all sorts of doors, the more exciting since some of them were forbidden.

Classical texts for use in schools were naturally chosen circumspectly and often bowdlerized, but the interested student did not have to look far beyond his set authors to find those accounts of pagan practices or amorous encounters that had been carefully omitted from his school book. Ovid's clarity and simplicity as a stylist ensured that selected extracts from the *Metamorphoses* were commonly read in the upper forms of grammar schools, then as now. Montaigne, whose education began exceptionally early and was remarkably liberal, recorded that 'the first taste I had for books came to me from my pleasure in the fables of the *Metamorphoses* of Ovid. For at about seven or eight I would steal away from any other pleasure to read them.' The variety of magical and mythical narratives naturally appealed to a child, but the adolescent reader was more likely to be impressed by the series of divine and human rapes and seductions, described in the graphic detail that is Ovid's hallmark as a poet. The account of Philomela's violation and mutilation at the hands of Tereus, for example, has a dark imaginative force that overflows into Shakespeare's *Titus Andronicus*, while his two poems *Venus and Adonis* (1593) and *The Rape of Lucrece* (1594), in their different ways, both reveal the Roman poet's influence. Ovid's most notoriously erotic poems were the *Ars Amatoria* ('The Art of Love') and his *Amores*, usually known as the *Elegies* at this time. Christopher Marlowe translated the latter with great verve in the late 1580s, thus providing a model for John Donne's *Elegies* written in the next decade. Marlowe's poetry, more than Shakespeare's, reveals a deliberate and self-conscious eroticism, not merely in the translated elegies where it was clearly called for, but also in his somewhat academic version of the Vergilian story of *Dido and Aeneas*, as well as in the tantalizingly bisexual treatment of Ovid's best-known love story, *Hero and Leander*. Like that of Pyramus and Thisbe, this story was already so familiar that any treatment of it was likely to be mock-heroic; this approach characterizes Nashe's version in *Lenten Stuffe*, and Ben Jonson's puppet play, at the end of *Bartholomew Fair*, where Sestos and Abydos are prosaically translated into the South Bank and Puddle Dock, and the lovers into comically indecent Cockneys.

Marlowe clearly recognized the potentially dangerous character of classical education. He introduced the subject into his tragedy *Faustus*, where the hero's disturbingly various aims are to some extent unified by the classical spirit that underlies many of his impulses. At the outset Faustus, speaking of himself, declares

> 'This word "damnation" terrifies not him,
> For he confounds hell in Elysium.
> His ghost be with the old philosophers.'   (I. iii. 58–60)
>
> *ghost*] spirit

a misconception passionately repudiated by Mephostophilis. Latin, here the language of magic rather than religion, is used for Faustus's long conjuration of the devil, while his absorption in classical culture is apparent in his reference to Elysium, his summoning of Alexander and his paramour, and fully voiced in his worship of Helen, at once a succubus, a demonic spirit who will steal his soul by having intercourse with him, and an embodiment of the fatal enchantment of the antique world:

> 'Sweet Helen, make me immortal with a kiss:
> Her lips suck forth my soul, see where it flies.'   (V. i. 99–100)

As the minutes finally draw on towards the consummation of his diabolic pact, Faustus's thoughts impart an ironic twist to the line from Ovid's *Elegies* where the poet, in his mistress's arms, begs night's horses to run slowly:

O lente, lente, currite noctis equi!   (v. ii. 135)

Faustus, in spiritual agony and anticipating physical torment, utters the same words. In desperation his mind reverts to those myths of the 'old philosophers' which had originally encouraged his scepticism as to the existence of that hell whose reality is about to swallow him up:

'Ah, Pythagoras' *metempsychosis*, were that true,
This soul should fly from me, and I be chang'd
Unto some brutish beast.
All beasts are happy, for when they die
Their souls are soon dissolv'd in elements;
But mine must live still to be plagu'd in hell.'   (v. ii. 168–73)

Marlowe's sense of the corruptingly sensual charms of classical literature was by no means peculiar to him. Something of the same reaction is reflected in Milton's poetry, while at a prosaically administrative level the ecclesiastical authorities were not at all happy about the proliferation of erotic poetry and satire in the 1590s, both of which derived their licentiousness from classical models. In 1599 copies of the most notorious of these, including Marlowe's Ovidian *Elegies*, and Marston's and Guilpin's satires (alongside the vituperative correspondence of Thomas Nashe and Gabriel Harvey) were called in and publicly burnt, on episcopal orders from London and Canterbury, which laid down that 'no satires or epigrams be printed thereafter'. It was also possible to resent the predominant classical bias of education on entirely different grounds, to find its oppressive influence increasingly irrelevant to the modern world – an attitude that later in the seventeenth century developed into the full-scale dispute between 'ancients' and 'moderns'. Spenser's headmaster, the educationalist Richard Mulcaster, commented – perhaps with a touch of exasperation – 'It is no proof because Plato praiseth it, because Aristotle alloweth it, because Cicero commends it, because Quintilian is acquainted with it, or any other else . . . that therefore it is for us to use.'

While education might afford the incidental pleasures of speculation or scurrility, these were very far from constituting its main source of attraction. According to the humanist view, education was necessary for governing well. Sir Thomas More in his *Utopia* had emphasized the need for scholars to steer the traditional ship of state, to participate in government while recognizing the far-from-ideal character of power politics. Tudor monarchy increasingly aimed to assemble an efficient administration. Royal advisers had traditionally been great noblemen or powerful ecclesiastics, trained in canon law, who had reached the top of their profession, but for various reasons the pattern of government was changing: Henry VIII's break with Rome put an end to the line of great ecclesiastical lawyers, of whom Wolsey was the last and perhaps the greatest representative, and while noblemen continued to contribute importantly to the country's government, the Tudors were alert to the dangers of any one individual becoming too powerful. They were thus more inclined to play them off against one another, or against their own protégés, men like Thomas Cromwell, Francis Walsingham and William Cecil, of humble or minor gentry origins, who had worked their way up to positions of power and responsibility largely through their intelligence, energy and competence. Education, eagerly pursued, provided the initial openings for such men, and a few Elizabethans of middling backgrounds sought success through government administration – Spenser is an example of one who, to some extent, achieved this goal: educated at Merchant Taylors School, and graduating from Pembroke Hall, Cambridge, he became secretary first to the Bishop of Rochester and then to Lord Arthur Grey, whose fall he survived. John Donne, educated at university and the Inns of Court, obviously hoped for a career within government circles when he became secretary to Sir Thomas Egerton, Keeper of the Great Seal and subsequently Lord Chancellor. From the sixteenth century onwards, noblemen were constantly advised to take their sons' education seriously, lest as a class they found themselves ousted from positions of trust and responsibility by their better-informed inferiors. The humanist Richard Pace warned old-fashioned aristocrats that if they continued to regard hunting and hawking as more gentlemanly pursuits than studying, 'Then you . . . must be content that your children may wind their horns and keep their hawks, while the children of mean men do manage matters of estate.'

The Tudor political stage was no longer a setting for amateurs. While the upper classes were always anxious to dissociate themselves from any occupation that smacked of the market-place, they were not slow to respond to the demand for better education in administrative circles, or to the improvement in standards at grammar schools and universities, previously the resort of clerks and scholars rather than gentlemen. Traditionally the gentry had employed private tutors for their children at home, later sending them to great households to acquire good manners and such courtly accomplishments as dancing, sports, and military exercises. Thus even before boarding schools arrived in any numbers, the English aristocracy had commonly educated their children away from home. Later, young men might have two or three years of foreign travel, to 'finish' them: under the guidance of an older person they would visit France and Italy, a habit deplored by those who, like the pedagogue Roger Ascham, considered the Italians capable of any and every vice. Although this pattern continued, and William Cecil's household provided formal schooling for a number of wealthy young aristocrats (many of them court wards), grammar schools and universities were increasingly patronized. Sir Philip Sidney and Fulke Greville attended the free grammar school at Shrewsbury, reputedly the largest of its day and one that included the teaching of Greek in its statutes. Like most young gentlemen of their generation, they then proceeded to university, though probably without remaining long enough to graduate. The need to adapt to changing patterns of government produced widespread concern over the appropriate education for the ruling classes, and an extensive literature, considered in the next chapter, developed around the subject.

It is difficult to judge how far the desire for education was associated with social aspiration, partly because our own society so readily assumes a direct link that would have been less obvious to an Elizabethan. David Cressy neatly identifies one aspect of the problem when he points out that 'literacy unlocked a variety of doors but it did not necessarily secure admission.' Society was committed to the view that men best served the commonwealth in the position allotted them by birth, that the gentry must rule and the rest obey. There seems to have been a profound reluctance even to acknowledge the extent of existing social mobility. Lear's fool warned his master that a madman is 'a yeoman that has a gentleman to his son; for he's a mad yeoman that sees his son a gentleman before him' (III. vi. 12–14). The deference due to parents could be challenged, as the rest of society's structure might be, by a sudden change of status: Lear, by abdicating, had produced a comparable degree of insubordination in his daughters. At the same time it is hard to believe that the bourgeois aspirations of the Yellowhammers in Middleton's *A Chaste Maid in Cheapside*, inordinately proud of their son Tim, 'the

Cambridge boy', were not characteristic, in their way, of the rising middle classes. Hopes of achieving high office in the central administration were most unlikely to be realized without the right family connections or strings to pull, yet the sudden elevation of a few lucky or gifted people may have acted as an incentive to others, and under James money more obviously became an aid to the acquisition of status.

At a far lower social level, the ability to read, write and keep accounts was usually a practical help, as well as advancing a man's professional or vocational standing. While it was most unlikely to have figured as a prudential consideration, literacy might save a man found guilty of committing a felony (any serious crime) from the gallows, since the ability to read the 'neck verse' (commonly the Latin text of the first verse of the fifty-first psalm) enabled the transgressor to plead 'benefit of clergy' and have his sentence commuted. Unless the felon was actually in holy orders, in which case different rules applied, he would be branded on the thumb, to prevent him from escaping death if he ever committed a second offence. Ben Jonson, found guilty of killing an actor in a fight, pleaded thus and was thus branded. Estimates of literacy are always controversial, but it seems likely that there was a strong correlation between literacy and social status in early modern society, and that the further down the social scale a man stood, the greater the likelihood that he would be illiterate. London, however, may have provided an exceptional environment, for it seems that half or perhaps more of its male population could read. Elsewhere, about a third of men in the home counties could sign their names, and a high proportion of these could probably read as well. In more isolated districts, literacy rates fell sharply, and remained very low among women everywhere. Only in aristocratic and exceptionally religious or intellectual households does there seem to have been much effort to educate them.

Basic literacy, writing and simple arithmetic were taught in the petty school, or less frequently in the preparatory classes of a grammar school. Children learnt to read by reciting the vowels and consonants, and then spelling individual words before they actually attempted to read them in a passage, or write them. At every level there was an enormous amount of rote-learning whose application would only become apparent at a later stage. The imposition of such tedious exercises was justified as a necessary part of memory-training, then held to be a vital element in eduation. There existed elaborate techniques for training the memory systematically, and various features of Elizabethan life witness the effects of such training, from the extensive literary borrowings of a writer like Webster to the large number of plays that an acting company could perform in repertory.

The complex issue of spelling ('orthography') tended to encourage bees in pedagogic bonnets. The schoolmaster Holofernes in *Love's Labour's Lost* holds forth on

'such rackers of orthography, as to speak "dout", fine, when he should say "doubt"; "det", when he should pronounce "debt" – *d, e, b, t,* not *d, e,t*: he clepeth a calf, "cauf"; half, "hauf"; neighbour *vocatur* "nebor"; neigh abbreviated "ne". This is abhominable – which he would call "abominable".'   (v. i. 19–24)

The intrusive 'h' in 'abominable' was one of many inappropriate additions made on the basis of dubious, and sometimes entirely false Latin derivations. This one did not survive, but many other such graftings were successful, contributing to the widening gap between written and pronounced English. Holofernes's spelling, if not his pronunciation, of 'doubt', 'debt' and 'neighbour' has survived to the present.

The majority of petty school pupils would have neither wished nor needed to progress beyond basic schooling to the study of good Latin that was the main educational objective of the grammar schools, so called because the children began by learning Latin grammar. In *The Merry Wives of Windsor*, William Page recites early lessons before the Welsh schoolmaster Sir Hugh Evans, to the uncomprehending amusement of Mistress Quickly (IV. i. 21–79). If they stayed the course, pupils then progressed to a mastery of Latin composition. Teaching methods traditionally involved the use of corporal punishment for mistakes. The jester in Nashe's play *Summer's Last Will and Testament* declares himself 'an open enemy unto ink and paper. . . . Nouns and pronouns, I pronounce you as traitors to boys' buttocks. Syntaxis and prosodia, you are tormentors of wit, and good for nothing but to get a schoolmaster twopence a week.' More imaginative educationalists increasingly hoped that instruction might come to appeal to the child for its own sake, rather in the same way as certain Calvinist preachers presented their doctrines as comforting and reassuring rather than exploiting the deterrent of hellfire. Roger Ascham began writing his treatise *The Schoolmaster* (1570) after a debate on school punishment occasioned by some frightened pupils running away from Eton College in 1563. He was particularly opposed to 'cruelty in schoolmasters in beating away the love of learning from children', believing that the young might sooner be brought to enjoy their lessons by patience and love than by punishment. Such enlightenment, however, was rare, and the majority of schoolmasters continued to whip their pupils, just as many preachers continued to threaten their congregations with eternal damnation.

To accommodate various ages and levels of progress, schools were divided into between three and seven classes, each of which would work on different texts and tasks, though often within one or two rooms only, depending on the size of the school. The bottom class studied only grammar, later beginning to read simple Latin texts, specially written colloquies or versions of Aesop or Cato, a favourite author for beginners since the Middle Ages. They would then work their way up the school, studying selected passages from the Roman dramatists, perhaps Cicero's *De Officiis*, on to Ovid, Horace and Vergil at the top of the school. A master who was capable of it might also begin Greek with his upper forms. Which texts were to be read was often laid down in the school's statutes, though the master might vary these a little at his own discretion and according to availability. The humanists believed that it was part of the schoolmaster's function to discourse to his pupils on the texts they were studying, introducing information about ethics, history, geography or astronomy, as each seemed relevant. How many masters were actually capable of giving such wide-ranging extempore lectures one cannot tell. Children were encouraged to develop their powers of expression in Latin, and to this end Erasmus recommended that they made collections of notable sayings as they came across them in their reading, grouping them under appropriate headings in a commonplace book. His own collection of adages may be seen as a sophisticated extension of the same principle. Many Elizabethans habituated to the practice made similar compilations in English as well, sometimes publishing them, as Ben Jonson did his, under the title of *Timber or Discoveries*, timber being the raw material from which the architect creates his structures. The dull curate Sir Nathaniel, like an obedient pupil, takes out his table-book to write down one of Holofernes's more choice epithets (in *Love's Labour's Lost*, v. i. 15), while on an altogether more memorable occasion, Hamlet calls for

> 'My tables – meet it is I set it down
> That one may smile, and smile, and be a villain!' (I v. 107–8)

Note-taking was ubiquitous, and was soon facilitated by the various techniques of shorthand or stenography available, which made the copying down of sermons or the pirating of plays for unauthorized publication an altogether simpler undertaking.

A good Latin style was acquired by translation, whether from the child's own composition in English or, according to Ascham's double translation method, from a passage already translated into English out of a Latin original, so that the pupil's Latin version could later be compared stylistically with that of the author he was studying. Mastery of Latin led to mastery of rhetoric, the linguistic skill used to win friends and influence people and generally get your own way in the world. The teaching of rhetoric was broken down into its constituent technical devices, and pupils practised writing on different topics, sayings or proverbs, or marshalled arguments for one side or another of a debatable proposition. Recitations and debates, sometimes dramatized in the form of playlets, were used in schools to promote rhetorical skills. Shakespeare's mastery of the academic exercise of 'varying', or finding different terms of praise for a particular object, is revealed in the Dauphin's self-conscious encomium on his horse (*Henry V*, III. vii. 11–37). Examples of speeches debating two sides of a proposition abound in his work – indeed such conflict may be felt to be the essence of dramatic writing: in the first act of *Richard II*, Gaunt urges patience on his exiled son in the speech

> 'All places that the eye of heaven visits
> Are to a wise man ports and happy havens.'

while the latter replies

> 'Oh, who can hold a fire in his hand
> By thinking on the frosty Caucasus?' (I. iii. 275–6, 294–5)

In a very different vein, but ultimately derived from the same old school rhetoric exercise, are Leantio's two contrasting speeches on the secret joys and miseries of marriage in Middleton's *Women Beware Women* (III. ii. 1–27, 190–214). Much of the time grammar-school education suffered from being dull, harsh and sometimes brutal, but there were nevertheless elements within it that were especially suited to producing a generation of great dramatists.

From our own point of view, the Elizabethan school day was appallingly long, though it needs to be seen in the context of the far longer working day that was the norm in early modern society. It began at six or seven in the morning, continuing until the children went home for their lunch at about 11.00. Work resumed at 1.00, and lasted till five or six in the evening, for six days of the week. No wonder some preferred to go bird's-nesting. Morning and afternoon breaks of fifteen minutes were sometimes advocated, often as a kind of carrot, so that slow or disobedient children could be kept in instead of being whipped. School holidays were far shorter than today, although there tended to be more single day holidays. Despite long hours and a dauntingly dry programme of studies, an outstanding schoolmaster might have a lasting influence on his pupils and occasionally command their affection as well as respect. Richard Mulcaster, high master of Merchant Taylors School for twenty-five years, taught Spenser (who referred to him as Wrenock in the December eclogue of *The Shepheardes Calendar*), as well as Thomas Kyd (author of *The Spanish Tragedy*), the writer and poet Thomas Lodge and the preacher Lancelot Andrewes. John Webster also attended the school, though probably after Mulcaster's departure in 1586. William Camden taught Ben Jonson at Westminster School, and the latter remained a devoted pupil, dedicating his 1616 folio of works to him and addressing him as

> Camden, most reverend head, to whom I owe
> All that I am in arts, all that I know . . .

From Camden, Jonson acquired scholarly habits of mind, a sound knowledge of Latin and some Greek, an unusual accomplishment in a man who had not attended university.

Oxford and Cambridge in the sixteenth century were undergoing a period of transition, as older methods and techniques associated with the medieval predominance of scholastic theology increasingly came to be considered out-of-date, and the study of canon law was abandoned altogether. The other advanced faculties, civil law, medicine and divinity, were, however, still available, but before embarking on these specialized courses of study, the scholar had to obtain the degrees of Bachelor and Master of Arts, a matter of four years' study followed by a further three years. Together they constituted a programme of seven years' work analogous to the seven-year period served by apprentices to various skills and trades (the only technological training currently available). The Bachelor of Arts degree included the traditional subjects of logic and rhetoric, a certain amount of Greek, mathematics (arithmetic, geometry and some optics), music and a little philosophy. In order to graduate the student was required to demonstrate his mastery of logic and rhetoric practically, by making speeches and engaging in public disputations ('wrangling'), defending or attacking a particular position and answering any objections that might be raised against his argument. The degree of Master of Arts involved further work in Greek and geometry and introduced the student to astronomy. The three branches of philosophy (natural, moral and metaphysical) also figured importantly.

The organization of the university was gradually changing: students had once lived mainly in halls. Now the colleges, which had previously consisted of small groups of graduates, took in students in increasing numbers and began to provide individual tuition for them. Undergraduates tended to be a year or two younger than today, and sometimes rather more than that. College tutors often took on responsibility not only for their intellectual guidance but also for supervising their behaviour, and even the state of their wardrobe and their laundry arrangements; they sometimes shared a room with their pupils, visited them in the vacation, and received fees and allowances directly from the parents. The movement away from university-based teaching may have encouraged extensions of the syllabus beyond the statutory requirements, so as to include more modern authors and topics, on the initiative of individual tutors. There were also several university appointments, notably the Savilian professorships of mathematics and astronomy established at Oxford in 1619, which introduced students to important recent discoveries such as those of Kepler and Galileo, as well as the use of logarithms in making calculations. But traditional subjects and methods still made up the most part of the four-year Bachelor of Arts degree.

It has been estimated that by 1640 as many as 2½ per cent of the annual male seventeen-year-old population went on to higher education (as compared to around 15 per cent today), though it was a far smaller number that finally graduated. Some failed to complete their studies because they could not afford the fees – this may have happened to Thomas Middleton, who went up to Queen's College, Oxford, but left without graduating. Poor students could become sizars, servants working for the college or for wealthier students, or take time off to accumulate the wherewithal for fees, but only if their families could afford to dispense with their earning capacity for some years. Catholics were debarred from graduating since this involved subscribing to the Thirty-nine Articles of the Anglican faith. John Donne, brought up a Catholic, studied at Oxford and probably also at Cambridge for several years and then, like so many of the gentry, went on without a degree to round off his general education at the Inns of Court. The latter offered a professional legal training and were commonly regarded as the third university. Litigation was almost a way of life for a number of Elizabethans who could afford to indulge in this unpredictable pastime, and fathers were anxious for their sons to pick up at least a smattering of legal terminology so that they might know what to expect when in due course they went to law themselves or alternatively administered it, sitting on the bench as local Justices of the Peace. Students at the Inns had, if anything, a worse reputation for wild behaviour than university undergraduates, a reputation which Shakespeare's Justice Shallow is touchingly anxious to perpetuate (see *2 Henry IV*, III. ii. 14–34, 194–218).

The increase in the numbers of gentry attending grammar schools and universities occasioned frequent complaints that the well-to-do were ousting the talented and deserving poor from scholarships and fellowships through the misuse of wealth and influence. While this may well have been the case, the early years of Elizabeth's reign were characterized by a drive to raise the supply of poorer graduates in an attempt to build up the numbers of the clergy, which had fallen drastically in the years following the Reformation. Endowment of scholarships and the number of places at university grew and student numbers rose steadily, at least until the difficult years of the 1590s, after which they continued to grow. It has been argued that the outcome of this expansion was ultimately to provide more hopeful clergymen than there were satisfying positions for them to fill, and that their disappointment and alienation subsequently contributed to the disruptions of the 1640s. As Mulcaster had written in his *Positions*, 'all may not pass to learning which throng thitherwards, because of the inconvenience which may ensue, by want of preferment for such a multitude.' Bacon endorsed this view in his essay 'Of Seditions and Troubles', where he commented particularly on the problems of 'an overgrown clergy', 'when more are bred scholars than preferments can take off'.

The literary historian is especially conscious of the problems of young men overeducated for their likely position in life since such youths, if they had no vocation for the church and were insufficiently well-connected to clamber on to the lowest rung of the administrative ladder, sometimes turned to writing pamphlets and plays as a means of supporting themselves. The rewards of the literary profession were, however, both inadequate and unreliable, for there was no system of royalties, and printers made outright payments for manuscripts (typically around £2), sometimes to their current possessors rather than to their authors. The habit of manuscript circulation, especially common in select circles, facilitated such misappropriation. Success was thus unlikely to benefit the author directly. On the face of it, the theatre looked more financially promising, but in practice the university men were often less versatile than the full-time professionals such as Heywood, Dekker or Shakespeare, and here too it was less profitable to receive an outright payment for a particular play (Henslowe paid a flat £6) than to be a company shareholder, regularly in receipt of a fixed proportion of the takings (as Shakespeare was), even if – as Greene is reputed to have done – one managed to sell the same play twice over.

Christopher Marlowe's career reveals the predicament of a young man whose education left him in a social no-man's-land. His father was a Canterbury shoemaker, a respectable artisan comparable in social position to the glove-maker John Shakespeare. Both playwrights were born in 1564. Marlowe won a scholarship to King's School, Canterbury, and then a further scholarship, intended to enable the sons of poor men to graduate at Cambridge and take holy orders. It had been endowed by Matthew Parker as part of a wider effort to cope with the acute shortage of clergymen which he had encountered as Elizabeth's first Primate. Marlowe completed his BA and proceded to the MA, which he took in 1587. By this time he seems to have begun working, at least intermittently, as an anti-Catholic spy, and his first stage success, *Tamburlaine,* was probably performed in the same year by the Admiral's Men. Marlowe's temperament was volatile and reckless. He would have been ill-suited to the monotonous, demanding and frequently underpaid life of the average parson, and he lacked the sobriety and discretion required in the corridors of power, at least of underlings. The government was only willing to employ him in an irregular and clandestine capacity.

A man in Marlowe's position who had been through university and might style himself a gentleman and a Master of Arts was uprooted. He could scarcely take up the shoemaker's tools and undergo a seven-year apprenticeship to the trade; he could not accept the church, and the administrative system would not accept him, so what was he to do? The same problem affected a number of young men of his generation, educated far above their parents' social level. Some undoubtedly drifted, as Marlowe had done, into part-time employment as a spy, and the literary figure of the malcontent, commonly a melancholy, disaffected intellectual, was often associated with comparably dashed hopes. Bosola in Webster's *The Duchess of Malfi* seems to have been driven by penury first to spying, and then to murder. Delio remembers him in early days:

'I knew him in Padua, a fantastical scholar, like such who study to know how many knots was in Hercules' club; . . . he hath studied himself half blear-ey'd, to know the true symmetry of Caesar's nose by a shoeing-horn: and this he did to gain the name of a speculative man.'   (III. iii. 40–6)

Of the three 'Parnassus' plays performed at Cambridge between 1598 and 1602, the second two, the first and second parts of *The Return from Parnassus*, depict the rake's progress of a group of university graduates who cannot find suitable employment in a world that has no use for their abilities. Ingenioso (who may represent Nashe) talks of putting his wit out to interest to 'make it return two pamphlets a week', but he is dismissed by his affected patron, and the hard-headed publisher Danter is only attracted by the offer of libellous satires. Even the actors Burbage and Kempe turn up their noses at such uncommercial talents, complaining (not without justification) that their plays 'smell too much of that writer *Ovid*, and that writer *Metamorphoses*, and talk too much of Proserpina and Jupiter'. The graduates are reduced to whipping dogs out of churches and administering enemas. In their own way, these plays offer an interesting commentary on the contemporary vogue for satire and social criticism.

Those bright young men, sometimes referred to as the 'university wits', who attempted to wrest a living from the literary scene in the 1590s seem to have been rather less than successful in so doing. Little is known about Marlowe's financial situation, but the fact that he was discovered in the Netherlands in 1592 attempting to forge English money scarcely suggests that he was comfortably off. Greene, on his own admission a drunkard and a spendthrift, apparently died in misery and want, while Nashe confessed that when 'the bottom of my purse is turned downward . . . I prostitute my pen in hope of gain.' Other writers were to abandon the profession of letters for the comparative security of the church, as did the dramatist John Marston, and his fellow-satirist Joseph Hall (later to become Bishop of Exeter). John Donne and George Herbert also turned to the church after the failure of more worldly careers, though this fact need not cast doubt on the conviction with which they did so.

Education, then, might afford a means to a literary career that could scarcely be relied upon to provide financial security, unless one was exceptionally lucky or exceptionally talented. Yet though the predicament of the 'university wits' is particularly vivid, it was probably the grammar schools rather than the universities which constituted the most vigorous and influential element in the system. They made the strongest impact on the urban bourgeoisie, from whose ranks nearly all the great dramatists were drawn – Marlowe, Shakespeare, Jonson, Middleton and Webster, as well as the epic poets Spenser and Milton, and such lesser talents as Nashe, Greene and Lodge. If the acquisition of education did not necessarily fulfil worldly hopes or bring wealth or status, it was nevertheless the high road to 'Parnassus', the prerequisite for creativity, regarded by the humanists as the most divine of human gifts, whose possession conferred a freedom and mastery far transcending anything afforded by more worldly pomp and circumstance. Elizabethan writers came to hover uneasily between a value system of which literary inspiration was the focus, and the mercantile world into which they had been born, and from which they had to wrest a living. Needless to say, the latter had little time for such an unmarketable commodity as inspiration.

5 The Court and its Arts

*Man is a noble animal, splendid in ashes, and pompous in the grave, solem-
nizing nativities and deaths with equal lustre, nor omitting ceremonies of
bravery in the infamy of his nature.*

'The most striking feature of the great nation states of the sixteenth
and seventeenth centuries', it has been claimed, was 'the enormous
expansion of the court and the central administration'. Among the
more obvious results were the development of a primitive civil
service, an increasing concentration of wealth and aristocracy at
court and the self-conscious cultivation of an extravagantly 'courtly'
mode of life, intended to impress foreign statesmen and the lower
orders. The court was to be regarded as an object of national pride,
while its doings were of permanent interest to outsiders. Like Holly-
wood film-stars, Queen Elizabeth figured in men's unconscious
fantasies, if the secret diaries of the astrologer Simon Forman are
anything to go by: his dream of arguing with her and kissing her
forms a prosaic equivalent to Prince Arthur's platonic dream of
Gloriana (*The Faerie Queene*, I. ix. 13–15). A great deal of literature
was written for the court, either directly inspired by its doings or
referring to it in other ways, for it was a natural cultural focus as well
as a potential source of financial support for the aspiring writer.
Images of courtliness and court life, embodying either a unique
refinement of manners and morals or alternatively an unacceptable
level of corrupt privilege and pervasive vice, are to be found in most
contemporary literature.

Of course courts had provided, and would continue to provide, the
obvious, though by no means the only, setting for literary activity
and patronage – Chaucer and Gower at the court of Richard II or
Dryden at the court of Charles II are cases in point – but
Elizabethan culture was particularly centred upon the court and the
capital city, London, whose links with, interest in and resentment of

this grossly overgrown household in its midst were still being forged. Great aristocrats who might have afforded rival establishments were actively discouraged from independence – Elizabeth preferred to have her nobles about her and know exactly what they were doing; if she thought herself neglected, she was liable to insist on their prompt return. It was, moreover, in their own best interests to remain close to the throne, strengthening their position by establishing their own clientele in key offices rather than letting their rivals steal a march on them (for there was still strong rivalry between powerful aristocratic families such as the Dudleys and the Howards). Influential peers would try to put their own supporters in for positions such as groom of the privy chamber or the provisorship of the horse (held by Bosola in *The Duchess of Malfi*); for places on the bench or the Council of the North; for secretaryships or captaincies of garrisons (like Leantio in *Women Beware Women*) or at a more everyday level, for pastoral livings, college fellowships or jobs as clerks or royal park-keepers. The client, bound by gratitude or merely obligation, did what he could when he could to advance his patron's interests or prestige. Occasionally, like Bosola, he would be required to provide 'intelligence', i.e. inside information. There existed a wide range of such offices, from the most influential to the most menial, and some might profitably be farmed out or sub-let, a fixed proportion of their income returning as rent to the formal office-holder. Few of these positions carried adequate remuneration, since the crown seldom bothered to ensure that this kept pace with inflation, nor was it necessary to do so since with most official positions it was the extras that made them financially worthwhile. Bribery and graft were endemic, and the state's reluctance to pay its servants appropriately only ensured that they continued to be so. When Francis Bacon, by then Lord Chancellor, was impeached for accepting bribes in 1621, he made no attempt to deny the charge, merely insisting that he had never allowed them to influence his judgements. Although patronage was most vital for those who lacked the requisite wealth or connections, even noblemen tended to form into factions, 'packs and sects of great ones', the lesser seeking out the protection of the greater.

As well as offices to be held, the court had other glittering prizes to hand out, both in terms of status and opportunities to make money: there were knighthoods, even peerages to be won, though Elizabeth was notoriously meaner with these than her successor: Raleigh received a knighthood only, while James's two great favourites became Earl of Somerset and Duke of Buckingham, the latter promotion causing deep resentment since it gave the holder automatic precedence over all the inherited titles of the kingdom. On the financial side, there was a variety of benefits to be had, ranging from government pensions through the leasing of royal lands on generous terms to more complex, often more dubious privileges: the right to collect customs fees on particular goods, exemption from certain export regulations, monopolies to make and distribute certain commodities, patents to develop new products. Most of such rights might be resold at a profit. There was widespread enthusiasm for new projects and patents that might corner a valuable market. The absurdity of many of these schemes is parodied in Jonson's *The Devil is an Ass* (1616), where the projector Meercraft proposes to make wine out of raisins, take out a patent on toothpicks and drain the Fens, thus conferring on the gull Fitzdotterel the title 'Duke of Drowned Lands'. The last turned out to be too near the mark, however, and Jonson told Drummond of Hawthornden that 'the King desired him to conceal it'. Most dubious among the royal handouts were the guardianship of wards, the rights to collect recusant fines (honourably turned down by Sir Philip Sidney) or to investigate the payment of state rents or debts. With no formal system of tax collection, monarchs were liable to hand over the rights to reclaim awkward debts as a form of reward, so that their collection then depended upon the energy and tenacity of the beneficiary.

While there were pickings to be had at court, it was in general a sweepstake, where losses were commoner than gains. Like a very grand hotel, the court provided luxurious meals and lavish entertainment; in return the courtier had to maintain himself in a style appropriate to the setting, in expensive clothes, with well turned-out servants and a coach and horses. According to Jonson's Carlo Buffone, 'To be an accomplished gentleman, that is, a gentleman of the time, you must give o'er housekeeping in the country, and live altogether in the city amongst gallants' (*Every Man Out of His Humour*, I. ii. 37–9). Greater obligations might fall on more influential courtiers – entertainment to be offered to the Queen and her entourage on her annual progresses, diplomatic missions abroad, even military expeditions to be undertaken, all of which could prove cripplingly expensive and for which any official payment was unlikely to cover the actual costs. Despite the numerous gifts to come their way, many of the greatest nobles died desperately in debt: Elizabeth's favourite Leicester owed more than £35,000 (perhaps two or three million pounds in today's terms) to the crown alone, while Essex was in serious financial straits when he lost the Queen's favour; his rebellion in 1601 was the gesture of a man at his wits' end with nothing more to lose. The Queen may sometimes have used debts as a means of enforcing her more potent nobles' dependence, despite the resulting inconvenience. Unfortunately the burden of extensive debts was felt not merely by the noblemen themselves, but by hosts of small tradesmen and suppliers who had little hope of being reimbursed; aristocratic privilege exempted peers from debtors' prisons but not their unpaid grocers or bootmakers. Shakespeare's *Timon of Athens* provides a graphic account of extravagance and generosity suddenly turning to penury and bad debts – Timon is more of an Elizabethan than an Athenian aristocrat. Yet whatever gains or losses might be incurred, the court remained a focus of wealth and authority, and there alone might Hobbes's 'perpetual and restless desire of power after power' find fulfilment.

The beginnings of national self-consciousness, the increase in centralized power, and a recognition that the court might crucially influence the evolving state were accompanied by the development of a body of theory, humanist in origin, as to how such influence might most effectively be deployed. The earliest treatises addressed themselves either to princes or to the ruling classes in general, the courtier and the governor (who might be either prince or magistrate), extending by degrees down the social scale to 'The Compleat Gentleman' (the title of Henry Peacham's guide of 1622). Handbooks on statecraft might easily degenerate into books on etiquette, since rules for political and social conduct were not as distinct as they are today; indeed political attitudes were commonly reflected in terms of ceremonial or its absence: Antony's whipping of Caesar's messenger, Thidias (III. xiii. 93), or Cornwall's stocking of Lear's servant, the disguised Kent (II. ii. 125), would originally have carried sharper implications, when the treatment of messengers or servants was a measure of the respect accorded to their masters. Different gradations of society were reflected in different gestures of deference, bowing or courtseying, standing bareheaded or kneeling in the presence of a superior. Similarly special modes of address distinguished the monarch, as well as a host of other offices ('your majesty', 'your highness', 'your honour', 'your grace', etc.), superiors in general being 'sir' or 'madam'. Apart from God Himself, only one's nearest and dearest, lovers, children or obvious social inferiors were addressed by the old-fashioned singular 'thou'. Kent's use of that singular to address both King Lear and later the Duke of Cornwall would certainly have produced a *frisson*, being an impertinence sufficient to justify Lear's fury and Cornwall's punishment, a deliberate attack on court protocol.

Handbooks for princes generally presupposed some form of monarch, and followed Plato in assuming that a better society would be achieved through wiser rule, ideally through that of a philosopher king, failing which philosophical counsellors might do much. More's *Utopia* (1516) is concerned with the creation of an ideal society, while rather bypassing the question of how this was to be achieved. The first book, written in the Platonic form of a dialogue, discusses the need for wise men to involve themselves in politics. In the same year, More's friend Erasmus composed *Institutio Christiani Principis* ('The Education of a Christian Prince') which advocates a humanist education, with due emphasis on the individual's obligation to the state, as set out in Cicero's *De Officiis*. The prince's primary aim, according to Erasmus, was to act as a Christian, and in his view the good Christian was essentially a pacifist:

If you cannot defend your kingdom without violating justice, shedding much blood and injuring the cause of religion, give up your crown and yield to the necessities of the time ... prefer rather to be a just man than an unjust prince.

Something of the impracticability of this gentle, passive and unworldly ideal comes out in Shakespeare's *Henry VI* trilogy. Three years earlier Machiavelli's *The Prince* (written 1513, published 1536) had considered the ruler's obligations to his people in the face of competition from unscrupulous operators from a very different standpoint – indeed, the book had caused consternation and alarm by refusing to judge political problems in terms of Christian ethics at all, offering instead a pragmatic analysis of how the ruler might most effectively achieve strength and stability within the state. Machiavelli assumed a certain toughness and ruthlessness was necessary in a ruler, and he permitted his prince to lie, pretend and break his word as 'reasons of state', that is, the state's best interests, demanded. Although he was often caricatured on the English stage as the mentor of all cynicism and atheism, it required no great perception to acknowledge, as Bacon did, that 'we are much beholden to Machiavelli and others, that write what men do and not what they ought to do.' *The Prince* vividly reflected changing patterns of power politics in the sixteenth century. Although no English translation was published until 1640, it was widely read in Italian, French or one of several manuscript translations, and its assumptions about the need for effective leadership underlie the historical dramas of Shakespeare, Marlowe and Jonson.

Different again from Erasmus's sophisticated Christianity or Machiavelli's pragmatism was Castiglione's *The Courtyer* (*Il Libro del Cortegiano*, completed by 1518, published 1528 and first translated by Sir Thomas Hoby, 1561). Here little attention is paid to the prince's moral dilemmas and less to his political ones. Instead Castiglione concerns himself with the courtier as a social being, and this is reflected in the structure, made up of four dialogues, between the chief courtiers at Urbino in 1507, in which they attempt to define their ideal. While traditional morality is upheld, much of the emphasis falls on personal accomplishments, both indoors and out; in addition to the central art of speaking well, on display in the dialogue, the courtier should be able to write gracefully, both in prose and verse, draw and paint, play music, sing and dance. It is some evidence of the durability of this scheme that well over a century later Molière's *Bourgeois Gentilhomme* was still attempting to master these arts in his erratic progress towards gentility. It was inevitable that handbooks for courtiers or gentlemen should be consulted by the socially aspiring – perhaps especially by them; the growth of a new urban gentry contributed to their popularity.

Sir Thomas Elyot's guidebook, *The Boke named the Governour* (1531), reflects Castiglione's influence and recommends similar lists of accomplishments, but writing for a more suspicious and less cultivated audience, Elyot has to persuade them of the value of humanist educational ideals in the first place. He does so partly by using the traditional argument that without it their talents are threatened by more bourgeois, clerkly learning, but he then changes tack, hastily reassuring his readers that the practice of the arts to beguile leisure hours is essentially different from that of the craftsman, forced to earn his daily bread:

I intend not ... to make of a prince or nobleman's son a common painter or carver, which shall present himself openly stained or imbrued with sundry colours.   (Book I, ch. viii)

The distinction between living to play and playing to live remained crucial and was reflected in a variety of ways, for example in the upper-class reluctance to publish literary productions. Manuscript circulation remained the normal mode of dissemination for the Elizabethan gentleman. Courtiers composed poems to be sung at court, passing them on to musicians to provide the settings; later such lyrics might be published anonymously in songbooks, appearing under the composer's name. Dowland's collections contain poems now attributed to some of the leading courtiers of the day, among them the ill-fated Earl of Essex, Sir Edward Dyer, Fulke Greville, William Herbert third Earl of Pembroke, George Clifford Earl of Cumberland, and Sir Henry Lee. In general the standard of writing in songbook lyrics is impressively high, although it is still difficult to establish the individual provenance of many of the items that appear in them or of those in other contemporary manuscripts. Prose as much as verse would circulate in manuscript, as did Sidney's *Arcadia* before its publication in 1590.

The professional aspect of music also embarrassed Sir Thomas Elyot since, despite the pleasures of technical achievement, 'a gentleman playing or singing in a common audience impaireth his estimation.' He clearly felt on safer ground in recommending more traditional courtly pastimes, such as riding, hunting and other outdoor sports. Dancing, in particular, occupies four chapters (xix-xxii), being considered delightful in itself as well as a potent symbol of universal harmony. Unlike the great chain of being, the dance provided an image of active participation in society and the universal order, that implied the conscious acceptance of one's allotted role. The only alternative was to break time and measure, a rejection which might spoil the efforts of one's fellow-dancers. The dance figures repeatedly in Renaissance literature, bringing comedies to a formal end (as in *Much Ado About Nothing*), uniting the courtly performers and their audience in a masque, even providing a theme for cosmic rhapsodies in Sir John Davies's poem *Orchestra* (1596). The latter associates the creative efforts of the individual with the divinely ordered creations of God, as does the passage in *The Faerie Queene* where Calidore stumbles upon the dance of the Graces on Mount Acidale (VI. x. 10–17). The popularity of the dance as an image was connected with its almost universal appeal, from peasants stamping out their traditional rounds to the Queen performing a galliard, while, as Elyot explained, the motions of the universe seemed to the disciples of Plato to take the form of 'dancing or saltation'. In Jonson's masque *Pleasure Reconciled to Virtue* (1618), the archetypal creator Daedalus alludes to such idealizing associations when he sings

'For dancing is an exercise
  Not only shows the mover's wit,
But maketh the beholder wise,
  As he hath power to rise to it.'   (240-3)

If dancing as an exercise could also signify the right ordering of society, riding, another courtly accomplishment, might figure the triumph of reason or intellect over man's insubordinate animal passions and, by extension, his benevolent mastery over the more violent aspects of the natural world. As Stephen Orgel has observed, 'To bring the destructive energies of nature under control, both within and without, was the end of Renaissance education and science.'

Castiglione, much less conscious of the social or political aspects of courtiership than Elyot, constantly directs his discussions towards personal goals of self-improvement rather than towards the improvement of society as a whole. His courtier's skills are ideally to be displayed with a certain graceful negligence, *sprezzatura* or *grazia*, which will make them more pleasing than if they appeared studied, the outcome of deliberate effort. His elaborate definition of this desirable 'simplicity or recklessness' (in Hoby's slightly odd phrase) nevertheless suggests the art that conceals art, ultimately contradicting the possibility of that very spontaneity it seeks to promote, producing instead a self-consciousness that may, in its turn, shade dangerously into insincerity, even dissimulation. Yet the ideal of self-forgetfulness, of absorption into something beyond the self is potent within *The Courtyer* and is nowhere presented more forcefully than in Pietro Bembo's discourse on divine love at the end of Book IV, where the speaker enacts the self-forgetfulness he recommends. This last book gives some consideration to the purpose of the courtier's acts and, in an attempt to present them as something more than delightful pastimes, they are claimed to be a means of winning princely favour and thus of influencing the ruler to do good. Practical justifications, however, figure insignificantly in the book as a whole and the final pages provide a rapt exposition of Platonic or Neoplatonic love doctrines (mainly derived from the school of

Florentine Neoplatonists – see p. 4) which were strongly to influence Elizabethan love poetry. Here Bembo challenges the conventional distrust of physical beauty as a snare, insisting that all manifestations of beauty in the world, including feminine beauty, result from the presence of spiritual or heavenly influences, so that such beauty, rightly understood, ought to lead men not to sensual indulgence but to a rational or intellectual love focused on the heavenly elements within that earthly beauty. The lover can then cease to depend upon sexual gratification, or even the loved one's physical presence, progressing up the stairway of love, as Socrates had taught in Plato's *Symposium*, to the contemplation of all beauty and goodness wherever they are to be found on earth, and finally to beauty (or virtue) itself, in its most ideal and transcendent form. Such a contemplation would carry a man out of his body and up to heaven, and even as Bembo is speaking he seems to be '(as it were) ravished and beside himself . . . without once moving, holding his eyes toward heaven as astonied', as if in an ecstasy. When Emilia Pia touches his robe, he comes to himself, scarcely knowing where he is.

The Neoplatonic concept of the heavenly elements present in all beauty was to become a commonplace of love poetry, recurring, in one form or another, in all the major poets of the age. Sidney's sonnet sequence *Astrophil and Stella* often employs it as a point of departure. Sonnet V acknowledges that

> true beauty virtue is indeed,
> Whereof this beauty can be but a shade,
> Which elements with mortal mixture breed . . .

while Sonnet XXV cites Plato's authority for the view

> That virtue, if it once met with our eyes,
> Strange flames of love it in our souls would raise . . .

an image which Bembo had also borrowed: 'What happy wonder . . . that taketh the souls which come to have a sight of the heavenly beauty? What sweet flame?' Donne was another poet who made extensive use of Neoplatonic ideas and imagery, while characteristically endowing them with jokes, twists or paradoxes of his own. He used the concept of the ecstasy as an experience of spiritual love in the poem of that name, and regularly distinguished between sensual lust and the spiritual love that survives consummation and absence, even though he insisted (in contradiction to the received view) that

spiritual love required sexual fulfilment for its completion. Like
Bembo, he glimpsed in the loved one 'the true image of angelic
beauty'. Although the exact extent has been debated in each case,
Sidney, Spenser and Donne were all strongly influenced by Neoplatonism, with its notions of an ideal love, or divine aspiration, and
of the soul imprisoned in the retarding body (for matter was regarded
as inert, even negative if unredeemed by spiritual influences).
Michael Drayton revealingly entitled a sonnet sequence *Idea* (1593),
and of the many enchanting love songs that exploit these concepts,
Campion's experiment in classical metrics is one of the loveliest:

> Rose-cheeked Laura, come
> Sing thou smoothly with thy beauty's
> Silent music, either other
> Sweetly gracing.

> Lovely forms do flow
> From consent divinely fram'd;
> Heav'n is music, and thy beauty's
> Birth is heavenly.

While the doctrine of love was probably its most familiar and
vulgarized aspect, Neoplatonism pervaded Renaissance thinking in a
variety of forms. Although Plato had been read and revered during
the Middle Ages, a fresh impact was made by the rediscovery of his
texts in Greek and a renewal of interest in his Christian disciples,
especially Plotinus and Porphyry. The fifteenth-century Florentine
scholar Marsilio Ficino translated the Platonic dialogues into Latin,
regarding Plato as one of the transmitters of a repository of secret
wisdom, the so-called ancient theology, a tradition of mystic, even
magical thought believed to have been handed down from the Jewish
patriarchs through Moses and Zoroaster, by way of the Egyptians to
Pythagoras, Socrates and his pupil Plato. Especially important to
those interested in this mystic system were a group of writings associated with a mythical figure, Hermes Trismegistus (see p. 25), and
considered of great antiquity, though in 1614 correctly dated to the
early Christian era by the scholar Isaac Casaubon. By then the views
expounded in these Hermetic texts had been influential for well over
a century; they emphasized the power and potential of man to do and
become whatever he wished, to dominate the natural world through
the exercise of will and imagination, at a time when changes in the

existing power-structure encouraged such aspirations. Scholars like Ficino also found in them intimations of a darker power to be gained by self-discipline and the acquisition of a secret knowledge, the knowledge of 'natural magic', power over the elements that made up the natural world.

The figure of the Neoplatonic mage, whose lamp still burnt at midnight in Milton's 'Il Penseroso', found its noblest representation in Shakespeare's Prospero, its basest in Jonson's fraudulent Subtle, the eponymous villain of *The Alchemist*. Prospero is a particularly intriguing figure because in him are united the age's three most potent images of the power to transform: as mage, he can control the disruptive elements and spirits of the natural world and subdue them to his nobler purposes; as king, though he failed once, he is given a second chance to restore and redeem corrupt society through the benevolent use of his authority; and as an artist, the transforming images of his art, exemplified in the masque he calls up, can work on the audience's mind, leading them delightfully towards personal virtue and self-control. A belief in the power of the imagination to transform the world by projecting its images onto actuality was common to both the natural magician and the Renaissance artist, endowing both roles with a special authority. Associated with natural magic, though independent of it, was the belief that the beauty of nature might figure or manifest the secret processes and workings of God, an idea that inspired some of the finest seventeenth-century nature poetry, including lyrics by Marvell and Vaughan. An admiration for earthly beauty within a system as transcendent and otherworldly as Plato's seems, as has been observed (p. 4), to verge on the paradoxical, yet the fruitfulness of Platonic philosophy largely consisted in its flexibility and versatility: Castiglione could draw on Plato as a structural model for his dialogue, as a political philosopher who, in *The Republic*, laid down guidelines for a just society, and as the ultimate authority on transcendent love.

The man whom contemporaries saw as approximating most closely to Castiglione's ideal courtier by virtue of his fine moral and intellectual qualities and his numerous accomplishments was Sir Philip Sidney (1554–86). Outstanding poetic gifts were accompanied by a (probably self-conscious) element of careless grace or *sprezzatura*. Writing in *A Defence of Poetry* of the title of poet, he modestly observed 'as I never desired the title, so have I neglected the means to come by it. Only overmastered by some thoughts, I yielded an inky tribute unto them.' A similar approach is to be found in *Astrophil and Stella*, where Sonnet XC asserts

> In truth I swear, I wish not there should be
> Graved in mine epitaph a poet's name . . .

In general the sequence strenuously subordinates artistic self-consciousness to the force of self-forgetful emotion from the first sonnet where, amidst the throes of frustrated creativity, '"Fool," said my Muse to me, "Look in thy heart and write."' Sidney may have practised a comparable courtly negligence in life: his decision to leave off the thigh-pieces of his armour when fighting at Zutphen in the Netherlands, possibly made in a similar spirit, was to prove fatal. He was exceptional among Elizabethan noblemen in losing his life on the battlefield.

Castiglione's careless grace in achievement was combined in Sidney with a thoroughly English earnestness, a deeply humanist conviction that to teach was even more important than to entertain. In *A Defence of Poetry* he insists that the poet's primary responsibility is to instruct, to set before his reader the finest models that might be: 'so true a lover as Theagenes, so constant a friend as Pylades, so valiant a man as Orlando, so right a prince as Xenophon's Cyrus, so excellent a man every way as Vergil's Aeneas'. Epic, or as Sidney calls it, 'heroical poetry' is the 'best and most accomplished kind' since it 'inflameth the mind with desire to be worthy, and informs with counsel how to be worthy.' Spenser in the dedicatory letter to Raleigh that accompanied *The Faerie Queene* endorsed this view, stating that his 'general end' had been 'to fashion a gentleman or noble person in virtuous and gentle discipline' and adding how 'much more profitable and gracious is doctrine by example than by rule'. The similarities between Sidney's precept and Spenser's practice may owe as much to mutual discussions in the late 1570s as to prevailing opinions on the subject of epic poetry. Sidney too attempted the heroic vein, though not in verse – indeed, he did not consider verse an essential attribute of poetry (or 'making') at all:

It is not rhyming or versing that maketh a poet . . . But it is that feigning notable images of virtues, vices, or what else with that delightful teaching, which must be the right describing note to know a poet by.

His revision of the prose romance he had written to amuse his sister, the Countess of Pembroke's *Arcadia*, was clearly intended to turn it into something approaching a heroic poem, incorporating the moral lessons that the genre implied for him. The earlier 'Old' *Arcadia* had been very different, a literary version of a five-act tragi-comedy in a pastoral setting, its characters strictly limited in number, its action often farcical, its outcome a comic reversal of fortune. The heroes, Pyrocles and Musidorus, overmastered by passionate love, are so unable to separate the sensual from the spiritual that the mere force of their feelings seems to them sufficient excuse, first for irrational, then for dishonest and licentious behaviour. Pyrocles seduces the innocent Philoclea, while Musidorus's intended rape of Pamela is only prevented by the timely (or untimely) arrival of a band of rebels, themselves symbolically linked with his dangerous and insubordinate emotions. Their author in part concurred with Castiglione's Master Bernard who had observed,

'Truly, the passions of love bring with them a great excuse of every fault, yet judge I (for my part) that a gentleman that is in love, ought as well in this point as in all other things, to be void of dissimulation, and of upright meaning.'

The three books of the revised or 'New' *Arcadia* that Sidney had written before his death are very different in tone, and their traditional completion in the last two books of the Old produces a startlingly inappropriate finale, since among other changes the heroes become more virtuous, so that their trial no longer seems justified. The revised text is structurally far more complex, weaving together various plot strands that had previously been mere digressions, if they had figured at all. In accordance with the more evident didactic purpose the heroes are endowed with a new stoicism and personal integrity which at once makes them more worthy of emulation, but also simplifies our reactions to them; attention now focuses on the tormented Amphialus, a marginal figure in the earlier version, whose unrestrained passions cast him as the victim of a series of cruel tricks of fate.

In accordance with the general shift towards the heroic mode, the pastoral character of the Old *Arcadia* gives place to a stronger emphasis on politics, war, and the panoply of war. In the revised Book I there is a pageant followed by formal jousting in which Phalantus defends the beauty of his love Artesia, in Book II a full-scale tournament to celebrate the wedding anniversary of the Iberian queen, and in Book III a series of carefully staged single combats which take place during Amphialus's war against Arcadia. In each of these episodes, Sidney describes the elaborate fancy-dress armour worn by the participants, and the *impresa* or device depicted on his shield which combined with the knight's outfit to express the symbolic role he had chosen to play. Tournaments of this kind were actually staged at Elizabeth's court, part of the fun being to see what roles the challengers would adopt. In later years, the Queen regularly celebrated her accession day, 17 November, with a fancy-dress tilt, and Sidney himself seems to have participated: Sonnet XLI of *Astrophil and Stella* has Astrophil carrying off the prize on one occasion, while in LIII he makes himself a laughing-stock by gazing at Stella when he should be riding to meet his opponent at the barriers. In the Iberian tournament described in *Arcadia* Book II the shepherd knight Philisides (another persona of Sidney's), dressed in a conspicuously expensive imitation of rustic garb, rides against Lelius, a name used elsewhere for Sir Henry Lee, Queen Elizabeth's Champion at Tilt until 1590, and the main inspiration behind the accession-day tourneys. Records show that in 1581 and 1584 Sidney, and Lee were matched against each other at this event, and on the latter occasion opened the proceedings. The Iberian tournament of Book II may thus be seen as a fictional version of a real event in which Sidney had taken part, nor was he the only poet to make literary use of these romantic festivities.

Apart from the straightforward accounts in verse by George Peele ('Polyhymnia', 1590, and 'Anglorum Feriae', 1595), Spenser seems to have had the accession-day celebrations in mind when he described his conception of the general structure of his epic, in the dedicatory letter to Raleigh: 'The Faerie Queene kept her annual feast xii days, upon which xii several days, the occasions of the xii several adventures happened.' A manuscript found at Ditchley and probably written by Sir Henry Lee contains speeches for a 'damsel of the Queen of the Fairies', a clownish knight and a hermit, apparently intended for presentation at an accession-day tilt, though when and if they were actually used is not known. Spenser's scheme in the letter to Raleigh also includes a 'tall clownish young man' who later turns out to be Redcross, the knight of holiness, and a hermit or palmer who will accompany Sir Guyon on the adventures of the second day. Of course Gloriana's annual feast is also modelled on Arthur's traditional assembly of the Round Table at Pentecost, and clownish knights and hermits, as well as fairy damsels, are stock romance properties; nevertheless, Spenser himself declared that Gloriana represented the Queen, and Elizabethan writers seem to have excelled at transposing real events into occasions for imaginative compliments. Oddly, the structure expounded in the letter to Raleigh is not actually reflected within the poem itself, though as we have it, it is incomplete. Possibly the letter included more specific allusions than Spenser was willing or able to incorporate into his text.

The strongest link, however, between Spenser's poem and the entertainments staged before Elizabeth lies less in any particular reference than in a prevailing nostalgia for the world of medieval romance, the deliberate re-creation of a lost style of chivalric knighthood being offered for courtly emulation. Roy Strong has observed that 'it is one of the great paradoxes of the Elizabethan world ... that an age of social, political and religious revolution should cling to and deliberately erect a façade of the trappings of feudalism.' Formal jousting may have been one way of disguising the sordid reality of contemporary warfare, deprived of heroic potential by the use of gunpowder and the sacrifice of 'cannon fodder'. There is certainly a stark contrast in the New *Arcadia* between heroic single combat and the mangled corpses of a full-scale battle that 'uglily displayed their trailing guts'. But the traditions of medieval chivalry were also a way of encouraging ideals of personal integrity and loyalty in her courtiers, as well as endorsing Elizabeth's rights to their homage as coming of a great and ancient lineage, the heir of English kings and, through her grandfather, of a line of Welsh princes who claimed descent from the legendary King Arthur. Much of the imagery associated with her was designed to reinforce these claims, and it is no accident that the hero of Spenser's epic is the young Prince Arthur. Sometimes Elizabeth's descent was even traced back to Brut, the mythical Trojan founder of Britain. A madrigal written by Thomas Watson and performed before the Queen in an entertainment of 1591 at Elvetham alludes to this, praying

> O beauteous Queen of second Troy,
> Accept of our unfeignèd joy.

If the sanctions of her right to rule were thus indirectly invoked in the medieval imagery of the tilts, there were also religious claims to be made for Elizabeth as the godly prince, the protestant leader who stood against the antichristian figure of the Pope, and this aspect of her authority was emphasized in Foxe's *Acts and Monuments* (see p. 75) as well as by her preachers. Accession day was not merely an occasion for court celebrations, though the tilts, complimenting the Queen and displaying the foremost courtiers, were open to the public as a kind of archaic winter Wimbledon. All over the country a popular holiday, the first truly protestant holiday, was celebrated. The popish festival of St Hugh had become Elizabeth's day, marked by sermons and thanksgiving services, as well as feasting, bell-ringing, bonfires, and cannonades. Latterly celebrations extended to the Queen's birthday (7 September) and Armada Day (19 November).

Elizabeth's virginity, which had once so much distressed those advisers with an eye to the succession, became part of her mystique as she grew too old for child-bearing. She spoke of being 'wedded to her people', combining the role of wife and mother to her country with the peerless chastity of a Diana or a Tuccia, the vestal virgin who miraculously carried water in a sieve. That sieve, like the spotless ermine and the single self-renewing phoenix, became a favourite emblem in royal portraits. Shakespeare gracefully alludes to this quality in *A Midsummer Night's Dream* where Oberon describes how Cupid loosed his arrow in vain

> 'At a fair vestal throned by the west . . .
> But I might see young Cupid's fiery shaft
> Quench'd in the chaste beams of the wat'ry moon,
> And the imperial vot'ress passed on
> In maiden meditation, fancy-free.'   (II. i. 158, 161–4)

It looks as if the cult of the Virgin Queen was promoted as a substitute for the officially outlawed worship of the Virgin Mary whose combination of chastity and motherhood Elizabeth apparently imitated. A song in Dowland's *Second Book of Songs* (1600), usually attributed to Sir Henry Lee, actually proposes (one hopes light-heartedly) the singing of a

> Vivat Eliza for an Ave Mari!

Some of her portraits as Astraea show her crowned with stars, and memorial poems occasionally allude to her heavenly assumption and coronation.

Such an attitude of worship – fanciful, yet not wholly so – is reflected in the prologue to Dekker's play *Old Fortunatus* (1599), whose speakers are two old men:

1. Are you then travelling to the temple of Eliza?
2. Even to her temple are my feeble limbs travelling. Some call her Pandora; some Gloriana; some Cynthia; some Belphoebe; some Astraea; all by several names to express several loves. Yet all these names make but one celestial body, as all those loves meet to create one soul.
1. I am of her country, and we adore her by the name of Eliza.

The alternative names suggest classical goddesses, often worshipped under different titles in different cities, and they indicate the range of literary homage paid to the Queen. 'Pandora', meaning 'all gifts', referred to the benefits she conferred on her happy people. Gloriana and Belphoebe were her personae in Spenser's *Faerie Queene*, as the author explained in his letter to Raleigh. Cynthia was a name for Diana, 'Queen and huntress chaste and fair', in particular as the moon, ruler of the waters, and often with a glancing reference to the defeat of the Armada. Elizabeth first figured as Cynthia in Lyly's play *Endymion* (1588), and subsequently in Raleigh's unfinished and obscurely solicitous 'The Ocean to Cynthia'. Raleigh, whose name Walter was pronounced 'water', punningly becomes the Ocean, and it was as the Shepherd of the Ocean that he appeared in Spenser's *Colin Clout's Come Home Againe* (1595), where the Queen was still Cynthia, as she was in Jonson's *Cynthia's Revels* (1601). Astraea was the name of the goddess of Justice who had long ago abandoned the earth, thus terminating the golden age, but whose return, prophesied by Vergil, would restore that happy time, as Elizabeth had done. She figured as Astraea in George Peele's pageant *Descensus Astraeae* (1591), in the complimentary masque that ends John Marston's play *Histriomastix* (1599), and as the subject of Sir John Davies's *Hymns to Astraea* (1599), a series of twenty-six poems based on the acrostic 'Eliza-betha Regina'. As plain Eliza, she was the 'Queen of shepherds all' in the April eclogue of Spenser's *Shepheardes Calendar*, as well as in a host of lesser pastoral poems, many of which are collected in the anthology *England's Helicon* (1600). As Zabeta she received Paris's apple, awarded to the fairest in Peele's *Arraignment of Paris* (1581), as she had also done in Hans Eworth's painting at Hampton Court, while in *The Lady of May* she herself was expected to decide between rival suitors, a shepherd and a forester, for the Lady's hand. This was an entertainment written by Sidney to be played before the

Queen as she walked through the gardens at Wanstead, his uncle Leicester's house, where Elizabeth was staying on a royal progress in the late 1570s.

One of the odder features of Elizabeth's reign is the way in which the demand for showy and artificial entertainments designed to flatter the ageing Queen and provide her with settings in which to star, far from producing an undistinguished series of weary, flat, stale and unprofitable panegyrics, instead contributed substantially to the ideal tone and imagery of some of the greatest poems of the age. Elizabeth herself possessed an unerring instinct for self-presentation, and despite harsher realities, the roles she assumed in poems, plays and portraits continued to captivate men's imaginations; she was seen as reigning over a golden age of peace and plenty. When the rest of Europe was at war, the English, according to Lyly's *Euphues and his England* (1580), were 'neither to be molested with broils in their own bosoms, nor threatened with blasts of other borderers; but always, though not laughing, yet looking as through an emerald at others' jars'. This distorted view of things tended to increase, rather than diminish, after her death.

As time wore on, however, the flattering addresses grew more and more out of step with reality. The Guise in Chapman's play *Bussy D'Ambois* (1604) complains of the English

> 'making semi-gods
> Of their great nobles; and of their old Queen
> An ever-young and most immortal goddess.'   (I. ii. 11–13)

Although 1588 saw the miraculous victory over the Spanish Armada, the 1590s were years of plague, dearth and civil unrest, culminating in the embarrassing folly of Essex's rebellion in 1601. Morley's collection of madrigals, *The Triumphs of Oriana*, presented to the Queen in the same year, were not happily named, for all their allusion to Spenser's Gloriana. Oriana means 'rising'; in truth Elizabeth was sinking, growing old, ugly, and more than ever unreliable in temper; only her notorious meanness was increasing. To men of Shakespeare's generation, born close to her accession, it must have seemed as if she had reigned forever, and the shadow of that old, moody, quick-tempered ruler who had governed time out of mind falls across *King Lear*. Beneath the myths of her semi-divinity lurked harsher truths, just as behind the courtly welcomes to great houses – for example at Lee's Ditchley in 1592 –

> Happy hour, happy day
> That Eliza came this way

– we glimpse Sir Henry himself prophesying ruin on hearing that 'Her Majesty threatens a progress and her coming to my houses.'

A similarly unromantic chasm opens up between the projected images of the great patrons of art, men like the Earls of Leicester and Pembroke, lauded by clients as the Maecenas of their day, protector of the faith or generous benefactor, and the miserable shifts to which such men were regularly driven in order to maintain their status and influence. The Earl of Leicester acquired the rights to customs dues on a variety of Mediterranean imports, as well as reclaiming, with apparent harshness, lapsed royal rights in the Forest of Snowdon, while the third Earl of Pembroke bought one of the great sinecure offices in the Court of Common Pleas. The old ideals of generous and open housekeeping and patronage could no longer be maintained without recourse to whatever dubious capitalist enterprises were currently available. Literature, proliferating rapidly, was particularly in need of subsidies, and not merely for creative writing: histories, sermons, translations and learned discourses were hawked about in search of patrons, whose attitudes were hardening in the face of too frequent requests. When Richard Robinson presented Sir Thomas Egerton with a learned theological translation he had made, the great man demanded 'What have we here? Begging letters?' Fulsome dedications became the order of the day, designed to obtain some financial gift in return (about £2 was average) or perhaps a more durable reward, for example a place in a household as tutor, clerk or even secretary. The old system of individual patronage of particular authors by noblemen no longer operated under the new conditions produced by the printing press, which had created so many new readers and writers; yet the author's receipts were commonly inadequate to support him; a few were even obliged to pay to have their books printed at all. Far larger numbers of writers now expected rewards from both readers and patrons that too often were simply not available. By the end of the sixteenth century a host of poetasters were urging unwanted dedications on reluctant patrons. Nashe in *Pierce Penniless* (1592) warned his friends to be more circumspect in the matter:

Alas, it is easy for a goodly tall fellow that shineth in his silks, to come and outface a poor simple pedant in a threadbare cloak, and tell him his book is pretty, but at this time he is not provided for him.

Though Nashe's sympathy is with the poor pedant, unsolicited dedications could be a nuisance, especially when accompanied by a demand for prompt remuneration. If Dekker is to be believed, there were rogues who printed up pamphlets with elaborate dedicatory epistles into which they inserted, by hand-printing, the names of a number of different noblemen, in the hopes of being reimbursed by as many as possible of the dedicatees. Dekker calls this trick 'falconry'.

Some writers found the system of sycophantic dedications so repellent that they made fun of the whole thing, as did the satirist John Marston. His first book, *The Metamorphosis of Pygmalion's Image* (1598) was dedicated 'To the world's Mighty Monarch, Good Opinion', his volume of satires 'To his most esteemed and best beloved self', while his play *Antonio and Mellida* was published in 1602 with a full-blown dedication

To the only rewarder and most just poiser of virtuous merits, the most honorably renowned Nobody, bounteous Maecenas of poetry and lord protector of oppressed innocence.

Obviously the only dedication that did not expose itself to the charge of insincerity was one to a friend or colleague from whom no financial return was expected, and so in 1604 Marston dedicated his best play *The Malcontent* to his friend Ben Jonson. Under such circumstances, Francis Bacon's tart dismissal of the whole convention seems amply justified:

Neither is the modern dedication of books and writings, as to patrons, to be commended: for that books (such as are worthy of the name of books) ought to have no patrons but truth and reason.

(*Of the Advancement of Learning*, Book I, A. 3. ix)

Bacon, however, could better afford such a view than some of his contemporaries. Although Shakespeare and a handful of other popular playwrights supported themselves adequately on their stage earnings, the coterie dramatists apparently had a more difficult time. Lyly wrote a desperate letter to the Queen when he was in serious financial difficulties at the end of his life. Jonson, who mainly depended on court commissions, also seems to have encountered difficulties latterly, to judge by 'The Humble Petition of Poor Ben' and several other elegantly begging verses. In addition to his royal pension of a hundred marks (about £33 per annum), Jonson was also granted a pension of £25 a year for books by the Earl of Pembroke. The poets Michael Drayton and Samuel Daniel depended on private patronage for most of their lives, while John Donne, in the difficult years at Mitcham, was glad of the patronage of Sir Robert Drury, whose daughter's death he celebrated so extravagantly in *The First Anniversary* (1611). Spenser was awarded a royal pension of £50 a year on the strength of *The Faerie Queene*. Earlier he had obtained the position of secretary to Lord Arthur Grey, probably through the good offices of Leicester or Sidney. Spenser's administrative position at Dublin is a good example of one of the difficulties inherent in the whole question of patronage, since it is uncertain whether it was intended partly as a sinecure, allowing him a certain amount of spare time to write his projected epic poem, or whether it was intended to make serious demands on the known capabilities of a competent official. The habit of courtly compliment, incidentally, was so deeply ingrained in Spenser that he published *The Faerie Queene* with sixteen dedicatory sonnets addressed to different courtiers; even this looks restrained beside the ninety-three different dedications of Geoffrey Whitney's *The Choice of Emblems* (1586).

Although Spenser was one of the age's worthiest recipients of patronage, he clearly had few illusions about the workings of the system as a whole. *Mother Hubberd's Tale* vividly evokes the frustration of the gifted man compelled to wait on the whims of the more privileged:

> Full little knowest thou, that hast not tried
> What hell it is, in suing long to bide:
> To lose good days that might be better spent;
> To waste long nights in pensive discontent;
> To speed to-day, to be put back tomorrow;
> To feed on hope, to pine with fear and sorrow;
> To have thy Prince's grace, yet want her peers';
> To have thy asking, yet wait many years;
> To fret thy soul with crosses and with cares;
> To eat thy heart through comfortless despairs;
> To fawn, to crouch, to wait, to ride, to run,
> To spend, to give, to want, to be undone.

Unhappy wight, born to disastrous end,
That doth his life in so long tendance spend.   (895–908)

For Spenser's disillusioned self-portrait, Colin, in the October eclogue of *The Shepheardes Calendar*, the days of patronage are over: 'Maecenas is yclad in clay.' Courtly corruption is vividly portrayed in *Colin Clout's Come Home Againe*, even if the Queen herself and a few others are excepted. Despite his idealizing celebrations, Spenser remained firmly in touch with the harsher realities of his day. Though Gloriana represented the Queen and *The Faerie Queene* was dedicated to her, within it she appears only as a fleeting ideal, and even her fairy knights are carefully distinguished from human knights, and have their own genealogy (consulted by Guyon in Memory's chamber, II. x. 71–6). Book V, the most topical, begins with a warning of the injustice of the degenerate world (see page 36), and here Elizabeth figures as Mercilla, reluctantly accepting the guilt of Duessa, driven by a grim necessity rather than revelling in the joyous freedom that characterizes her other persona, the huntress Belphoebe. For Spenser, human courts were sad places, and his imagination is cheered and liberated when he releases his courtly knight, Calidore, into the pastoral world. The Faerie Queen's court at Cleopolis is another matter – a golden age dream, as desirable as it is unattainable.

The more the court was idealized and presented as the fountain-head of all order, culture and learning, the more obvious became the gaps between the illusion and the reality. The court was supposed to set standards for the rest of the country, and wicked courtiers, according to Castiglione, 'do infect with deadly poison not one vessel, whereof one man alone drinketh, but the common fountain that all the people resorteth to'. Ben Jonson took up this familiar metaphor in his dedication of *Cynthia's Revels*, which characteristically moves from compliment to scolding:

To the special fountain of manners the Court. Thou art a bountiful and brave spring, and waterest all the noble plants of this island. In thee the whole kingdom dresseth itself, and is ambitious to use thee as her glass. Beware then thou render men's figures truly . . . It is not powdering, perfuming, and every day smelling of the tailor, that converteth to a beautiful object: but a mind shining through any suit, which needs no false light, either of riches or honours, to help it.

Valuing men in terms of appearance rather than real worth was an error to which courtiers were particularly prone. Spenser commented on the tendency in *Colin Clout's Come Home Againe* (line 711), and Elizabeth herself, with her thousands of dresses, seemed to encourage such attitudes. She could not have been pleased when Thomas Drant preached to her of Adam and Eve's nakedness, and Sir John Harington reports her irritation with a bishop who touched 'on the vanity of decking the body too finely . . . Perchance the bishop hath never sought Her Highness' wardrobe, or he would have chosen another text.'

The fountain image recurs at the opening of Webster's *The Duchess of Malfi*, where Antonio describes the happy French court, but, like Castiglione, Webster is concerned with the fountain's capacity to pollute the whole of society:

> 'a Prince's court
> Is like a common fountain whence should flow
> Pure silver-drops in general. But if't chance
> Some curs'd example poison't near the head,
> *Death and diseases through the whole land spread.'* (I. i. 11–15)

Nor was this entirely a figure of speech. Webster's contemporaries commonly believed that God rewarded or punished a whole people according to whether he was pleased or displeased, not merely with their behaviour, but with that of their rulers, so that bad times, evil enough in themselves, might further indicate that something was wrong at the top. Certainly the wickedness of princes and their tendency to corrupt the rest of society were favourite themes of Jacobean tragedy.

The treachery and uncertainty of court life had long been commonplace poetic topics. In *Pierce Penniless*, Nashe quoted a tag from Seneca's *Hippolytus* (982), 'Fraus sublimi regnat in aula' (treachery reigns in the lofty palace), which he rendered more familiarly as ''tis rare to find a true friend in kings' palaces'. The second chorus of Seneca's *Thyestes*, dealing with a similar theme, had been effectively translated by Wyatt in the verses beginning

> Stand whoso list upon the slipper top
> Of court's estate . . .

Henry VIII's court poets, Skelton, Wyatt and Surrey, wrote particularly movingly on the instability of court life, no doubt because it was only too vivid to them, and Spenser's persona Colin Clout was adopted from Skelton's satire of that name. Sidney composed a pastoral in 'Dispraise of a Courtly Life', preferring the shepherd's simplicity to the insincerity and dissimulation of the court:

> Greater was that shepherd's treasure
> Than this false, fine, courtly pleasure,

while Raleigh composed a 'Farewell to the Court'. Nevertheless, much the most forceful criticisms of court life, outside sermons and pamphlets, were expressed in the drama, though necessarily indirectly, due to censorship, the courts shown usually being those of France or Italy, Denmark, Spain, or England at some remote date. The outrages regularly perpetrated may partly reflect a typical English chauvinism that saw abroad, especially Italy, as a paradise for poisoners and sexual perverts, a view that found some justification in the more melodramatic events of recent Italian history. Yet the depravity presented also had a more reflexive aspect, since flattery, spying, whispering, plotting, bribery, exploitation of status and privilege and general moral laxity were also characteristic of contemporary English court life, and were presumably intended to be recognized as such by those familiar with it. For some who were not, it is possible that any idealized conception of the court they may have had was undermined by what they saw on the stage; alternately they may have felt relieved that such violent events bore so little resemblance to the home life of their own dear Queen. There were occasions, however, such as the Essex rebellion or the murder of Sir Thomas Overbury, when life appeared to be imitating art. The popularity of dramatic exposés of scandal in high places is easy enough to explain: then as now, audiences revelled in the unrestrained wilfulness and glamorous self-indulgence of the great which simultaneously invited vicarious enjoyment and moral disapprobation.

A strong tradition held that one of tragedy's functions was to act as a mirror for princes, so that by presenting the vices of tyrants and the corruption of courts it might warn great men how important it was to carry out their duties justly and conscientiously, and listen to their wisest counsellors. Certain dramatists convey a deep conviction of the moral dangers incurred at court. In *The Revenger's Tragedy*, the sexual rapacity of the courtiers and the defencelessness of their victims is emphasized both through the action and in individual speeches. Vindice, testing his sister's virtue, urges the attractions of high life:

> 'Oh think upon the pleasure of the palace,
> Securèd ease and state; the stirring meats
> Ready to move out of the dishes
> That e'en now quicken when they're eaten;
> Banquets abroad by torchlight, musics, sports . . .
> Nine coaches waiting – hurry, hurry, hurry –'   (II. i. 195–9, 202)

Similar accounts of court life occur in Middleton's tragedy *Women Beware Women*, as well as in plays by Marston and Chapman. Antonio's last words in Webster's *The Duchess of Malfi* urge

> 'Let my son fly the courts of princes'   (V. iv. 71)

while Vittoria in *The White Devil* dies declaring

> 'Oh happy they that never saw the court,
> *Nor ever knew great men but by report.*'   (V. vi. 259–60)

In real life, similar words were sometimes spoken by those about to die on the scaffold, an appropriate moment for public repentance for a misspent life. Sir Walter Raleigh declared 'I have been a soldier, a sailor and a courtier; which are courses of wickedness and vice.' Two accomplices caught up in the Overbury murder trial harped on the same theme, Sir Gervase Elwes recalling how his father had 'charged him on his blessing that he should not follow the court', while Mrs Turner melodramatically exclaimed:

'O the court, the court! God bless the King and send him better servants about him, for there is no religion in most of them but malice, pride, whoredom, swearing and rejoicing in the fall of others. It is so wicked a place as I wonder the earth did not open and swallow it up. Mr Sheriff, put none of your children thither.'

The Overbury murder and trial (1613–15), though exceptional in many respects, suggests that courtiers could, on occasion, behave with all the passion, ruthless egotism and high-handed self-will exhibited on the stage. Frances Howard, seventeen-year-old daughter of a great family, insisted on divorcing her husband, the young Earl of Essex, in order to marry James's current favourite Robert Carr, now Viscount Rochester. She could only do so on the grounds of non-consummation, and James was obliged to set up a panel of bishops, including George Abbot and Lancelot Andrewes, which he coerced into declaring her a virgin. In her path stood Carr's confidant and secretary, Sir Thomas Overbury. She arranged for him to be imprisoned in the Tower, where she subsequently poisoned him, but the incident remained undiscovered until after her remarriage, when the murder trial revealed the young Countess's conduct in much salacious detail. She and her (perhaps innocent) husband were found guilty, but reprieved, imprisoned for a while and permanently exiled from the court. The lesser people who had acted as accessories – the Governor of the Tower, Sir Gervase Elwes, the go-between, Mrs Turner, and other unimportant tools – all died on the scaffold. Such exploitation of others, combined with personal exemption from the heaviest penalties, must have aroused deep resentment; a similar bitterness is often to be found among the tool villains and parasites of Jacobean drama.

The Overbury murder raises the important, if unresolvable question of whether James's court was in fact more loose-living than Elizabeth's, as a number of contemporary writers seemed to think. Sir John Harington, for example, wrote a hilarious account of court drunkenness on the occasion of a visit from the King of Denmark in 1606. A masque was intended, but the allegorical figures were past performing with any competence, and one accidentally threw her tray of sweetmeats into the Danish King's lap. Charity was the only member of the sacred triad sober enough to speak her lines, but she soon returned to 'Hope and Faith, who were both sick and spewing in the lower hall', while Peace 'much contrary to her own semblance, most rudely made war with her olive branch'. James's court certainly seems to have been more drunken and rowdy than Elizabeth's; she kept a tighter rein on misbehaviour, even disapproving of marriage among her favourites, though this probably encouraged secretiveness rather than greater chastity. Elizabeth's repressiveness or James's permissiveness were in any case only partial factors, the crucial attitudes of the courtiers themselves being harder to determine. While many of the tragedies depicting court debauchery were written under James, this may have more to do with the development of tragedy than with any exactly corresponding alteration in court behaviour. *Hamlet* (1601), antedating James's accession by at least two years, is the play of Shakespeare's that most vividly creates an atmosphere of court corruption, while Marston's Antonio plays of the same period satirize time-servers and sycophantic carpet-knights. In retrospect, however, Elizabeth's court probably seemed respectably old-fashioned.

In one area of taste, too, Elizabeth's court remained distinctly old-fashioned. Notwithstanding the genius of the miniaturist Nicholas Hilliard, Elizabethan painting as a whole tended to be stiff and icon-like, portraying an individual surrounded by the badges and emblems of office in a style that, despite a sharp eye for the detail of an embroidered dress, a jewelled ring, or a patterned carpet, looks primitive in comparison with most contemporary European painting. The art of depicting complex perspective, as well as the neo-classical influences on painting, sculpture and architecture, were largely introduced by James's brilliant protégé Inigo Jones. Music, however, like literature, was not affected by the parochialism that inhibited the development of the plastic arts at Elizabeth's court, and indeed this was a great age for English music. In 1588 Nicholas Younge published *Musica Transalpina*, a set of Italian madrigals with English words substituted for the Italian texts, and within a very few years English music had recapitulated the major developments that had taken place in Italian music over the previous century. Most secular music was written for performance at court, but there is evidence of the enjoyment of music as a pastime at every level: pedlars of the same type as Autolycus hawked new ballads to be sung, while the popularity of the court composer John Dowland extended well beyond court circles, if dramatic allusions are anything to go by: the grocer's wife in Beaumont's *Knight of the Burning Pestle* specially requests that his mournful pavane 'Lachrymae' be played, and the numerous references to it, and arrangements of it, suggest that it was a runaway success.

Dowland was versatile, but his special gift was for melancholy, introverted music. Like so many new tastes, the interest in music was fostered by the printer's art, part-songs often having their music printed in a square facing outwards, so that four participants could sit round a table and each read their music printed the right way up. Four-part music was particularly adaptable since the parts, soprano, alto, tenor and bass, might be sung, or played on consorts of recorders or viols.

Although the Elizabethans did not use the terms at all exclusively, it is convenient to divide songs up into airs and madrigals, the latter being part-songs written for four, and sometimes six parts, and it was in the arrangement of these that the Italian influence was most strongly felt. Composers rapidly developed a deeply satisfying complexity of rhythm and harmony, and a variety of decoration and invention – Byrd, Morley and above all Weelkes were the masters of the form. With several voices involved and comparatively little singing in unison, the madrigal usually consisted of a single stanza, often with greatly varied line-lengths, expressing simple emotions in repeatable phrases. The following, from a Morley songbook for five and six voices, is not untypical:

> O grief! e'en on the bud that fairly flowered
>   The sun hath lowered.
> And, ah, that breast which love durst never venture,
>   Bold death did enter.
> Pity, O heavens that have my love in keeping,
>   My cries and weeping.

It was part of the convention of song-writing that the music should underline the meaning by imitation. Thomas Morley directed the composer to 'depose your music according to the nature of the words which you are therein to express, as whatsoever matter it might be which you have in hand, such a kind of music must you frame to it.' He goes on to explain that sad words must be matched with minor keys, cheerful words with quick music and short notes, while 'when your matter signifieth ascending, high heaven and suchlike, you make your music ascend; and by contrary where your ditty speaketh of descending lowness, depth, hell and others such, you must make your music descend.' Such musical mimicry, though mocked by later composers, contributed to the entrancing plangency of much Elizabethan music, but while it was manageable in the madrigal, where only short phrases were repeated, it was harder to achieve satisfactorily in the air, a song for single voice accompanied by the lute or a keyboard instrument, and usually – not invariably – consisting of several stanzas performed to the same tune. The poet's skills here came into play, since it was necessary to maintain close parallels both in word-rhythms and meaning between the different stanzas, so that the same music would be rhythmically and significantly appropriate to each.

Perhaps the greatest exponent of this art was Thomas Campion, who composed settings for his own lyrics, though it is uncertain whether the tunes or the words were written first. He had a remark-

able ear for the rhythms of words and would make corresponding
lines in different stanzas of a song fit perfectly with one another. The
following, from his *Third Book of Ayres* (1617) is as typical as it is
graceful:

> Shall I come, sweet love, to thee
>   When the evening beams are set?
> Shall I not excluded be?
>   Will you find some feigned let?
> Let me not, for pity, more
>   Tell the long hours at your door.

In the musical setting, Campion makes the first two and the pen-
ultimate syllables of the first line short notes, while the three central
ones ('come, sweet love') are long, and in the succeeding two stanzas
he has to use phrases that can be fitted to an identical rhythmic
pattern:

> Who can tell what thief or foe . . .
> But to let such dangers pass . . .

The most complex musical treatment, however, is reserved for the
last line, which is actually sung as

> Tell the long, long hours, tell the long hours at your door.

Since 'long' is repeated, Campion uses it again in that position in the
second stanza, whose final couplet runs

> So may I die unredressed,
> Ere my long love be possessed.

In the last stanza, he progresses to an even longer vowel sound,
replacing 'long' with 'cold', which subtly reflects back on the sweet
love herself:

> Do not mock me in thy bed,
> While these cold nights freeze me dead.

Fitted to the same setting, the last line is actually sung 'While these
cold, cold nights, while these cold nights freeze me dead'.

   The necessity to adapt stanzas to fit one another so congruently,
both in terms of rhythm and meaning, encouraged close attention to

word-rhythms, and so did the practice of writing poems to fit existing tunes, as Nicholas Younge had done in *Musica Transalpina*. Earlier several of Sidney's songs in *Certain Sonnets* had been composed for popular tunes, as were several of Donne's *Songs and Sonnets*. Such attention clearly contributed to the technical achievement of lyric poetry during the period. Another exercise which developed metrical skills was that of writing Latin verses, as Campion, Donne, Herbert and others did. A few poets also began experimenting with English verse written in classical metres, forcing the irregular and accentual rhythms of English into the quantitative metrics of Latin. Scholarship had shown rhyme to be a late invention, associated with medieval Latin and unknown to the Greeks or the finest Roman poets. Might it not, then, be possible to restore the purity of unrhymed metrics in English? Some poets, notably Sidney and Campion (in his *Observations in the Art of English Poesie*, 1602), thought that it was, and though their attempts to do so remained unconvincing, their success in more regular forms is directly associated with an exceptional sensitivity to rhythm, no doubt refined by such exercises.

Sidney's experiments in classical metre were part of a wider concern with 'imitation' common to all serious writers. The critical canons of the day required that the poet follow his predecessors in certain important respects – in subject matter, form, style or treatment – while bringing to it some variation of his own. Originality thus was felt to consist in a fresh interpretation of some recognized and familiar element. Sidney was a great imitator, in that he adopted many European forms into English poetry, often for the first time; the enormously varied and experimental eclogues included in the *Arcadia* provided a treasury of models for later English poets to imitate in their turn. Here was the first formal epithalamium in English, the first formal pastoral elegy (unless Spenser's November eclogue precedes it), the first 'crown' poem (in which the last line of one stanza becomes the first of the next), and the first sestina. Of this demanding Provençal form, which rings changes on the six final words in a six-line stanza, Sidney wrote a plain version, a rhymed version and, in an extraordinary display of virtuosity, a double version. Nine different sonnet forms occur among the Arcadian verses, and the metrical variety is dazzling. The experiments in classical metres are mainly given to the disguised princes to speak, perhaps as the prerogative of the educated; these include elegiacs, sapphics and asclepiadics. An example of the last is Dorus's well-known song beginning,

Ō sweet woods, the delight of solitariness
O how much do I like your solitariness.

Pleasant though these opening lines sound, they do not convey the Latin rhythm with any great obviousness, and the choice of long and short syllables in practice tends to sound arbitrary, even though Sidney and others tried to evolve a system for deciding the length of particular syllables. A number of English polysyllables have a natural rhythm (e.g. 'delight'), but monosyllables vary in weight and emphasis according to sense, a quality that makes them conveniently versatile, but slippery where an exact configuration is required. Sidney and Campion (see p. 128) wrote delightful poems in classical metre, but unless the reader is thoroughly conversant with the models being used, these are usually only audible to modern ears when accompanied by a tune that imposes the right length on each note, as in Campion's hymn 'Come, let us sound with melody, the praises', from his first *Book of Ayres*.

As far as knowledge of the classics went, however, an Elizabethan poet might rely on familiarity at the very highest levels: Elizabeth knew Greek and Latin (she translated Boethius) and was proud of her fluency in the latter, as well as in Italian, nor was James notably her inferior in this respect. A scholarly and learned prince, he liked to cast himself in the role of Solomon, giver of peace and wisdom. What must have struck his new courtiers, accustomed to Elizabeth's parsimony, was his thoughtless extravagance. Although Elizabeth had patronized an acting troupe, from 1583 there is some doubt as to whether they actually received regular wages as an independent company, or whether they simply played together occasionally, on commission. Her entertainments were never on the grand scale of the next reign, and she encouraged her courtiers to foot the bill whenever she could gracefully do so. Formal tilts obviously involved large expenditures, but much of the cost fell on the contestants who were expected to provide their own outfits, horse, armour and whatever else might be required in the way of chariots, musicians or speakers to make an impressive entrance. James, by contrast, was a lavish entertainer and giver of gifts, showering money and titles on his favourites. Pursued by the solicitous and hopeful, he was once driven to exclaim 'You will never let me alone. I would to God you had first my doublet and then my shirt, and when I were naked I think you would give me leave to be quiet.' The privileges of great men did not include privacy or peace. But James's money was not invariably ill-spent; one of his earliest actions was to adopt Shakespeare's company, the Lord Chamberlain's Men, as his own, so that they became the King's Men, Grooms of the Royal Chamber. Shakespeare alluded gracefully to his new master in *Macbeth* where the line of kings descending from Banquo and stretching out to the crack of doom included James and his family. His plays were popular at court and performed there regularly both before and after his death.

Like the allusion to the 'imperial votaress' of *A Midsummer Night's Dream*, that to James in *Macbeth* is merely a brief bow, contrasted to those elaborately designed vehicles for applauding the royal family and their entourage which rapidly became so popular with the Stuarts, the court masques. Mummings or masques, occasions when masked or disguised visitors made an imposing entry, accompanied by speeches or songs, had long been popular at court and in great men's houses. Shakespeare himself depicted such an occasion in *Henry VIII*, where the King and some of his people arrive at Wolsey's palace masked and 'habited like shepherds' and the King, incognito, leads Anne Boleyn into a dance. Elizabeth herself had often witnessed similar events, some of them staged out of doors on her summer progresses. But the Jacobean court masques passed far beyond their simple prototypes. Combining the most elaborate spectacle and the finest music, poetry and dancing of the day, they embodied courtly magnificence at its most expansive – and expensive. At the same time the theoretical underpinning of these 'worldly toys' took its origins from the highly unworldly philosophy of Plato and his disciples. Notions of Plato's philosopher king and more recent Italian accounts of the court as a storehouse of virtue and taste were presented to a courtly audience, both as an imaginative exemplification of themselves as they were, and as an ideal of what they might become, 'a kind of mimetic magic on a sophisticated level, the attempt to secure social health and tranquillity for the realm by miming it in front of its chief figure', as Jonas Barish has expressed it. Celebration and moral education were combined in the form, as Sidney had believed they should be in epic or heroic poetry, and as Spenser had combined them in *The Faerie Queene*. The excitement, splendour and action characteristic of the tilts combined with a poetry fusing epic, dramatic and lyric elements into a new form that voiced several of the main concerns of the age. This was the ideal mode for princely instruction, Sidney's 'delightful teaching' which, in the humanist tradition, combined usefulness with sweetness. The greatest exponent of the form, Ben Jonson, summed up the paradoxical character of the masque thus in his preface to *Hymenaei* (1606, composed for the ill-fated marriage of Frances Howard and the young Earl of Essex):

This is it hath made the most royal princes and greatest persons, who are commonly the personators of these actions, not only studious of riches and magnificence in the outward celebration or show, which rightly becomes them, but curious after the most high and hearty inventions to furnish the inward parts ... which, though their voice be taught to sound to present occasions, their sense or doth or should always lay hold on more removed mysteries.

Reading the printed texts of Jonson's masques, we are in danger of forgetting how unimportant the actual words were and how much was contributed by the brilliant costumes not only of the royal or aristocratic performers, but also of the courtiers who joined them in the dances, as well as by the singers, the music, and the increasingly brilliant stage scenery and machines designed and invented by Inigo Jones, of which his surviving drawings give some indication. An elegant proscenium arch (then unknown in the theatre) enclosed an idealized, but often realistically perspective set (also unknown in the theatre), which slid apart or suddenly became transparent to reveal further depths, the visual equivalent of Jonson's 'removed mysteries', a temple or a garden beyond. Machines would swing round or open up to reveal performers, or entries would be made in triumphal cars drawn on to the stage. Before Inigo Jones tucked such spectacles away behind the proscenium arch, with the perspective correctly aligned to the King's chair of state – that other, and even more important focus of courtly attention – masques had often been staged at different points within the hall. Jones introduced the first modern stage to England, and the first use of theatrical illusion, but oddly it was not until the 1630s that his system of stage sets was used for performing plays at all – for the time being these continued to be acted with a minimum of scenery, on platforms thrust out among the audience.

Ben Jonson's first attempt, written for Queen Anne, was *The Masque of Blackness* (1605), but *The Masque of Queens* (1609) was the first to make use of an antimasque, a dance of grotesques, put to flight or otherwise overcome by the heroic figures of the main masque. According to Jonson's preface, the suggestion for this 'foil or false masque' came from the Queen herself, here lauded as Bel-Anna, Queen of the Ocean, Jonson's equivalent of Spenser's Belphoebe. The antimasque was a crucial device for Jonson, providing a core of conflict, as well as an occasion for the comic or indecorous elements required to amuse the King. The antimasque commonly represented the chaos of nature or the material world before redemption by the spiritual powers figured in the main actors. The heroes and deities were played by courtiers whose idealized roles afforded elegant speeches for them to deliver, but did not require that they demean themselves at all by inappropriate behaviour. The antimasque and any other unsuitable parts were taken by professional actors, often from Shakespeare's company.

In 1610 Jonson composed a masque for Henry, Prince of Wales, the fifteen-year-old heir to the throne, already renowned both for his love of learning and his skill in martial arts. His excellence at tilting and fighting with the pike may have offered an attractive alternative to his father's studious pacifism. Jonson presents him as the heir to the medieval and Elizabethan traditions of chivalry, now fallen into decay. At the outset, Chivalry is sunk in sloth in her cave, until the Lady of the Lake, King Arthur and Merlin summon the young prince, at whose name Chivalry re-awakes. The centrepiece was not the usual dancing, but an indoor tournament at barriers, designed to show off the young prince's prowess. In the following year, the Arthurian (and Spenserian) imagery was taken a stage further in the masque of *Oberon*, in which Arthur's heir is presented in a triumph, and a band of wild satyrs submit to his authority. In November 1612 the popular young prince, patron of Chapman and the long-imprisoned Sir Walter Raleigh, 'the expectation and rose of the fair state', suddenly died, perhaps from typhoid.

At the centre of the two masques for Prince Henry lay the concept of transformation, for Jonson the heart of the matter. A basic tenet of Neoplatonism had been man's ability to transform both himself and his world, and such transformations were embodied in the actions of the masques as the drowsy figure of Chivalry awoke or the wild satyrs were tamed to the Prince's service; the playwright's faith in the potentiality of his myth to educate and thus to change the court is implicit both in the situations depicted and in the act of depicting them. His intention was to present philosophical truths delightfully – Sidney's old ideal later to be endorsed by the young John Milton in his masque of 1634, *Comus*. Jonson never forgot that it was primarily the poet's privilege to lead men to reformation, but even the humble engineer could participate, since it was his *machina versatilis*, his sliding flats and panels, that created the transformations in the most literal sense. Above all, the masque celebrated the power of the king to change society, restore ancient customs and lost integrity, reconcile pleasure and virtue, change winter to summer or night to day, as in *The Vision of Delight* (1617), where Wonder asks

> 'What better change appears?
> Whence is it that the air so sudden clears,
> And all things in a moment turn so mild?'

Fant'sy replies

> 'Behold a king
> Whose presence maketh this perpetual spring,
> The glories of which spring grow in that bower,
> And are the marks and beauties of his power.'   (163–5, 189–192)

Such myths of absolute power might have a dangerous effect on an imaginative man. Prince Henry's younger brother Charles appears to have succumbed to their influence, and in his years of rule without parliament, court masques, in which he played variants of the philosopher king, grew ever more lavish and elaborate. The astonishingly high costs of these ephemeral entertainments either exemplified the traditional virtue of magnificence or appalled by their wastefulness.

Although the dramatists Beaumont, Chapman and Middleton, and the poet Thomas Campion all wrote court masques with some success, it was Jonson who brought the full weight of his inventive genius to bear on this slight form, year after year turning out surprising and ingenious antimasques, and wonderfully lyrical songs. Perhaps his most extraordinary achievement was *The Gypsies Metamorphosed*, written for the favourite Buckingham when he entertained the King at his country seat in 1621. In some respects, it is nearer a playlet than a true masque, for spectacle is kept to a minimum – Jonson probably had few regrets about that. His long association with the designer Inigo Jones finally broke up in a quarrel in 1631. Jones won in the sense that he continued to design masques for new writers, while Jonson was left to vent his spleen in the 'Expostulation with Inigo Jones', which scornfully observes that

> Painting and carpentry are the soul of masque.　　　　(50)

In *The Gypsies Metamorphosed* Buckingham and his family are got up as a troupe of gypsies who, using the canting terms of the cony-catching pamphlets, proceed to tell the fortunes of the royal guest and his distinguished entourage. The piece exemplifies Jonson's audacity, since Buckingham himself played the chief gipsy (or 'jackman') and the masque breaks all the normal rules of decorum in presenting noblemen as a band of rogues and outcasts, even if rather magical ones. Needless to say, James was delighted with it, and it was performed on two further occasions by special request, with extensive rewriting to accommodate the new occasions and company.

Although the comic intimacy of this piece is exceptional, Jonson never ceased to take risks. In 1623, Prince Charles visited Spain with Buckingham in order to negotiate his own proposed marriage to the Infanta – James had unwisely conceived the project of balancing the marriage of his daughter Elizabeth to the protestant Elector Palatine by having Charles marry a Catholic princess. In the event, it came to nothing, to the enormous relief of most Englishmen, and the failure of Charles's mission was popularly celebrated with unembarrassed enthusiasm. Jonson composed for Twelfth Night 1624 *Neptune's Triumph for the Return of Albion*, which, although rehearsed and ready for performance, was cancelled at the last minute because of a precedence dispute between the Spanish and French ambassadors – the moment was a particularly delicate one since England was now on the brink of war with Spain. The choice of Neptune to figure James seemed, on the surface, obvious enough; England was a maritime power, and the Queen had long since become Bel-Anna, ruler of the waves, yet Neptune's role in the Spanish trip had hardly been propitious – indeed Charles had almost been drowned on the voyage ('How near our general joy was to be lost'). By identifying James as Neptune, the masque cunningly suggests that in all that had happened, his benevolent underlying purposes had reached fortunate fruition. Far from the truth though this was, it put the best possible face on an unsuccessful diplomatic mission by pretending that the happy outcome had been intended from the first – Jonson implies that Neptune had never really intended to drown his own son any more than he had intended to marry him to the Infanta. Instead,

> 'now the pomp of Neptune's triumph shines!
> And all the glories of his great designs
> Are read, reflected in his son's return!'   (253–5)

The only allusion to the real purpose of his mission presents Albion/Charles as escaping from the sirens' snares.

If the choice of Neptune as presiding deity was audacious, so too was the whole opening of the masque, which begins in the banqueting hall itself, empty but for two dedicatory pillars, where the poet, about to distribute leaflets giving the masque's argument, is interrupted and cross-questioned by the cook as to the principles of his art, and then ticked off for not supplying an antimasque; this the cook remedies, producing a giant cauldron full of dancing vegetables. The masque's movement from the familiar setting of the banqueting hall into the magical depths of Neptune's palace is characteristic of many of Jonson's later masques which, rather than moving from a wild and desolate scene to the formal beauty of a palace, as earlier examples had done, increasingly tend to begin in or around James's palace and move into an ideal location.

Jonson's cook demands of the poet

> 'But why not this till now?'

The poet replies

>   'It was not time
> To mix this music with the vulgar's chime.
> Stay, till th'abortive and extemporal din
> Of balladry was understood a sin,
> Minerva cried . . .'   (114–19)

Certainly there had been great popular acclaim for the failure of the mission, expressing itself in a variety of forms. Unquestionably the most striking was Middleton's outrageous satire *A Game at Chess*, staged in August 1624. By far the most successful play of its age, it ran for nine consecutive days to packed audiences (estimated at more than 3,000 on each occasion), after which the Privy Council closed the theatre and issued a warrant for Middleton's arrest. It had presented the events of the previous year, culminating in Charles's mission, and making particular fun of the unpopular Spanish ambassador Gondomar, a crony of James's and largely responsible for the initial negotiations for the match. He suffered from an anal fistula and had to be carried about London in a special litter equipped with a 'chair of ease'. On one occasion, ribald apprentices had shouted after him 'There goes the devil in a dung cart'; a fight ensued, and Gondomar had insisted on the reluctant city authorities exacting due punishment from the culprits. One of the apprentices had subsequently died as a result of the whipping they received. Now this hated figure was burlesqued on the London stage, his striking mannerisms exactly imitated, carried in the very same litter, which the actors had somehow or other obtained. The effect was sensational.

Perhaps to avoid giving too realistic an account of the royal and noble actors, Middleton distanced his action and gave it a simplified and allegorical outline by presenting it in terms of a chess game, in which the English, naturally, are white, the Spaniards black, so as to emphasize their respective virtues and vices. Like Jonson, Middleton presents Charles (White Knight) and Buckingham (White Duke – a contemporary term for the rook or castle) as heroes, omitting any reference to their intention of negotiating the Spanish marriage. Instead, they enter the black house to expose its plots which Gondomar (the Black Knight) is tricked into revealing, thus producing the familiar gambit 'checkmate by discovery'. Middleton, experienced as a writer of pageants and masques, probably intended his structure to approach the formality and impersonality of the masque, even though the latter normally provided a radically different experience from even the most elaborate indoor theatres. Unlike Middleton's other plays, this one makes no attempt to delineate psychology, perhaps because the author saw political or diplomatic behaviour as governed by a series of rules as arbitrary as those of the chessboard. Interestingly, in a tragedy that may have been written a year or two earlier, *Women Beware Women*, Middleton had used an onstage game of chess to parallel an offstage seduction, the different moves making the different stages explicit. This tragedy ends with a court masque whose order and dignity are interrupted by a series of vengeful murders enacted within the dramatic framework. Emphasis falls on the total hypocrisy of the roles undertaken: the marriage-destroying bawd Livia plays Juno the marriage goddess. She murders her votaress, and is in turn poisoned by the smoke of her offering. The corrupt Hippolito and Guardiano are dressed as those archetypal innocents, shepherds. Though the court here uses the masque to perpetuate its own self-deception, the drama exposes that function, as it occasionally did elsewhere. For example, Strato, in Beaumont and Fletcher's *The Maid's Tragedy* (1610), bluntly complains of masques that

'They must commend their king and speak in praise of the assembly, bless the bride and bridegroom in the person of some god; they're tied to the rules of flattery.'

By the early seventeenth century, if not earlier, the Renaissance ideal of the court as a place of special moral, intellectual and cultural virtues was becoming suspect. Many found the court to be on the contrary a place of greed, fierce rivalries, artificial excitement and widespread venality. To avoid permanent disillusion, the courtier had somehow to negotiate the gap between the ideal and the reality. To do so required either some degree of self-deception or the kind of conscious dissimulation to which the age was becoming increasingly sensitive. For Nashe, the Italian art of the courtier made a man 'a curious carpet knight; which is, by interpretation, a fine close lecher, a glorious hypocrite.' Others shared his opinion, and courtiers are increasingly presented as fops or sycophants, like Le Beau in *As You Like It*, Hotspur's 'certain lord, neat, and trimly dress'd' in *Henry IV* (I. iii. 33), Osric or Oswald, or alternatively old foxes like Polonius. Marston, a professional satirist, particularly harped on the theme of the sickening flattery that characterized courtly manners: *Antonio and Mellida* includes an absurd caricature of this type, called Castilio Balthazar (Baldassare Castiglione's name reversed). When Rosaline, to whom he pays court, spits at him, he hastens to assure her 'By my wealthiest thought, you grace my shoe with an unmeasured honour; I will preserve the sole of it as a most sacred relic, for this service.' Later he pretends to have received a love letter from her, but when the angry Feliche snatches it from him ('O you spoil my ruff, unset my hair', he complains) it turns out to be only a tailor's bill for taffeta to cover his old canvas doublet, itself a further image of worthlessness overlaid with ostentatious display. Marston's plays are full of images of courtly glitter that barely conceal the seething moral corruption beneath. In the same play, great men are surrounded by

'Troops of pied butterflies that flutter still
In greatness' summer, that confirm a prince' . . .   (IV. i. 49–50)

a familiar metaphor, later used by Lear in his joyous contempt for

'gilded butterflies . . . court news . . .
Who loses and who wins; who's in, who's out . . .'   (v. iii. 13–15)

as he happily anticipates imprisonment with Cordelia.

Despite *Hamlet*, Shakespeare tends to place less emphasis than such dramatists as Marston, Webster or Middleton on court corruption. As chief dramatist to the King's Men he may have considered such an emphasis indiscreet, or it may be that his generation took a less critical attitude. *Timon* focuses on flattery, but not at court. *Lear*, however, contrasts the unattractive truth-speaking of Kent and Cordelia with the unctuous flattery, the 'court holy-water' of her sisters, in a way that suggests that court ceremonial and polite lying are somehow inextricably linked, that the one may let you in for the other. Cordelia's insistence on seeing things as they really are breaks up the proceedings in a 'most admir'd disorder' that was not tolerable in a court environment, but what, then, was wrong with that environment that it could no longer tolerate plain speaking? Castiglione and Machiavelli took antithetical attitudes to moral compromise, but Castiglione was ethically naïve – even his recommendation of a careless grace in performance negated the possibility of its unselfconscious achievement. His view that the courtier should acquire accomplishments in order to charm and influence his prince was, as More had made Hythloday argue in *Utopia*, potentially compromising, for where was the courtier to draw the line in his anxiety to please his ruler? And instead of his virtues leading the prince towards goodness, might not the prince's vices deprave or corrupt the courtier's integrity? A later handbook for courtiers, Lorenzo Ducci's *Ars Aulica* (1601, translated by Edward Blount, 1607), written to show the courtier how to gain his prince's grace, recommends the use of 'praise and flattery'. A special position of trust can be achieved by satisfying the prince's less creditable and more furtive impulses, 'as of *ambition* in procuring some high degree of honour: or of *covetousness*, gaping after gain, or *wrath*, thirsting for immoderate revenge, or of *love*, longing impatiently for the fruition thereof.' Perhaps these instructions were intended to be ironic. In them, the art of Castiglione's courtier has been overtaken by a

Machiavellian duplicity, and the subordination of all moral considerations to the great arts of pleasing and getting on. A courtier whose accomplishments were directed to the winning of his prince's favour might find moral scrupulousness more of a liability than an asset.

As courts came to be peopled by sophisticated new men, there was no longer a place for the old, simple, heroic type who was actually what he seemed. Chapman's tragedy *Bussy D'Ambois* may be intended to delineate the fall of a man whose simplicity belongs to a more ideal world, and whose inability to compromise reveals him as out of step with a decadent and morally sluttish present: Bussy is

> 'A man so good, that only would uphold
> Man in his native noblesse, from whose fall
> All our dissensions rise'.   (III. ii. 90–2)

But *Bussy* is not just a lament for a type of primal nobleman for whom there was no longer room in Europe's modern courts. He was also Hamlet's antithesis, a type of unity and simplicity that a new intellectual self-consciousness had apparently swept away, replacing it with an awareness of the contradictions and inconsistencies that characterize the protean inner self. The ability to observe himself in the act of thinking might reassure man philosophically of his tenuous existence, but it also guaranteed that he was never entirely certain whether he was playing actor or audience of his own performances.

6 The Theatre

The world to me is but a dream or mockshow, and we all therein but pantaloons and antics to my severer contemplations.

As Shakespeare was the greatest writer of his age (perhaps of any age), so drama was the most representative of the age's forms, the most alive and responsive to the permanent variety of human emotions as well as to the particular theories, philosophies and attitudes of the day. Much of the drama's vigour derived from its commercial nature, which enabled it to absorb and reflect contemporary behaviour with few constraints, and largely freed it from voicing establishment views (unlike the literature that sought for court patronage), allowing it to respond to wider and, on occasion, more critical social forces. There was a price to be paid: the Revels Office imposed censorship on plays, and this might range from the excision of a few oaths to whole scenes (the abdication at Westminster Hall is omitted from the quarto text of *Richard II*), or sometimes to the suppression of an entire play, as seems to have happened in the case of *Sir Thomas More* (? 1595), whose scenes of rioting apprentices and sympathy for a Catholic martyr presumably worried the authorities. In general, however, censorship operated along fairly rigid and simple-minded lines, and plays which today might be regarded as profoundly subversive – Shakespeare's *King Lear* or Jonson's *Bartholomew Fair*, for example – seem to have passed substantially unchallenged. The drama was to develop into an exact and sensitive register of the age's most characteristic issues: the proliferating viewpoints, the consciousness of a gap between what men said and what they did, the increasing complexity of moral conflict, and new ideas about man's role in the universe, in society, and his sense of selfhood. It occupied a precarious and ambiguous position which aroused distrust, while conferring a special versatility and flexibility.

Burbage's Theatre, erected at Shoreditch in 1576, and its successors were the first commercial theatres to be built in this country, a new phenomenon both architecturally and economically speaking, and many of their features were anomalous in one respect or another. Their very location, put up outside the city walls in the so-called 'liberties' of Shoreditch or on the South Bank (technically Surrey), at Finsbury or in the suburbs of Clerkenwell, meant that they were at once part of London and yet outside the jurisdiction of the city fathers, who consistently attempted to control or even ban the players' activities. Then the mixed audiences of the public theatres represented an exceptional blend of nobility, respectable middle-class artisans, merchants and 'mere riff-raff', a social range that took in ambassadors and apprentices, peers, pickpockets and prostitutes. Differential prices attracted this varied clientele, which some have considered the essential precondition for Shakespeare's comprehensive achievements. The theatres themselves were simul-taneously under cover yet out of doors, the playing area and galleries being roofed, while the audience stood or sat in the open. The actors' status was similarly equivocal: according to the notorious statute of 1572, wandering players were to be classed with such other undesirables as masterless men, beggars, and vagrants, as 'rogues and vagabonds', but of course the professional acting companies were far from 'masterless', being licensed, and entitled to wear the livery of their patron. Shakespeare's patron, after 1603, was the King, and along with his fellow-shareholders he thus became a member of the royal household. The greatest actor of the age, Edward Alleyn, retired enormously rich, holding office as Master of the Royal Game, Squire of Dulwich Manor and founder of the charitable institution of Dulwich College. When his first wife died he married a daughter of the Dean of St Paul's, John Donne (who, it must be admitted, seems to have treated him with some contempt).

There were numerous other anomalies associated with the theatre: women's roles were always played by boys, while the plays them-selves had assimilated an extraordinary hotch-potch of sources, from native, predominantly biblical models to classical or closet drama. Its purer forms, as advocated by Aristotle and more forcefully insisted upon by Renaissance Italian critics, were never adopted on the English stage (despite the modern tendency to discuss Shakespearian heroes in terms of a 'tragic flaw' — Aristotle's 'hamartia'). English dramatists instead 'thrust in clowns by head and shoulders, to play a part in majestical matters, with neither decency nor discretion', as Sidney complained. Laughter was always inclined to erupt in the middle of tragedy, for this was an art as impure and unclassical as it was coarse and energetic.

The inclusion of a variety of viewpoints is, of course, characteristic of drama, which exploits conflicting voices. Its greatest exponents seized the opportunities provided by the medium, including the absence of any dominant authorial voice, to pose moral problems with all the complexity and insistency of life itself, further intensifying them by the subtle manipulation of audience responses. From the 1580s, dramatists concerned themselves with important issues, often presenting them with an exceptional open-mindedness that their critics have not always shared. The drama's readiness to debate such issues at length, and the conviction that such debates would hold an audience's attention, are related to the central position occupied by the art of rhetoric in the humanist tradition (see above, p. 112). Education was directed towards the discussion of political or moral issues, the assembling of evidence to form a telling argument, and finally the speaking of those sentiments whose aim was to persuade their audience. It produced the lawyers and politicians required by an expanding bureaucracy, and was soundly based on Cicero's forensic eloquence, the aspiring rhetorician's ultimate model. Since rhetorical training included the art of delivery as well as of composition, students practised formal speech-making, both at school and university, and plays were performed as exercises in memorizing, correct pronunciation, and the effective matching of actions to words, a component of speech-making as well as an essential dramatic skill. Some of the most powerful scenes in Elizabethan drama seem to have their roots in school rhetoric exercises: the contrasted speeches of Brutus and Antony in the forum, in Shakespeare's *Julius Caesar*, recall, however distantly, the kind of school exercise in which pupils were required to attack or defend Brutus's murder of Caesar.

Greater familiarity with different philosophies or outlooks, and the evident gaps between the different primitive, classical or Christian attitudes they embodied, meant that dramatists could present particular issues or situations from inconsistent, or even opposing angles. In *Hamlet*, for example, suicide is seen from the outset as a sin, specifically forbidden by God and properly excluding the victim from burial in consecrated ground, until Horatio proposes to die with Hamlet at the end, when it suddenly becomes an act of stoic fortitude. Revenge, which features in a whole genre of tragedies, can similarly be regarded as an act of justice required by society to right a secret wrong, as part of a primitive obligation to a murdered kinsman, or as specifically forbidden by the biblical assertion, 'Vengeance is mine; I will repay, saith the Lord' (Rom. 12:19). The first half of this familiar sentence (in Latin, *vindicta mihi*), however, took on quite a different meaning in the mouth of the revenger, where it might become an assertion of his personal right to take matters into his own hands, repudiating all other claims on him. Although contemporary laws punished premeditated murder harshly, this seems to have had little effect on the actions of the plays themselves, which generally assumed that the audience would sympathize with the revenger, at least up to a point.

Perhaps the very centre of the theatrical experience is an anomalous one, for the performance challenges the audience to believe and disbelieve simultaneously, to involve themselves in what they see and be self-forgetful, and yet to let the play work upon them, involve them, even change them. It requires a sophistication of response, which a child may give readily and unthinkingly, but any pause to consider the nature of the theatrical illusion makes its paradoxes appear lumpily unresolvable. They certainly worried some of Shakespeare's contemporaries, who saw the stage as an industry for the deliberate manufacture of lies, tricks and falsehoods. While this obviously overstates the deceptive intention of the medium, Dr Johnson's enlightened insistence that 'it is false that any representation is mistaken for reality' seems, in its turn, to understate it. By offering a complex experience and demanding a complex response, the theatre was uniquely placed to voice more relative ways of thinking and feeling, as well as the consciousness of simulation and dissimulation, both within the self and in others. At the same time so much anomaly, so much marginality, so much that was so difficult to categorize conveniently, aroused suspicion and even alarm, as did the very novelty of its premises, both literal and metaphorical. Like the various philosophies presented, drama seemed to threaten older certainties, now felt to be in danger of disappearing beneath an inextricable tangle of argument, logic and casuistry. Such suspicions were justified, for the dramatists soon evolved ways of saying whatever they wanted, usually without arousing official censure, and from the outset they were fascinated by ethical dilemmas and extremes of behaviour. Their rapidly expanding moral horizons aroused the disapproval and distrust of those who would have preferred to turn the clock back. One motive behind the closing of the theatres in 1642 may well have been a desire to dispose of such awkward and uncomfortable institutions, part of a more general attempt to recover the lost simplicity and certainty of the saints.

The development of the commercial theatre in London was disturbing to many people, and not merely to puritans, because it was so wholly without precedent. While the validity of entertainment for its own sake had long been accepted in courtly circles, and defenders of the arts could invoke doctrines of teaching by pleasing, the franchise to enjoy themselves was less willingly extended to working people, and popular pastimes currently had more opponents than supporters. They were widely under attack throughout Europe, and it was not merely in protestant countries that playing, profane dancing, and May Games (or their equivalent) were being energetically suppressed. There seem to have been no earlier attempts to justify the existence of popular drama, since the moral and religious elements had been self-evident in most plays, and secular playing or mumming had not yet come under serious scrutiny. Official medieval drama had begun under the auspices of the church, had been acted by respectable members of town guilds, made no profit, and was performed for the glory of God: in general, it might be supposed to be edifying. Even though rude jokes often counterbalanced the moral message, the latter always had the last word and evil was invariably discomfited. Indeed, it was the didactic potential of drama that impressed the early reformers, men like John Bale or George Buchanan, who saw in its popular appeal useful opportunities for propaganda. The more academically minded might also have justified its value by citing Aristotle's high claims for this particular literary form, yet both responses would have seemed inappropriate to the first commercial theatres, whose primary commitments were by no means to moral or artistic goals; they were only too patently dedicated to the more sordid ambition of attracting an audience prepared to pay for their seats.

Burbage's Theatre at Shoreditch in 1576 was followed a year later by the little Curtain, on the opposite side of the road, but the next group of playhouses were built south of the river, on Bankside. Here stood the Rose (1587), managed by Philip Henslowe whose diary is the most important of all the surviving documents concerned with the Elizabethan stage; the Swan (1595), famous for its elegant furnishings, and from 1599 Shakespeare's Globe, constructed from the timbers of the earlier Theatre at Shoreditch, which was pulled down and re-erected on its new site, following a disagreement with the original landowner. Burbage's son Richard was the star of Shakespeare's company, and the great tragic roles were all written for him. Two more open-air theatres were built, the Fortune (1600) at Finsbury and the Red Bull (1606) – notorious for its rowdy audiences – at Clerkenwell, then a red-light district.

At the apex of the open-air theatres stood the stage, sheltered by a canopy which protected the actors' costly and elaborate costumes, commonly purchased second-hand from courtiers. At the back of the stage and concealed by a wall or curtain was the 'tiring house' or dressing room, and above ran a gallery used by the actors for castle walls or overhearing scenes, and sometimes by the audience too, who also sat on the stage on occasion. Above the gallery was another room used for sound effects, musicians, the trumpeter whose fanfare announced that the play was to start, and for heavenly descents. The open yard before the stage was occupied by the groundlings who stood or sat on the ground or on hired stools, those 'under-standers', so notoriously lacking in understanding, of whom the dramatists regularly complained. This open area was surrounded by a horseshoe-shaped building consisting of roofed galleries, accessible by stairs, with wooden seats and occasional private rooms like theatre boxes that were hired out to wealthier or more fastidious patrons. The whole structure is likely to have been larger than most modern theatres, and seems to have held more spectators, perhaps 2,000 or more when packed to capacity. Costs were comparatively low at first – a penny to enter and stand in the yard, another to enter the sheltered galleries, and a third for a cushion or more comfortable seat, sums of money that would have been well within the range of a London merchant. Even day-labourers, when working, received three or four pence a day, though few were employed on a regular basis. These costs, current in the 1580s and 1590s, rose in the next reign and by 1614 Jonson was referring to seats costing sixpence, a shilling and half-a-crown, one indication of the effects of inflation.

London, with its increasing trade and bureaucracy, was capable of supporting several commercial theatres and actors' companies competing against one another. An astoundingly large repertoire of plays was maintained, a different one being performed each day, according to the diary of Philip Henslowe, which recorded the takings for each play for several months at a time. Higher entrance rates were probably charged for new plays, and takings naturally went up on public holidays, and perhaps prices too. Although Sunday had traditionally been the day for presenting plays, and Elizabeth might still command a court performance then, legal steps were taken to prevent public playing on the sabbath. Complaints about Sunday acting and some rather inconclusive evidence from Henslowe's diary make it conceivable that the ban, like so much Elizabethan legislation, did not always prove effective.

Despite the popularity of certain well-established favourites (*The Spanish Tragedy* and *Hamlet* are often mentioned), there was, as with television today, a tremendous demand for new plays, and of the many that were acted, most have probably sunk without trace, while others are known to us only by name (often from Henslowe's diary), no text or manuscript having survived. Others again have survived only by chance, often in single copies, and this is partly the result of the commercial theatres' low standing in the estimation of the literary world as a whole. The professional playwrights seemed to belong to the sordid world of business transactions, rather than cultivating art for its own sake as the aristocratic closet dramatists, Fulke Greville, Sir William Alexander or Sidney's sister, Lady Pembroke, had done; they were regarded as incapable of self-respect, worthless commercial hacks who had bartered their talents for bread, and their writings were consequently assumed to be negligible. Sir Thomas Bodley, instructing his agent to collect books for his great new library at Oxford in 1612, with a maddening lack of foresight insisted that such 'idle books and riff-raffs' as 'almanacs, plays and proclamations' should be left out, lest they lay his collection open to the charge of lack of discrimination: 'The more I think upon it, the more it doth distaste me that such kind of books should be vouchsafed a room in so noble a library.'

When, a few years later, Ben Jonson published sixteen plays in a folio volume of his collected works, his action was regarded with a mixture of admiration and disapproval of the arrogance it implied. Previously plays had only been published in small quarto editions, retailing at sixpence and scarcely differing in appearance from conycatching pamphlets, accounts of contemporary scandals and similar ephemeral writings, even though their content – in some cases at least – might be very different. The Shakespeare folio of 1623 was only the second such volume to appear in that large and imposing format accorded to such works as the Bible, Foxe's *Acts and Monuments*, sermons or classical texts. Both folios contributed to the gradual reassessment of the drama and its authors that took place during the seventeenth century.

The commercial success of the theatre brought substantial rewards to some of its more notable contributors, and with these, social status, but it was probably less the success or respectability of particular individuals than a gradual change in the audiences that helped to improve its standing. By the early seventeenth century, forward-looking theatrical companies were beginning to make use of indoor theatres, in addition to the big public playhouses, traditionally the haunt of criminals, vulgar tobacco-smoking 'stinkards' and loud-mouthed watermen (the sixteenth-century equivalent of taxi-drivers). The indoor theatres – the Blackfriars (used by Shakespeare's company after 1608), the Phoenix and the Salisbury Court – were much smaller, more expensive and altogether more select. They originally charged sixpence for admission, but as public theatre prices rose, entrances went up to a shilling, and half-a-crown for the special seats allotted to members of the aristocracy. Certain plays were written with these special audiences in mind. A few, like Francis Beaumont's *The Knight of the Burning Pestle*, made gentle fun of the naïve patrons of the public stage, and a significant number of highly mannered dramas were written for the companies of child actors (Hamlet's 'little eyases') who became fashionable at the end of the sixteenth century, and who contributed to the demand for indoor theatres, where their small stature and voices did not tell against them (see below, p. 180).

Although the private theatres to some extent evolved their own repertoire as the seventeenth century wore on, several of Shakespeare's plays were written for performance outdoors at the Globe, indoors at Blackfriars, as well as within the even more exclusive confines of the court, and the repertoires of indoor and outdoor playhouses often overlapped. Court patronage of actors and plays further helped to raise their status, and the King's obligation to provide amusement for the court might have been considered some justification of the form. Certainly the substantial contribution of London's several theatres to the life of the city seems to have been recognized as exceptional; it made a deep impression on foreign visitors who were often overwhelmed by the richness of clothes, both of actors and audience, as well as by the size and scale of the whole proceedings. The point was not lost on Thomas Heywood, who in his *Actor's Apology* of 1612 asserts that 'playing is an ornament to the City, which strangers of all nations, repairing hither, report of in their countries, beholding them with some admiration.' English dramatic skills seem to have been in demand abroad, and several English companies toured Europe in the early seventeenth century, performing their repertoire in English.

Despite gradual improvements in status, the theatre had many critics, and the playhouses had always operated outside the city's boundaries in order to evade the jurisdiction of the authorities, who, as its most consistent and militant opponents, had made unsuccessful attempts to close the theatres down at least once in each of the three final decades of Elizabeth's reign, in addition to enforcing temporary closures when plague casualties rose, as in 1593–4. The city fathers regarded the playhouses as potent sources of moral and physical infection. In addition to spreading illness, they might promote sedition or subtler moral contagion since the actions presented were commonly so undesirable, 'nothing else but unchaste fables, lascivious devices, shifts of cozenage and matters of like sort', as Lord Mayors regularly complained to the Privy Council, adding, so as to pre-empt the standard defence, that they drew the audience 'into example of imitation and not of avoiding the said lewd offences'. Plays further encouraged idleness and time-wasting, especially among the young, in whom the virtues of thrift and hard work required to be inculcated. The skiving of apprentices to visit plays was particularly resented since it cost their masters money and time. Economic and religious motives mingle uncomfortably in the complaint that plays 'draw apprentices and other servants from their ordinary works and all sorts of people from the resort unto sermons and other Christian exercises, to the great hindrance of trades and profanation of religion'. Thomas Nashe, in the most intelligent and penetrating defence of the theatre to be written, characteristically in a few throw-away paragraphs near the end of *Pierce Penniless his Supplication to the Devil* (1592), comments that the actors would happily do without apprentices since, like modern football hooligans, they were inclined to indulge in vandalism. The apprentice holidays, Shrove Tuesday and May Day, were not infrequently occasions for destructive rampages.

More seriously, the theatres provided a natural focus for criminals:

thieves, pickpockets and whores plied their trades among the crowds, aided by the audience's permanently diverted attention, and even the mere numbers assembled might in themselves seem threatening. Two thousand people, excited to fever pitch by the deliberate manipulation of their emotions, embodied the very worst fears of the authorities, while a public theatre provided an ideal platform for inspiring seditious sentiment, as the performance of *Richard II* at the Globe on the eve of the Essex rebellion implied. Henry Crosse in *Vertues Commonwealth* (1603) demanded

For what more fitter occasion to summon all the discontented people together than plays? . . . at a stage play . . . the horrible rebellion of Ket and his accomplices, by a watch-word given, broke out, to the trouble of the whole kingdom.

This was the threat that made the censorship of the Revels Office so vital: the establishment had to know exactly what was going to be said on the stage beforehand, and if necessary remove any dangerous or dubious passages. In the face of such natural fears as these, it was useless to insist that plays more often propounded moral than immoral sentiments, more often reinforced authoritarian attitudes than subverted them. The church regarded the playhouses as rival concerns, drawing potential sermon audiences away from the truths that really mattered, at evensong or on holidays. Actually playwrights surprisingly often endorsed the moral lessons of the clergy, as they occasionally pointed out, but such infringement only gave further offence. I. G. in *A Refutation of the Apology for Actors* (1615) insisted

God requireth no such thing at their hands, that they should take it upon them; . . . God gave authority to instruct and preach, to correct and anathematize, only to the Apostles and to their successors, and not to players . . .

Although opponents might challenge and denouce the drama's claims to edify, the age's religious teachings are often vividly reflected within it. By showing the bad ends to which bad rulers and bad men might come, drama reflected the pulpit's characteristic preoccupation with self-indulgence, sexual licence, irresponsibility, extravagance and hypocrisy. Tragedy commonly enacted exactly those providential lessons that committed protestants were so eager to point out to doubters, sometimes in books whose very titles implied the theatrical nature of their revelations (see pp. 77–8).

The traditional opposition between strong protestant views (which disapproved of entertainment and similar frivolous distractions) and the theatre, with its harsh caricatures of puritans, certainly existed, but needs to be modified by the recognition that both dramatists and patrons might themselves be 'puritans', and that pilloried stage puritans were commonly separatists, disliked and disapproved of by almost everybody else (see pp. 81–2). Thomas Middleton was particularly associated with the ultra-protestant city fathers, for whom he wrote pageants and Lord Mayor's Shows (see p. 62). Several of the great protestant patrons also took an active interest in the theatre: the Earl of Leicester had his own company of actors, while William Herbert, third Earl of Pembroke, paid Ben Jonson a pension, and with his brother Philip was joint dedicatee of the Shakespeare first folio. A number of important parliamentarians patronized the theatre in the 1630s, the most articulate of whom, John Milton, indirectly professed his admiration for Shakespeare and Jonson, and in 1634 wrote his own masque, *Comus*, partly inspired by memories of Jonson's *Pleasure Reconciled with Virtue* (1618).

In addition to the comparatively straightforward objections, there were several complaints that derived from a general unease about the position of playhouses in society and what went on there. One source of offence already mentioned was the playing of female parts by young boys, which might have been thought to encourage homosexuality, even if the Old Testament had not specifically forbidden such transvestism. To Nashe, however, the English convention was more respectable than having 'whores and common courtesans to play women's parts'. Another objection raised was to the kind of economic parasitism that the theatres seemed to represent. Citizens earned good money which, instead of being ploughed back into trade for the general benefit, came to rest in the undeserving pockets of the players. Nashe made a tart reply:

As for the hindrance of trades and traders of the city by them, that is an article foistered in by the vintners, alewives, and victuallers, who surmise, if there were no plays, they should have all the company that resort to them lie boozing and beer-bathing in their houses every afternoon.

It was nevertheless hard, from a utilitarian point of view, to see what the actors gave of measurable value in return for all those pennies taken. Far from providing anything of recognizable worth for your money, the boards merely afforded an opportunity for any young upstart who fancied himself to chuck up his job and indulge in showing-off as a profession, swaggering about in the fine clothes of his betters, a potential threat to the whole order and fabric of society:

We are commanded by God to abide in the same calling wherein we were called, which is our ordinary vocation in a commonweal. ... So in a commonweal, if private men be suffered to forsake their calling because they desire to walk gentleman-like in satin and velvet, with a buckler at their heels, proportion is so broken, unity dissolved, harmony confounded, that the whole body must be dismembered.

insisted Stephen Gosson in *Plays Confuted in Five Actions* (1582). For critics like this, drama as a whole was based upon the principles of lying, pretence and deception, and, what was worse, elevated these sins into a commercially rewarding practice.

Elizabethan defenders of the form – with the notable exception of the clear-thinking Nashe – were singularly ill-equipped to answer such charges, largely because they themselves were confused as to how commercial drama fitted into accepted social and economic patterns. It was so awkwardly unprecedented except at the negligible level of travelling minstrels, who had never commanded respect and were now classified as vagabonds within the terms of the 1572 statute. Moreover, something of the general unease seems to have rubbed off on the dramatists themselves. Revenge tragedy, in particular, developed a range of imagery which, though primarily directed against the illusion and artifice of court life, as suggested in the previous chapter, also questioned the nature of the medium within which it operated. Over and over again, pretence and hypocrisy are condemned ('Seems, madam? Nay, it is, I know not "seems"', *Hamlet*, I. ii. 76); affected courtiers like Osric or Marston's Castilio Balthazar are mocked, and face-painting, common to actors and fast women, is satirized ('I have heard of your paintings . . . God hath given you one face and you make yourselves another', *Hamlet*, III. i. 142). Role-playing and disguise are often imposed on the hero by his situation, but they are also burdensome, prompting inner confusion and self-doubt – for where did one draw the line between necessary or politic dissimulation, and treacherous or Machiavellian simulation? The very word 'hypocrite' originally meant simply an actor. The perception of hypocrisy was particularly acute at this time. For Thomas Adams, in a famous sermon of 1612, it was 'the White Devil' that had eaten through the whole of Jacobean society. Plays-within-plays were often sinister in purpose, providing occasions for murders which the stage audiences watched as impassively as their real counterparts; both acted as willing accomplices in establishing a world that rejected reality for a glitteringly dangerous deception. In its own way, comedy too indicted its audiences for their inability to distinguish between truth and illusion: Jonson's work is full of confidence-tricksters, versatile performers whose easy manipulation of their victims echoes the players' deception of their audience, eagerly thronging to be imposed upon for three hours, and perhaps, like the on-stage fools, have their pockets picked and their purses cut into the bargain. The age's two greatest dramatists both seem at times to have felt a revulsion against their chosen medium, expressed indirectly in some of the symbolism of their plays, more directly in the more personal voice of lyric poetry:

> O, for my sake do you with Fortune chide . . .
> That did not better for my life provide
> Than public means which public manners breeds.
> Thence comes it that my name receives a brand,
> And almost thence my nature is subdued
> To what it works in, like the dyer's hand.   (Sonnet III)

It is hard for modern bardolators even to conceive that Shakespeare ever felt ashamed of the profession that gave us his work, as this sonnet implies. Jonson's great ode 'Come, leave the loathed stage' is, characteristically, more irascible. Whether it was the artificial nature of the medium itself, with its assumption of alien clothes, roles, and face-painting, the fact that it was undertaken for pay rather than for its own sake, or the low esteem in which the profession was held, that prompted such reactions cannot now be decided, but it is striking that two playwrights of such stature, on occasion, concurred with their detractors.

The distinction between truth and illusion or deception was felt to be crucial but was in practice extraordinarily difficult to define. Sidney, in his *Defence of Poetry*, confidently dismissed accusations of lying by insisting on the accepted separation of reality and make-believe: 'What child is there, that, coming to a play, and seeing *Thebes* written in great letters upon an old door, doth believe that it is Thebes?' Thomas Heywood, however, in his *Apology for Actors*, blurred Sidney's proposed distinction by suggesting that the actor's power to convince an audience of the reality of the dramatic experience might be of value, especially if it produced fortunate side-effects which might redound to the credit of the profession; he proceeds to relate several instances of these. Heywood's confusion on this subject is the more striking since he was the most prolific dramatist of the age. Eight years before his death he admitted to having written or 'had a main finger in' 220 plays, only 56 of which can now be identified. As a spokesman for the stage, he can scarcely be considered inexperienced.

For Heywood, Hamlet's belief

> 'That guilty creatures sitting at a play
> Have by the very cunning of the scene
> Been struck so to the soul, that presently
> They have proclaim'd their malefactions . . .'   (II. ii. 589–92)

is an item of faith. He reports two episodes involving women who had secretly murdered their husbands, and publicly gave themselves away by crying out in the middle of a theatrical performance. A play in which a murderer is haunted by her husband's ghost made one guilty woman believe she had seen a *real* ghost since her own murdered husband's 'fearful image personated itself in the shape of that ghost'. As well as conflating real and simulated experience, Heywood's story suggests the peculiar power that the presentation of the supernatural on stage might still have while belief in it remained strong. Ghosts and demons were especially alarming since even their pretended presence might somehow accidentally invoke the real thing. Modern stage superstitions about *Macbeth* dimly echo this attitude. An incident at Exeter during a performance of Marlowe's *Faustus*, an exceptionally satanic play, triggered off a full-scale panic among nervous actors and audience:

As a certain number of devils kept every one his circle there, and as Faustus was busy in his magical invocations, on a sudden they were all dashed, every one hearkening other in the ear, for they were all persuaded there was one devil too many amongst them; and so after a little pause desired the people to pardon them, they could go no further with this matter; the people also understanding the thing as it was, every man hastened to be first out of doors.

A different sort of confusion occurred in a further incident reported by Heywood, when a band of Spaniards landed at Cornwall 'with intent to take in the town, spoil and burn it'. Fortunately some actors were presenting a battle on stage at the time and 'struck up a loud alarm which the enemy hearing and fearing they were discovered, amazedly retired, made some few idle shots in a bravado, and so in a hurly-burly fled disorderly to their boats.' A clearer thinker than Heywood would have realized that the accidental alarm of a raiding party was in no way meritorious; instead he seems inclined to credit the actors with the conduct of a successful military operation. Elsewhere he reduces the critical commonplace that comedy promoted self-examination to its most elementary terms when he explains that the clown's 'slovenly and unhandsome behaviour' should make men 'reform that simplicity in themselves which others make their sport'. Heywood's naïve approach to theatrical experience resembles that of Simon Forman, the astrologer, who after seeing a performance of *The Winter's Tale* in 1611 concluded (apropos of Autolycus), 'Beware of trusting feigned beggars or fawning fellows', a lesson he might just as well have learned from the average cony-catching pamphlet.

Yet despite widespread intellectual uncertainty as to the nature and morality of dramatic illusion, in practice dramatists manipulated with the utmost skill and confidence a wide range of techniques that openly acknowledged or even drew attention to the mechanics of that illusion: prologues, framing devices, asides, soliloquies, plays-within-plays, moving instinctively within a well-established tradition of give-and-take with an audience. Indeed they had been confidently blending theatrical illusion with reality, deliberately reminding the audience that they were watching a play, and generally employing alienating techniques from the beginnings of medieval drama, the religious basis of which implied the mingling of the great and permanent truths of the Bible with the particular here-and-now of the audience's conscience. Mystery plays explored both these aspects, moving freely between local references and the biblical settings of their stories, conflating Christ's inquisitors with types of contemporary ecclesiastical corruption, making Herod directly threaten the mothers of young children in the audience. Justification for such an approach lay in the way that the universal truths of Christian history were always particularizing themselves in the life of the individual.

The complex deployment of theatrical illusion evolved remarkably early. Henry Medwall's humanist play *Fulgens and Lucrece*, written at the end of the fifteenth century, employs some exceptionally sophisticated devices. Its main presenters are two young men (referred to only as A and B) who at first seem to be members of the audience, chatting as they wait for the play to begin. A assumes from B's dress that he is an actor, a suggestion firmly repudiated by B. Later they decide to participate in the play's action, becoming servants to the main characters, so that they move from being (supposedly) members of the audience, to becoming commentators, to participating in the unfolding events, rather as the Vice character was to move backwards and forwards within the interludes. More than a hundred years later, Jonson's induction to *Bartholomew Fair* begins with a comparable simulation of reality as the stage-keeper, broom in hand, chats familiarly to the audience, warning them of the worthlessness of the play they are about to watch, since, in his opinion, the playwright knows nothing of his subject: 'He has not hit the humours, he does not know them.' Framing devices such as these were used to cross the gap between the reality of the audience settling in their seats and cracking their nuts (the Elizabethan equivalent of rustling sweet papers), and the illusion that must follow. There were no house lights to be dipped on the afternoon stage and so it was all the more important that the impact of the first scene should establish the right atmosphere. Many plays simply start straight into the action – the platform at Elsinore at midnight or the wordless tussle that opens Jonson's *The Alchemist*: when the antagonists have recovered sufficient breath to speak, Face threatens Subtle – 'Believe't, I will' – who contemptuously replies, 'Thy worst. I fart at thee.'

Alternatively, plays could begin with expository dialogues (*Lear*, *Othello*), with lengthy and informative soliloquies (*Richard III*, *Volpone*, *The Revenger's Tragedy*) or with a chorus or narrator (*Henry V*, *Pericles*). In addition to actors pretending to be members of the audience, as in *Fulgens and Lucrece* or Beaumont's *Knight of the Burning Pestle*, a prologue might involve a distinct set of characters who were neither audience nor participants in the main action, as in the Christopher Sly episode that opens *The Taming of the Shrew*, or in Kyd's *The Spanish Tragedy*, where the ghost of Don Andrea and Revenge have come to witness the drama, and remain on the stage throughout the succeeding events. They are awaiting satisfaction for

Don Andrea's untimely death, but events initially baffle, rather than fulfil, their expectation. This whole play is a Chinese box of dramatic tricks, many of which deliberately draw attention to the theatrical character of the action. In addition to the standard addresses to the audience by means of soliloquy or ironic asides, there is a central overhearing scene in which the villains eavesdrop on the lovers as they make a rendezvous, interjecting threatening but, to the lovers, inaudible asides. With a rhetorical neatness that is almost operatic in its effect, contrasted purposes blend into a single poetic unit:

BELIMPERIA. Why stands Horatio speechless all this while?
HORATIO. The less I speak, the more I meditate.
BELIMPERIA. But whereon dost thou chiefly meditate?
HORATIO. On dangers past, and pleasures to ensue.
BALTHAZAR [*hidden above*]. On pleasures past, and dangers to ensue.
BELIMPERIA. What dangers and what pleasures dost thou mean?
HORATIO. Dangers of war, and pleasures of our love.
LORENZO [*similarly concealed*]. Dangers of death, but pleasures none at all.
BELIMPERIA. Let dangers go, thy wars shall be with me.   (II. ii. 24–32)

In this scene the audience watch Revenge and Andrea's ghost (whose presence is recalled by Horatio's reference to the 'dangers of war' in which Andrea was killed) watching Lorenzo and Balthazar (presumably on the gallery above the stage) watching Horatio and Belimperia. A similarly complex effect is produced when Hieronymo performs his play of Soliman and Perseda before the court, in which the murders are not merely mimed but actually carried out, and the play is thus used to cloak the killing of Lorenzo and Balthazar.

The use of plays-within-plays, as in *Hamlet*, continued to be a popular device in revenge tragedy, whose consistent exploration of the relations between appearance and reality rendered it appropriate. As masques became the characteristic mode of court entertainment, these were often incorporated into plays as well: a wedding masque is staged in Beaumont and Fletcher's *The Maid's Tragedy*, while in Middleton's *Women Beware Women* (see p. 156) and Ford's *'Tis Pity She's a Whore*, it provides an opportunity for murder, as the play had done in *The Spanish Tragedy*. Deaths inflicted within the context of elaborately formal occasions, such as masques or banquets, tend to disturb modern critics because of their artificiality, but their frequent use by successful dramatists suggests that they had the reverse effect on original audiences, for whom the inevitable and uninterruptable sequence of an enacted ritual heightened excitement, rather as accompanying music might in the cinema today. The powerful demands that ritual could make are indicated in Ford's *The Broken Heart*, where Calantha receives a sequence of heartbreaking messages during a dance, but refuses to break step, declaring

> 'it is methinks a rare presumption
> In any who prefers our lawful pleasures
> Before their own sour censure, to interrupt
> The custom of this ceremony bluntly.' (v. ii. 24–8)

Though strictly unrealistic, this technique does not seem to have disturbed audiences who were accustomed to it, and on whose emotions it worked subliminally.

Plays-within-plays were not, of course, limited to tragedy, but figure with comparable frequency in comedy, as can be seen from Shakespeare's *A Midsummer Night's Dream* and *Love's Labour's Lost*, or Middleton's *A Mad World, My Masters* (where it is used as a cover not for murder but robbery). Jonson's comedies are full of play-acting of different kinds: *Bartholomew Fair* includes a puppet show, while Volpone's household act out little dialogues for him. Overhearing scenes such as that in *The Spanish Tragedy* also provided favourite comic effects, for example in *Much Ado About Nothing* or *Twelfth Night*. Comedy, even more than tragedy, had numerous ways of obliquely reminding the audience of their status as onlookers.

Earlier sixteenth-century drama had paved the way for this in being notably uninhibited about addressing an audience directly, and manipulating their reactions. The figure popularly employed for this purpose was the Vice, a comic character who simultaneously acted as presenter and participant, but unlike A and B in *Fulgens and Lucrece*, played an unequivocally evil part in the proceedings. Ambidexter in Thomas Preston's *Cambises* (1561) is a typical Vice, chatting up the audience and asking a girl in the front row, 'How say ye, maid? to marry me will ye be glad?' At the same time he falsely persuades the tyrant Cambises that his brother is harbouring plans to supplant him, and should therefore be disposed of. He participates in the comic subplot as well, getting into scraps with Meretrix and the nicely named Marion May-Be-Good, and the audience are taken into his confidence as he comments on the unfolding action. After one of several horrible murders, he pulls them up sharply as he jumps from noisy grief to coarse jesting:

'A, a, a, a! I cannot chose but weep for the Queen! . . .
Oh, oh, my heart! Oh, my bum will break!'

The rapid — here too rapid — movement from tears to harsh laughter was to remain characteristic of the drama's powerful, if occasionally insufficiently discriminating, blend of tragedy and comedy. Much of Marlowe's work was written in this tradition of rapidly alternating, even overlapping moods, and it attained sublimity in *King Lear*. The difference between Shakespeare and such forgotten antecedents as Preston lies less in the techniques they used than in the mastery of those techniques.

For later dramatists the loose and unrealistic tradition within which the Vice had functioned was no longer viable. Earlier sixteenth-century drama had unfolded comparatively haphazardly, and had been peopled largely by personified abstractions rather than individualized characters. Marlowe and Kyd display an intermediate phase, in which a far more psychological drama might still include the odd allegorical figure — Revenge in *The Spanish Tragedy*, the unnamed old man who represents something like conscience in *Faustus*, the poor men who stand for the common people at the outset of *Edward II*, and the Death-like mower who betrays the King in hiding. Shakespeare, however, seems always to have possessed the knack of endowing the most minor figures with personality. The criminal Barnardine in *Measure for Measure*, whose forfeited head is to be substituted for Claudio's (and is, in Shakespeare's source), holds up the action by his stubborn insistence: 'I swear, I will not die today for any man's persuasion' (IV. iii. 59–60). Such recalcitrant individuality in a walk-on role conduces enormously to our sense of lived life within the plays. Although Elizabethan dramatists never regarded realism as a desirable effect, they grew increasingly interested in unfolding comparatively complex stories in persuasive and carefully orchestrated detail, so that the presence of a character like the Vice, whose essence was his disruptiveness, could no longer be tolerated, providing too constant a threat to the integrity of the action. The Vice's role had largely been functional, to move between audience and actors; the main purpose of his cheerful mischief-making had been to amuse while he broke up the sequence of actions into manageable units, suited to the audience's comparatively short concentration span. The London theatre, however, educated its audiences to accept not only a far more demanding form of entertainment, in terms of expression and ideas, but also to give their sustained attention to a complex sequence of events such as was never presented to earlier audiences. There are many references to the figure of the Vice in Elizabethan drama, but, with the exception of a few old-fashioned and largely forgotten plays, there was no significant attempt to revive the looser and more open structure within which he had operated. Occasionally characters might be used who stood both within the action and slightly outside it, in order to control or comment on it, figures like Vincentio or Prospero, Marston's *Malcontent*, or Vindice in *The Revenger's Tragedy*. But these never possessed the Vice's protean unpredictability, nor exercised the compère's role as fully and freely as he had done.

Although Elizabethan drama evolved from episodic earlier forms towards greater coherence and intensity, these were never achieved at the expense of variety; the sense of a clear linear development, of a single action implicit in the Aristotelian ideal, could not have been further from English creative habits. Shakespeare's late play, *The Tempest*, located on a single island and acted continuously, has a diversity of action that belies all claims that it fulfils the three unities, and none of Jonson's major plays, for all his classicism, possesses a simple outline. The taste for variety went very deep, and though audiences did learn to concentrate on complicated stories with different groups of characters interacting, sustained over two or three hours, dramatists were still inclined to change mood so abruptly as to leave a modern audience or reader quite disconcerted. Middleton does this with the appearance of the succubus and Sir Penitent's abrupt repentance in *A Mad World, My Masters*, while the subplot of *The Changeling* required a careful justification by William Empson (in *Some Versions of Pastoral*) before it was accepted as anything other than the collaborator's clumsy interpolation.

Developments towards greater coherence and psychological consistency went hand-in-hand with a comfortable acceptance of the artificial nature of the medium, and no particular desire to disguise its nature, or heighten its realism. Modern critics, however, accustomed to a tradition of naturalism, sometimes fail to recognize that the Elizabethan theatre was as joyously and openly artificial as opera, and that melodramatic conflicts and heavily ironic juxtapositions were of its essence. Indeed the stage itself, often outdoors, lacking lighting or substantial scenery to enhance the illusion, lacking, too, the high boots and masks of Greek theatre, required actors to magnify facial expression, words and gestures accordingly. When Christopher Ricks, in a persuasive critique of certain Jacobean dramatists, censures an overhearing scene in *The White Devil* for being more 'stagey' than a comparable scene in *Othello*, he is making a point that would have been meaningless to Shakespeare's contemporaries, who never realized that one important aspect of the dramatist's art might be to disguise the nature of the medium in which he worked. They were more accustomed to playwrights deliberately exaggerating the artificial qualities of the drama, as they did when writing for the children's companies, whose charm lay in the piquant contrast between what they were and what they played.

In the first phase of the boy actors' popularity, during the 1580s, John Lyly had composed for them formal, elegant and unrealistic comedies, often on classical themes, with witty dialogue and plenty of songs to show off their choirboy voices. The songs were often bawdy, but stage children seem to have been credited with an unusual precocity, or perhaps their very inappropriateness was considered amusing. Certainly by the end of the sixteenth century, plays for children's companies focused more and more on obviously adult passions, involving ˜sex and violence and exploiting the incongruity of the small interpreters. John Marston wrote chiefly for the boy companies, and his plays are full of absurdly exaggerated feeling and language, as well as lines that deliberately break the theatrical illusion, as when, after a peculiarly horrid soliloquy in *Antonio's Revenge*, the courtier Balurdo comes on with his beard half-off, complaining 'the tiring man hath not glued on my beard half fast enough. God's bores, it will not stick to fall off' (II. i. 30–1).

The earlier of Marston's two Antonio plays, like Jonson's *Cynthia's Revels*, begins with an induction in which the boys, with cloaks thrown over their costumes, discuss each others' roles, arguing and scrapping among themselves. It is difficult to decide exactly how Marston's numerous references to the illusory character of the stage were intended to affect his audience. Were they an assertion of the author's confidence in the power of the boy actors to carry them off, an act of bravado comparable to Shakespeare's in *Antony and Cleopatra*? Here the boy playing Cleopatra, anticipating her capture by the Romans, must say

'The quick comedians
Extemporally will stage us . . . I shall see
Some squeaking Cleopatra boy my greatness
I' the posture of a whore.'   (v. ii. 216–17, 219–21)

One speech from *Antonio's Revenge* makes a comparable use of dramatic irony as the equanimity of an elderly stoic, Pandulpho, breaks
down in the wake of his son's murder; he compares his vain attempt
to preserve an impassive calm to that of a child actor struggling to
maintain a heroic posture:

'Man will break out, despite philosophy.
Why, all this while I ha' but play'd a part,
Like to some boy that acts a tragedy,
Speaks burly words and raves out passion;
But when he thinks upon his infant weakness,
He droops his eye.'   (IV. ii. 69–74)

Marston here suggests an analogy between role-playing and self-
deception in real life, and the conscious pretence of the theatre. Unlike Cleopatra's lines, however, the tendency of Pandulpho's speech
is to undermine the theatrical illusion rather than to reinforce it.

   In the modern theatre and cinema, frame-breaking of this kind is
acceptable in comedy, while being regarded as inappropriate in a
serious context. Groucho, gagging a train driver in *The Marx
Brothers Go West*, can comment 'This is the best gag in the whole
picture', just as Fabian in *Twelfth Night* (but again with a reinforcing
rather than undermining effect) can comment in an aside, 'If this
were played upon a stage now, I could condemn it as an improbable
fiction' (III. iv. 127–8). Modern critics like Christopher Ricks
accordingly find the intrigue, deliberate artificiality, even absurdity,
of Renaissance comedy more acceptable than the use of the same
effects in tragedy: 'The situations of comedy, like the language of
comedy, draw attention to themselves more directly than do those of
tragedy. We relish the very unlikeliness of comedy.' This comment
directs us precisely to those characteristics of Renaissance tragedy
that modern readers find most difficult to accept. Renaissance
tragedy draws attention to its situations just as openly as comedy,
and these are often bizarre or heavily ironic: we are even expected to

relish the element of the grotesque when the mutilated Lavinia in
Titus Andronicus picks up her father's severed hand between her
teeth (her own hands having been cut off), while he picks up one of
the two severed heads of his sons in his remaining hand, saying to
Marcus:

'Come, brother, take a head,
And in this hand the other will I bear;
And, Lavinia, thou shalt be employ'd;
Bear thou my hand, sweet wench, between thy teeth.'   (III. i. 279–82)

The comparative lack of interest in *Titus* today contrasts with its
early popularity: in the induction to *Bartholomew Fair* of 1614
Jonson refers to *The Spanish Tragedy* and *Titus* as the great
favourites of old-fashioned playgoers. Gruesome business with a
severed hand also occurs in *The Duchess of Malfi*, where the heroine
is left holding one in the dark. This, like the scene in *The Atheist's
Tragedy* where the lovers lie down to sleep in a graveyard, using
skulls as pillows, is clearly a situation consciously drawing attention
to itself. On the whole, Shakespeare's great tragedies conform to
modern taste considerably more than those of his contemporaries,
and this may be one aspect of his superiority – but Shakespeare too
rejoiced in artifice and often used it as startlingly as they did. When
the alien traditions exploited by his contemporaries encourage us to
write them off too easily, it reflects more on our own limited
sympathies and tastes than on any innate failure in them. The self-
asserting characteristics of comedy were, at this period, shared by
tragedy; both made extensive use of devices such as inductions,
plays-within-plays, elaborate intrigues, disguises, overhearing scenes
and similar tricks and traps laid for the unwary. Both forms
exploited without inhibition a variety of linguistic devices often very
far removed from everyday speech.

Tragedy from its inception in the 1580s had expressed its intensest
moments in highly self-conscious and deliberately patterned
language – the stronger the emotion, the more highly worked
became its form of expression. Hence Hieronymo's lament over his
murdered son in *The Spanish Tragedy* approaches a Petrarchan
sonnet in its elaborate rhetoric:

> 'O eyes, no eyes, but fountains fraught with tears;
> O life, no life, but lively form of death;
> O world, no world, but mass of public wrongs,
> Confus'd and fill'd with murder and misdeeds . . .'   (III. ii. 1–4)

Indeed Petrarch's Sonnet CLXI includes the lines

> 'oi occhi miei (occhi non già, ma fonti) . . .'

Shakespeare also in his early work sometimes represented intense feeling in elaborately repetitive figures: in *Richard III*, Queen Margaret iterates

> 'Tell over your woes again by viewing mine.
> I had an Edward, till a Richard kill'd him;
> I had a Harry, till a Richard kill'd him;
> Thou had'st an Edward, till a Richard kill'd him;
> Thou had'st a Richard, till a Richard kill'd him.'   (IV. iv. 39–43)

In later and greater works, Shakespeare moved away from such over-formal devices, though not always towards looser or more naturalistic modes of expression. He discovered a different kind of complex rhetoric in which to express intense feeling, a complexity that lay altogether closer to 'the quick forge and working-house of thought', though it was still highly wrought and very far from normal speech patterns. It is characterized by the use of thickly laden imagery. Macbeth, in soliloquy before the murder of Duncan, anticipates the consequences:

> 'his virtues
> Will plead like angels, trumpet-tongu'd, against
> The deep damnation of his taking-off;
> And pity, like a naked new-born babe,
> Striding the blast, or heaven's cherubin, hors'd
> Upon the sightless couriers of the air,
> Shall blow the horrid deed in every eye,
> That tears shall drown the wind.'   (I. vii. 18–25)

Of course Shakespeare's mature work employs a variety of means to convey intense emotion. Sometimes it is deflected into indirect expression, as when Desdemona tells of her unshaken love for Othello by means of the willow song. Sometimes it is expressed laconically, as at the climax of *Lear*, whose heroine notoriously could not heave her heart into her mouth:

> LEAR. If you have poison for me, I will drink it.
>   I know you do not love me, for your sisters
>   Have (as I do remember) done me wrong:
>   You have some cause, they have not.
> CORDELIA. No cause, no cause.   (IV. vii. 71–4)

In Cordelia's mumbled response, psychological truth and dramatic convention marry, as they do so triumphantly in much of Shakespeare's work. The difficulty of speaking coherently, even of speaking at all, at moments of intense feeling coincides with a dramatic tradition deriving from Seneca that 'light griefs speak, but heavy ones are silent' ('Curae leves loquuntur, ingentes stupent', *Hippolytus*, 607), an insight wonderfully dramatized at the climax of *Titus* where the hero breaks a long-held pause, after receiving a series of unbearable pieces of news, by bursting into hysterical laughter.

A further affinity between Elizabethan tragedy and comedy is that both were inclined to play off the exceptional against accepted social norms, so that both focused, on occasion, on overweening pride, the classical 'hubris': Tamburlaine, Faustus, the Guise or Mortimer in Marlowe's plays, Coriolanus or Jonson's Sejanus and Catiline invite social or supernatural retaliation as surely as, in a different mode, do Volpone and Mosca, or Malvolio. The Jew of Malta or Leontes of *The Winter's Tale* display singular presumption within indeterminate forms, plays that possess the characteristics both of comedy and tragedy. In fact the distinctions normally drawn often look arbitrary when applied to Elizabethan drama where, apart from 'mongrel tragi-comedy' or chronicle plays, rambling historical sagas which cheerfully borrowed elements from both traditions, there are a number of pieces which seem undecided about which category they belong to. Preston's *Cambises*, referred to earlier, is typical of the kind of confusion that can occur: its story relates the fall of a tyrant, an event appropriate to tragedy as commonly defined, and the title page, with unconscious aptness, styles it a 'lamentable tragedy', but the presence of the Vice Ambidexter and the knock-about farce elements justify the running-head description of it as a comedy. Nor is it merely negligible plays like *Cambises* that exist in this limbo of uncertain status. Shakespeare's *Troilus and Cressida* poses similar problems. Hector's death may imply a tragic ending, and the first folio editors seem originally to have intended it to stand among the tragedies, but some accident during printing finally placed it between the tragedies and the histories. The 1609 quarto, while describing it as a history on the title-page, includes an address to the reader insisting that it is 'passing full of the palm comical', and reminding readers of Shakespeare's achievements in that mode. Modern critics often treat it as a history since this is a conveniently indeterminate term. Though Elizabethan critics would offer definitions of tragedy and comedy readily enough, the forms had much in common with one another, and they were not regarded as mutually exclusive until the general adoption of neoclassical rules in the second half of the seventeenth century.

One explanation of the extensive overlap between the two forms is that in England tragedy had developed out of comedy and never entirely outgrown its parent – this is the historical reason why English tragedy continued promiscuously to mingle kings and clowns and match funerals and hornpipes until the closing of the theatres in 1642. Comedy as the parent form derived its structure from medieval drama which, being essentially Christian, took as its overall pattern the divine comedy in which the tragic falls of Lucifer and Adam had provided the happy occasion of God's intervention to save man. The biblical cycles included moments of intense grief and horror, as Christ was scourged and crucified, and Mary lamented beside him, but these were eventually subsumed in the joy of the Resurrection and the wild farce of the harrowing of Hell, played for laughs with the devils beating one another and letting off fire-crackers. Many other biblical episodes were developed comically, and even sinister figures such as Cain, Herod or Christ's interrogators were exaggerated so that their terror was leavened by absurdity. Non-biblical plays also import much extraneous comic stuffing in the process of asserting God's charity to man. The meaning of the Christian message and the natural tendency of popular entertainment to invite audience-response through laughter combined to make comedy the dramatic prototype.

Elizabethan critics like Puttenham and Webbe recognized that this was the case, but were inclined to express their perceptions of the way drama had developed in terms of the evolution of the more authoritative classical dramatic forms: native traditions, such as the acting of plays on wagons led about the streets, are attributed to ancient Greece. Tragedy was regarded very much as a late development, while Webbe saw it as evolving out of a form closely resembling the morality play, whose style he implausibly associated with Aristophanes:

Comedies took their name ... to go a feasting, because they used to go in procession with their sport about the cities and villages ... But not long after ... they began to invent new persons and new matters for their comedies ... and from these they began to present in shapes of men the nature of virtues and vices, and affections and qualities incident to men as Justice, Temperance, Poverty, Wrath, Vengeance, Sloth, Valiantness and such like, as may appear by the ancient works of Aristophanes. There grew at last to be a greater diversity between tragedy writers and comedy writers.

(A Discourse of English Poetrie, 1586)

Inaccurate though this is as an account of the development of Greek drama, it throws some light on how the history of sixteenth-century drama looked to late Elizabethans. In their view, tragedy constituted a particular type of plot, but not a distinctive set of dramatic techniques, since these had simply been inherited from comedy. This accorded with the medieval conception of tragedy as a particular sequence of events – the fall of a great man from prosperity into misery; no one literary form was considered more appropriate than another for such a plot. In fact, before the 1580s tragedy most often took the form of narrative in verse such as Chaucer's *Troilus and Criseyde,* Lydgate's *Fall of Princes,* or Sackville and Buckhurst's *Mirror for Magistrates.*

Since tragedy had no peculiar techniques of its own, earlier dramatists like Marlowe fell back on the devices of comedy, padding out their tragic structures with comic episodes that were to give offence to later critics, accustomed to 'purer' tragic forms. Even in Shakespeare's work the primacy of comedy is still evident. His first essay in the form, *The Comedy of Errors,* has a certainty of touch, exploiting audience sympathy and responses more confidently than, say, *1 Henry VI*; it is more obviously characteristic of Shakespeare's developing art, anticipating in certain aspects a late play such as *The Winter's Tale,* a claim that cannot be advanced for *1 Henry VI.* Shakespeare's skills were not slow to show themselves, but the competence of the early comedies is nowhere matched in the early tragedies. Despite its lack of a single obvious source, *Titus Andronicus* feels substantially more derivative than *The Comedy of Errors* does, and the play is less successful in its own terms. A second essay in pure tragedy, *Romeo and Juliet*, drew extensively on his experience of Italianate comedy, and its most memorable figures are comic. Between them, Shakespeare, Kyd and Marlowe effectively created the tragic genre that was to blossom so suddenly and so fully under James. It was Nicholas Brooke who first demonstrated that Marlowe lacked precursors, and that his

supposed line of descent from a type of play trying hard to provoke pity and fear, but lapsing from sheer incompetence into absurdity is a complete fiction ... There was no English tragedy before Kyd and Marlowe outside the Inns of Court, where it was amateur, private and incredibly dull.

Yet even though comedy, unlike tragedy, belonged to a well-established tradition and Shakespearian comedy seems to have sprung fully armed from his head, many of the earlier comedies, written before the establishment of Burbage's Theatre in 1576, still sound extraordinarily primitive, even childish. The reason has less to do with structure than with the type of humour employed, which tended to be vulgar, and was often insistently scatological. This aspect of morality plays and interludes was understandably largely ignored by earlier editors. Indeed the text of *Mankind* edited in a collection of early drama made by J. Q. Adams in 1924 omitted as unprintable all but the opening lines of the song in which the audience are invited to participate. The comedy here is of a knock-about variety, with frequent references to bodily functions. A favourite comic situation is produced by the inability to control these under threat, particularly of the supernatural. This naïve scenario provided a popular source of laughter for more than a hundred years, from *Mankind* (1465–70) to Ulpian Fulwell's *Like Will to Like* (1568) where the Vice Nichol Newfangle is so terrified of Lucifer that he befouls himself. A slightly earlier though far more sophisticated comedy, *Gammer Gurton's Needle* (1552), culminates in the same joke within a structure derived from Plautus. Even in his translation of an Italian comedy, *Supposes*, presented to the comparatively select audience of Gray's Inn in 1566, George Gascoigne could not resist a quibble on 'supposes' and 'suppositories' in the final speech. If it is true that laughter commonly reveals a society's inner tensions, early Tudor audiences must have been as preoccupied with self-control and the indignity of failing to achieve it as the average nursery-school class; more probably, the failure of physical control stands as a metaphor for a failure of moral control in the presence of temptation.

After the establishment of the professional theatres, however, London audiences seem to have acquired altogether more refined tastes. Nervous incontinence was no longer considered amusing, and though the clowns might be allowed the occasional low joke – Launce's dog in *Two Gentlemen of Verona* misbehaves himself noisomely – excremental humour was fairly rapidly succeeded by an altogether wider range of laughing matter. Many jokes now involved subtle social distinctions, while others reflected the growing taste for sexual innuendo. By the early seventeenth century, dramatists like Middleton, Marston, Webster, and Tourneur were presenting extended scenes based on *double entendres*. An especially tedious example from *The Atheist's Tragedy* moves from botany (medlars, poppering pears and bachelor's buttons) to music: '*Mi* is a large there; and the prick that stands before *mi*, a long . . . Here's a sweet close – strike it full . . .', etc.

One explanation of this substantial shift in taste may be that a different type of audience was now being addressed. London society was itself evolving and becoming manifestly more sophisticated than the provincial audiences for whom so much medieval drama had been performed. From the first, the professional dramatists seem to have introduced elements of delight as well as laughter into comedy through the use of romance, a vein that had only appeared sporadically before. Medwall's *Fulgens and Lucrece*, in so many respects in advance of its time, had employed it, as had Italian comedies like *Supposes*, which ultimately derived from Roman New Comedy, with its plots of divided lovers. Morality plays and interludes had seldom presented lovers at all, and one later dramatist, Ben Jonson, was to find himself in sympathy with their exclusion. The comedies of the 1580s often combined romantic interest with legendary material drawn from classical literature, contemporary fantasy (as Greene's *Orlando Furioso* was), or from native English fairy-tales. The most successful employment of the latter was in Peele's *The Old Wives' Tale* with its three sisters, oracular heads in the well, and its dead travelling companion. Such folk-tale elements continued to surface from time to time – Robin Goodfellow oddly materializing in a wood near Athens, while the fairies and Herne the Hunter are invoked, less surprisingly, in Windsor Forest.

Shakespearian comedy, which dominated the 1590s through its originality and inventiveness, preferred exotic locales to such English settings as Wakefield or Fressingfield, favoured by Greene.

The exception is *The Merry Wives of Windsor*, linked through its setting to the court, which may have commissioned it, and through Falstaff to the London tavern comedy of the second history cycle. It was here, rather than in his comedies, that Shakespeare presented the world of tapsters and hostesses, of bar-room heroics and tipsy practical jokes, that had long been such a notable feature of interludes. Later comedy was increasingly to abandon the idealized locales of Athens, Venice and romantic forest wastes for the familiar rough-and-tumble of Cheapside, Smithfield and Finsbury. London and recognizable London types – whores, rogues, ambitious merchants, pleasure-hating puritans, swaggering gallants – were to dominate the Jacobean stage, bringing with them a new immediacy and, occasionally, a degree of topical indiscretion unattainable in the fairy-tale or romantic comedies that preceded them (see pp. 62–4). Marston, Jonson and Middleton held up a looking-glass to London, and if some of the types they found there were only too predictable, they incorporated them into plays notable for their structural complexity and cohesiveness. It was as if the audience's detailed knowledge of their own city challenged the dramatists to synthesize the familiar material into freshly observed and ever more pointed inventions. The lasting success of this citizen comedy, which presented the audience with theatrical versions of themselves, is indicated by the fact that Restoration comedy, though often more obviously stylized, was nevertheless a continuation of this tradition. Meanwhile, the direct presentation of London life, obviously entertaining to Londoners who could pick up all the topical allusions and references, also closely fitted the traditional justification of comedy as a mirror of society, 'an imitation of the common errors of our life which he representeth in the most ridiculous and scornful sort that may be, so as it is impossible that any beholder can be content to be such an one', as Sidney expressed it.

The expectation that literature should justify itself by teaching a lesson applied to drama almost as forcefully as it did to epic and romance: Nashe defended chronicle plays on the grounds that they immortalized the great achievements of the past and stirred young minds to virtuous emulation. It was perhaps less obvious what lesson tragedy taught, other than that the whirligig of time brought in his revenges, or that Fortune's wheel, which carried the Scythian shepherd Tamburlaine to world conquest, and the tyrant Cambises to destruction, turned inexorably:

'Base Fortune, now I see, that in thy wheel
There is a point, to which when men aspire,
They tumble headlong down.'   (*Edward II*, v. vi. 59–61)

In these lines Mortimer deftly embroiders upon the platitude that great men always risk losing their prosperity. In order to point a lesson rather than assert an obvious commonplace, tragedy particularly addressed itself to tyrants and oppressors, affording a dreadful warning to corrupt princes and magistrates. This specialized didactic function is assumed by most of the critics of the age: for Sidney, 'the high and excellent tragedy ... openeth the greatest wounds, and showeth forth the ulcers that are covered with tissue; that maketh kings fear to be tyrants, and tyrants manifest their tyrannical humours.' (Tissue here has its original meaning of cloth of gold, rather than flesh.) His friend Fulke Greville asserted that the function of tragedy was 'to trace out the high ways of ambitious governors, and to show in the practice, that the more audacity, advantage and good success such sovereignties have, the more they hasten to their own desolation and ruin', while Sir John Harington saw tragedy as 'representing only the cruel and lawless proceedings of Princes, moving nothing but pity or detestation'.

The critic George Puttenham, in his *Arte of English Poesie* (1589), significantly entitled his chapter on tragedy 'In what form of poesy the evil and outrageous behaviours of princes were reprehended'. He then proceeded to describe how, when society began, men were 'in a manner popularly equal', but after a time certain individuals acquired power over the others, and 'having learned them all manner of lusts and licentiousness', fell into evil. Though feared while alive,

after their deaths, when the posterity stood no more in dread of them, their infamous life and tyrannies were laid open to all the world, their wickedness reproached, their follies and extreme insolencies derided, and their miserable ends painted out in plays and pageants, to show the mutability of fortune, and the just punishment of God in revenge of a vicious and evil life.

Puttenham's notion of the passive revenges that time and God might take on the tyrant afforded cold comfort to an age in which altering balances of power were reinforcing royal authority to an unprecedented degree. In England, the reformers had insisted that the church abrogate temporal power, thus simultaneously strengthening and enriching their prince. Moreover if the prince failed to attain the requisite godliness, traditional wisdom regarded this as God's punishment inflicted on an erring people, for who but God controlled the implanting of a future tyrant in his mother's womb? Tyranny must be borne patiently, with tears and prayers, and God would demand restitution in His own time and way. Some views even held the prince accountable for the state of his people's souls as well as their bodies – the point is discussed in Shakespeare's *Henry V* (IV. i. 132–58). Evil princes and their depraved courts were to become favourite subjects of Jacobean tragedy, and classical treatments of the theme were reinforced by its centrality as an issue of the day (see pp. 141–3). For those who recognized that their worldly obligations now began and ended with Caesar, the drama's postdated sanctions against tyranny could only offer vicarious satisfaction, yet even these may have been better than nothing. Caesar's murder on stage imaginatively enacted a revenge on absolute privilege and prerogative with which many of the audience must have sympathized. As the seventeenth century progressed, Englishmen recognized that they had more substantial defences against tyranny than its condemnation in tragedy, and grasping these, it seems as if they no longer needed the imaginary solutions that tragedy had held out. The Jacobean tragedy of state had no major descendants. It would, however, be misleading to suggest that tragedy was exclusively concerned with the great. Although contemporary tragic theory laid down that it should be, the professional dramatists never waited on any precedent but popularity. Ballads dealing with domestic violence were widely read, and their subject-matter was quickly accommodated to the stage in domestic tragedies, featuring bourgeois protagonists – *Arden of Faversham* (1591), Thomas Heywood's *A Woman Killed with Kindness* (1603), and *A Yorkshire Tragedy* (1606) being among the best-known examples of this type.

The extraordinarily varied and complex development of tragedy, once it arrived, suggests the fortunate coincidence of certain current feelings and concerns with a form well-adapted to express them. This kind of rapid development may be compared to that of the novel in the eighteenth century. The neutrality of dramatic form allowed playwrights to present the age's increasingly conflicting values and standards in terms of urgently opposed individual convictions, for the essence of drama is conflict, and a conflict of attitudes is more sustainedly interesting than any mere disagreement. Even in an early and in certain respects stiff and diagrammatic play like *Tamburlaine*, inclined to present contrasted viewpoints rather than dramatized conflict, various responses to the action are indicated. In becoming a world conqueror, the shepherd Tamburlaine breaks all accepted doctrines of hierarchy, yet his strength seems to be sanctioned by the heavens. He himself believes that he has mastered Fortune, as some Renaissance thinkers believed a man could, or else that he is God's scourge to punish the puny tyrants he overthrows. Arguments about his true nature are considered – is he really human? Tamburlaine himself understandably insists on the normality of human aspiration (which leaves the question of his singularity unresolved), but the world he rules so effectively continues to grow more cruelly and inhumanly oppressive – several individuals take the stoic's traditional escape-route from tyranny, through death. Marlowe nowhere suggests that there can be any simple solution to the problems posed by the conqueror's relentless ambitions, and the play demands the continuous exercise of judgement and sympathy in a stimulating and challenging way. While lacking something of the enlivening detail and psychological inwardness of later and greater successors, *Tamburlaine* is nevertheless a significant landmark in the development of the drama.

Though Tamburlaine is short on inner life – indeed he appears to have no personality, as distinct from his unremitting self-confidence, Marlowe here (as elsewhere) invites the audience to examine, and perhaps in the second part to feel compassion for a figure whom they can scarcely approve of. The playing off of an audience's sympathies against its moral perceptions was increasingly to become a feature of tragedy, allowing it to explore the hearts or minds of a ruthless usurper and tyrant in *Macbeth*, a murderous servingman and his morally enfeebled mistress in Middleton's *Changeling*, an incestuous brother and sister in Ford's *'Tis Pity She's a Whore*, and many other depraved characters. As in everyday experience, insight into the lives and motives of the characters involved might confer understanding, while in no way exonerating them. Elizabethan drama was not immoral, yet those critics who insisted on the immorality of the medium spoke truer than they knew. In the theatre audiences are always eager for action, and their sympathy and interest are commonly monopolized by the most dynamic figures before them, those who excite them most, irrespective of moral qualities. This factor, already evident in the popularity of the old Vice figure, was naturally exploited by dramatists like Marlowe and Shakespeare, through figures like the Jew of Malta or Richard III, while virtue, as represented by the Jew's daughter Abigail, was constantly in danger of appearing ineffectual, even comically so. Shakespeare alone found ways of endowing his virtuous characters with positive energy and vitality; in this, as in so much else, he remained exceptional.

Both tragedy and comedy were inclined to test the convictions of the heart against the unthinking assumptions of the day, and in so doing sometimes reached potentially subversive conclusions. Parents and relatives were commonly more interested in pursuing financial advantage in marriage than in promoting true love – a type of venality exposed as sharply in Middleton's *Chaste Maid in Cheapside* as in Webster's *The Duchess of Malfi*. On the other hand, young women were often unable to distinguish true love from passing fancy, and their unstable whims and lack of foresight laid them open to irreversible moral corruption as dramatized in Middleton's late tragedies, *The Changeling* and *Women Beware Women*. Perhaps the most consistent theme of tragedy outside Shakespeare was the depravity that accompanied power and privilege, the dangers of attendance at court with its servitude to ephemeral pleasure rather than eternal joy.

Jacobean tragedy, in examining different moral attitudes and relating them to the interests of their holders, seems to point towards some ultimate scepticism, a doubt that recalls Erasmus or Montaigne as to whether anything can be impartially judged or certainly known in this world. Yet, as with both philosophers, scepticism had accompanied firm religious convictions, so most plays, however radical some of their implications might be, came to rest in the traditional wisdom that God was not mocked nor could sin be indulged without punishment: thus the Cardinal at the end of *Women Beware Women*: 'Sin, what thou art, these ruins show too piteously'; or Giovanni, concluding *The White Devil*,

'Let guilty men remember their black deeds
Do lean on crutches made of slender reeds.'

In the meantime, the dramatist may have turned upside down or inside out many received opinions which would never look quite the same again. Vindice, for example, in *The Revenger's Tragedy*, gazes at his mistress' skull, remembering the fatal desire she had aroused in the Duke. As he does so, he wonders whether the whole lust-driven world, on-stage or off, is not really in the grip of some collective mania, and while this view has its roots in medieval indictments of worldly pleasure, its direct and horrified expression here is peculiarly Jacobean:

> 'Surely we're all mad people and they,
> Whom we think are, are not: we mistake those.
> 'Tis we are mad in sense, they but in clothes.'   (III. v. 79–81)

Such fundamental questioning of the most basic human assumptions was one outcome of the most exploratory literary form of that exploratory age.

Conclusion:
Divided and Distinguished Worlds

What is our life? A play of passion,
Our mirth the music of division;
Our mothers' wombs the tiring houses be,
Where we are dressed for this short comedy;
Heaven the judicious sharp spectator is
That sits and marks still who doth act amiss;
Our graves that hide us from the searching sun
Are like drawn curtains when the play is done.
Thus march we playing to our latest rest,
Only we die in earnest, that's no jest.

Sir Walter Raleigh's epigram on this favourite literary theme of the period combines an overall ease and grace of accomplishment (Castiglione's *sprezzatura* or *grazia*) with a sense of complex and concentrated meaning located in particular words (passion, judicious, act, playing, jest) which anticipates metaphysical poetry. Its tone is difficult to define, at once wry, detached and amused, and yet also serious, saddened at life's brevity, its known and pre-determined boundaries. Metaphors of life as theatre, appropriate enough on the stage itself, were so commonly used elsewhere as almost to constitute a literary cliché. Raleigh himself, in a stoical passage from the Preface to his *History of the World*, refers to God as 'the author of all our tragedies', who

hath written out for us, and appointed us all the parts we are to play ... Certainly there is no other account to be made of this ridiculous world than to resolve that the change of fortune on the great theatre is but as the change of garments on the less.

Later he refers to 'the false and dureless pleasures of this stage-play world'. All such metaphors drive home a sense of the individual's alienation from his allotted role, convey a sense of watching oneself at a distance which a man of Raleigh's searching and introspective habits of mind must frequently have experienced amidst the highly structured and determined routines of military and diplomatic missions, and the even more intense and demanding formality of court life. Within the established patterns of court ceremonial, and the more difficult, because less clearly formulated, games of compliment and flirtation around the Queen, Raleigh had his set part to play. His keen intellect, no less than his secret marriage to Bess Throckmorton, would suggest that he was unable to subscribe to these wholeheartedly.

In this, Raleigh, though gifted with qualities of mind, body and character far above the average, was a man of his time. The theatrical metaphor vividly expressed a more general unease at the increasing gap between public performance and private reservation. This might reflect a sense of indulged and deluded vanity –

> 'Like a strutting player, whose conceit
> Lies in his hamstring, and doth think it rich
> To hear the wooden dialogue and sound
> 'Twixt his stretch'd footing and the scaffoldage . . .'
>
> (*Troilus and Cressida*, I. iii. 153– 6)

or of total despair –

> 'Life's but a walking shadow, a poor player,
> That struts and frets his hour upon the stage,
> And then is heard no more.'
>
> (*Macbeth*, V. v. 24–6)

or of an intense anxiety that, perceiving all action in terms of acting, inhibits any –

> 'What's Hecuba to him or he to Hecuba,
> That he should weep for her? What would he do,
> Had he the motive and the cue for passion
> That I have?'
>
> (*Hamlet*, II. ii. 559– 62)

Anne Righter, in the course of a brilliantly sustained analysis of theatrical metaphor, has observed

A sense of futility, of the vanity or folly of human ambition, is characteristic of all meditative Elizabethan comparisons of the world to a stage. Even at their most cheerful, such descriptions manage to mock the seriousness of man's pursuits, to point out the somehow ludicrous nature of his perpetual activity.

Viewed in this way, such images are linked to similar manifestations of disaffection or alienation apparent in the contemporary vogue for satire, and the closely related figure of the malcontent, the cults of melancholy and of withdrawal from *negotium* to *otium*, from business to leisure, from the world of public concerns to privacy and retirement. In Sonnet XXX of Sidney's *Astrophil and Stella* the poet withdraws from the world of insistent political questions, confessing to Stella:

> 'I cumbered with good manners, answer do,
> But know not how, for still I think of you.'

Elsewhere such a withdrawal is embodied in the plot of the *Arcadia*. The conflict between an imposed, usually public, role, and allegiance to an inner life, a personal authenticity, was especially characteristic of the age. It was enacted within the individual psyche, even as it was being played out in the public events of European cultural, social and religious history.

The society implied in the concept of the 'Elizabethan world picture' was one that expressed itself and its values in terms of symbols, externalizing its convictions into carefully classified rituals that pervaded life at every level of experience: religion, literature, social structure from the family to the state, were expressed as a series of carefully graduated steps, within which stable framework an individual expected to find satisfaction in the fulfilment of his appropriate and allotted tasks – at first these were scarcely sufficiently distinguishable from him to be termed his role. But changes in society, structural, economic and demographic, were dividing it along new and untraditional lines, so that particular groups were now being differentiated in terms of common interests and shared values, and as these broke down, a cultural and religious movement developed which challenged the whole symbolic system as meretricious and artificial, a series of images wrongly valued for themselves and not for what they stood for. In future truth must be 'felt along the heart', not embodied in empty histrionic words and gestures that could be memorized and repeated without spontaneous feeling. The actors were no longer comfortable with their roles.

Large-scale changes in how a society sees and expresses itself occur over centuries rather than decades, and they are naturally accompanied by eager and sometimes frantic efforts to shore up existing systems and beliefs, creating little eddies or counter-currents against the long withdrawing tide of symbolic and sacramental modes of thought. That tide expressed itself in its most paradigmatic form in the protestant Reformation, which challenged the worldly hierarchy of the church and its images, the shared and routine observations, the material exchanges that symbolized spiritual acts, overthrowing them in favour of a faith in inner conviction which, in its extreme forms, repudiated a great many existing authorities: the diminution of the priest's role, Calvin's scheme of church government by elected elders, the Quaker hope of eliminating social distinctions by reviving the archaic intimate form 'thou' all pointed in this direction. Yet it would be an oversimplification to see the Reformation as anything more than an element in a wider reaction, equally typified by the Catholic reformer Erasmus who, before Luther, had attacked the mechanical aspects of prayer and observation, without wanting to see the church dismantled or in schism. Peter Burke has observed a parallel movement against traditional rites and rituals, against popular religious drama, holiday festivities, May games and carnival behaviour taking place on a European scale, and involving both Catholic and protestant regimes, and perhaps the Eastern church as well. Certainly both Reformation and Counter-Reformation tended in the long run to isolate the priesthood (and, less directly, the judiciary) from the symbolic life style of their simplest parishioners.

Another area in which hierarchy and its external expression came under criticism was at court. In general, the courts of Europe were increasing and consolidating their power in the sixteenth century, and were thus more than ever eager to demonstrate their influence in traditional displays of extravagance and munificence at a time when (apart from becoming more difficult to finance) the whole concept of display was beginning to cause unease. The more that was spent on self-presentation, the more its opponents railed against privileged pride, folly and vanity. An uncompromising opposition towards anything felt to be performance or pretence animated puritan and anti-theatrical propaganda throughout this period. It is characteristic of the presbyterian Martin Marprelate tracts of 1588-9, with their vituperative attacks on the bishops for failing to be what they seemed or set up to be: here the Mass is seen merely as playing to the gallery, its protagonists as 'these Mar-Martins, these stage-players, these prelates'. By focusing on that area between formal or official self-presentation and less flattering truth, the Marprelate tracts established the tone for most prose satire, and some verse, that was to follow; the gap between what we would be and what we are is a rich and natural vein for tough-minded comedy, and the Jacobeans were only too well aware that 'A dog's obey'd in office' (*King Lear*, IV. vi. 159). In the greatest and most comprehensive literature, as here, such an observation is balanced against the recognition that there may also be what Kent sees in Lear's countenance, 'that . . . which I would fain call master'.

LEAR. What's that?
KENT. Authority.   (*King Lear*, I. iv. 27–30)

In his Roman plays, particularly, Shakespeare was to explore the ways in which the traditional aristocratic virtues – martial honour, nobility and magnificence (with all its connotations of conspicuous generosity or display) – were no longer acknowledged as relevant by a younger, less imaginative and more materialistic generation. Yet only a decade or so earlier, Spenser had not only lauded them but made them central to the action of his *Faerie Queene*, which, for all its protestant sentiments, remains in essence an extended medieval romance, the last great poem to be written in the symbolic mode. It was left to Milton to clothe the new inwardness in its appropriate poetic garb.

Inevitably, since art is centrally concerned with structure and imagery, the full effect of the social and cultural opposition to their traditional domination cannot immediately and concentratedly be experienced through the medium of literature itself, and it is in the great puritan autobiographies, works such as Bunyan's *Grace Abounding* (1666), that such opposition is to be felt most intensely. In any case, there was a strong reactionary tendency to shore up the old cosmology and the values and ways of thinking that accompanied it, or to promote alternative emblematic systems, such as classical iconography or schemes of mystic hermetic correspondences that conflicted less directly with current iconoclastic impulses. Drama itself, opening with a fanfare and concluding with a jig, originating in church sequences and including ritualized exchanges and events, seems a characteristic product of an essentially symbolic and external way of thinking. Yet the variety of devices used to remind the audience of its artifice seem designed to draw attention to, and perhaps invite criticism of that aspect of the form, while the rituals so commonly enacted in revenge tragedy – masques, plays, banquets or duels (see p. 176) – are inevitably interrupted by private acts of self-authentication, personal declarations concerning the falsity of such occasions. Interventions of this kind, sometimes even taking the form of murders, were directed simultaneously against the particular rite enacted, and the more general hypocrisy of the decadent state whose false surface was being presented in terms of ceremonial. The need to discover or rediscover the self and its inner life within the desensitizing habits of convention is everywhere apparent in this period, in Montaigne's insistence on his own inconsistency (see p. 7), in the Shakespearian hero's search for himself –

> 'Who is it that can tell me who I am?'   (*King Lear*, I. iv. 230)

as well as in the deliberate retraction from poetic conventions that is first apparent in Sidney's *Astrophil and Stella*, and which, passing through Shakespeare and Donne, was to become so characteristic a feature of metaphysical poetry; here stock expectations are invited only to be evaded as the poet slips into some more personal and oblique variation on his theme.

In Sidney's sonnets, conventional attitudes of idealizing admiration are suddenly undermined by the unresolvable force of physical passion:

> So while thy beauty draws the heart to love,
>   As fast thy virtue bends that love to good:
>   'But ah,' Desire still cries, 'give me some food.'   (LXXI)

Shakespeare's sonnets take divided feelings a stage further by conveying opposing impulses within the same words, so that such final couplets as

> But here's the joy, my friend and I are one;
> Sweet flattery! then she loves but me alone.   (XLII)

or

> Therefore I lie with her, and she with me,
> And in our faults by lies we flattered be.   (CXXXVIII)

are simultaneously neat resolutions to the problems posed and un-answerable cries of anguish. In both the notion of flattery, associated with self-deception, turns out to have left the poet and his reader painfully undeceived. The external resolution and the internal lack of solution overlap exactly and unbearably, as they must often have done within the age's pained consciousnesses, attuned as they were to observing a comparable gap in their social and religious experi-ence. Many critics, impressed by such richness of thought and feeling, and, perhaps, by a recognition of conflicting awarenesses embedded, as in these final couplets, in a single matrix, have sought explanations for the plenitude so characteristic of Shakespeare's times. In 1921 T. S. Eliot proposed that a 'dissociation of sensibility' occurring in the mid-seventeenth century had broken up previously synthesizing habits of mind. While his account has been repudiated often and in detail, there is a sense in which Renaissance English literature has a fullness and intensity of response, both to ideas and experience, which is no longer the encyclopaedic or comprehensive fullness of medieval literature, nor yet the relaxed and felicitous treatment of *concordia discors*, harmonious confusion, to be found in Augustan literature,

> Where order in variety we see,
> And where, though all things differ, all agree.
>
> (Pope's *Windsor Forest*, 15–16)

Most characteristic is the sense of opposing visions inextricably intertwined: for Sidney, sexual desire is ultimately inseparable from Neoplatonic admiration, just as Othello's sordid suspicions are deeply bound up with his high-minded idealism, and Hamlet's sense of something rotten in the state is bound up with his own self-doubt. Jonson's pervasive ethical preoccupations cannot be separated from his sharp-eyed observation of what went on in London's booths and alleyways, any more than Donne's sense of love's spirituality can be isolated from his consciousness of its comedy, its absurd and banal carnality. It was the ability to retain such opposing perceptions in a volatile synthesis, the refusal to ignore contrary evidence or to reject refutations of one's strongest convictions that made the great Eliza-bethan and Jacobean writers so enduringly important. Such excep-tional honesty, though partly innate, was certainly fostered by the experience of growing up in a society whose deepest values and

modes of understanding had been called in question. It lent their
writings an extraordinary awareness of the conflicts inherent in the
human condition. As a later writer, Sir Thomas Browne, saw it,

'Thus is man that great and true amphibium whose nature is disposed to
live, not only like other creatures in diverse elements, but in divided and
distinguished worlds.'   (*Religio Medici*, part I, sect. 34).

Chronology

Unless otherwise stated, dates for works in prose and verse are those of publication. Dates of plays are those of first performances, as given in A. Harbage, *Annals of English Drama, 975–1700* (revised S. Schoenbaum, 1964).

1509	Accession of Henry VIII.
1517–21	Lutheran Reformation begins in Germany.
1531	Elyot, *The Boke named the Governour*.
1532	Henry VIII divorces Catherine of Aragon.
1533	Henry VIII excommunicated, marries Anne Boleyn; birth of Elizabeth I.
1534	Acts of Succession and Supremacy mark formal breach between England and Rome. Anabaptists take control of Münster.
1535	Execution of More and Fisher.
1536	Calvin's *Institutes* (first Latin version).
1536–9	Dissolution of monasteries.
1542–7	Henry VIII dissipates most of wealth taken from church on campaigns in Scotland and France.
1543	Publication of Copernicus's *De Revolutionibus orbium coelestium*.
1547	Death of Henry VIII; accession of Edward VI. Period of radical protestantism begins in English church.
1549	First protestant Prayer Book.
1552	Second Prayer Book. Birth of Spenser. Stevenson (?), *Gammer Gurton's Needle*.
1553	Death of Edward VI; accession of Mary Tudor. Catholic reaction begins in England.
1554	Mary marries Philip of Spain. Birth of Raleigh and of Sidney.
1555	Burning of Latimer and Ridley. Peace of Augsburg accepts domination of most of Germany by protestantism, by allowing individual princes and city governments to decide religion of their territories.

1556   Burning of Cranmer.

1557   *Tottel's Miscellany* (reprinted poems by Wyatt and Surrey).

1558   Death of Mary; accession of Elizabeth I.

1559   Acts of Uniformity and Supremacy (Elizabethan church settlement).

1560   Geneva Bible.

1561   Awdeley, *Fraternity of Vagabonds*; Castiglione, *The Courtyer* (trans. Sir Thomas Hoby); Preston, *Cambises*.

1562   French Wars of Religion begin; English troops sent to help protestants, but withdrawn following year.

1563   Thirty-nine Articles of Anglican church. Foxe, *Acts and Monuments* ('Book of Martyrs').

1564   Birth of Shakespeare and of Marlowe.

1566   Gascoigne, *Supposes*.

1567   Harman, *Caveat for Common Cursetors*.

1567–8 First revolt of the Netherlands suppressed by Spanish troops under Duke of Alva.

1568   The Bishops' Bible. Mary Queen of Scots flees to England. Fulwell, *Like Will to Like*.

1569   Revolt of northern Earls suppressed.

1570   The Pope excommunicates Elizabeth and declares her deposed. Ascham, *The Schoolmaster*.

1572   St Bartholomew's Eve massacre of French protestant leaders in Paris. Seizure of Brill and other towns by Sea Beggars inaugurates successful Dutch revolt. Birth of Donne and of Jonson.

1576   Sack of Antwerp by unpaid Spanish troops, followed by collapse of Spanish control throughout Netherlands. First steps towards new Poor Law System. Priests from Douai arrive in England. The Theatre built.

1577   Drake begins voyage around world. The Curtain and Blackfriars theatres opened. Harrison, *Description of England*.

1578   Lyly, *Euphues, the Anatomy of Wit*. Sidney, *The Lady of May*.

1579   Prince of Parma begins reconquest of southern Netherlands for Spain. Jesuit mission to England begins. Spenser, *Shepheardes Calendar*.

1580   Spenser goes to Ireland as secretary to Lord Arthur Grey; Raleigh also goes to Ireland. Lyly, *Euphues and his England*. Montagne, *Essais*, vols. i–ii. Sidney probably writing *Arcadia* and *Astrophil and Stella*.

1581	Recusancy laws against Catholic laity greatly strengthened. Peele, *The Arraignment of Paris*.
1582	Lord Arthur Grey returns in disgrace. All seminarists and Jesuits declared to be traitors. Raleigh becomes favourite of Elizabeth I.
1584	Assassination of William of Orange. Spanish ambassador Mendoza expelled from England. Puritan campaign through parliament for further reform of church reaches its peak, but is frustrated by Elizabeth's opposition. Lyly, *Campaspe* and *Sappho and Phao*.
1585	Leicester's expedition to the Netherlands inaugurates state of undeclared war with Spain.
1586	Babington Plot; trial of Mary Queen of Scots. Sidney killed fighting Spaniards in Netherlands. Webbe, *Discourse of English Poetrie*, Bullokar, *Bref Grammar of English*.
1587	Pope proclaims crusade against England. Drake's attack on Cadiz. Execution of Mary Queen of Scots. Kyd, *The Spanish Tragedy*; Marlowe, *Tamburlaine*.
1588	Defeat of Spanish Armada. Lyly, *Endymion*; Younge, *Musica Transalpina*; Montaigne, *Essais*, vol. iii.
1588–9	Marprelate Tracts.
1589	Catholic League takes over much of France; King Henri III assassinated; Henri of Navarre becomes king as Henri IV. Elizabeth makes alliance with him, and over next few years English forces are sent to aid him in reconquest of France. Raleigh visits Spenser in Ireland; Spenser returns with him to court. Marlowe, *Jew of Malta* and (probably) *Dr Faustus*; Puttenham, *Arte of English Poesie*.
1590	Beginning of major campaign against leading puritan ministers, under direction of Archbishop Whitgift and Bishop Bancroft of London. Peele, *The Old Wives' Tale*, Sidney, *Arcadia*; Spenser, *Faerie Queene*, Books I–III; Watson, *First Sett of Italian Madrigalls Englished*.
1591	Anon., *Arden of Faversham*; Peele, *Descensus Astraeae*; Sidney, *Astrophil and Stella*; Spenser, *Complaints*. Entertainment for Elizabeth at Elvetham.
1592	Raleigh's secret marriage to Elizabeth Throckmorton leads to his disgrace. Death of Greene. Marlowe, *Edward II*; Nashe, *Pierce Penniless* and *Summer's Last Will and Testament*; Shakespeare, *The Comedy of Errors* and *Henry VI*.
1593	Plague in London; theatres closed. Death of Marlowe. Hooker, *Laws of Ecclesiastical Polity*, I–IV; Shakespeare, *Venus and*

Adonis, Richard III and Two Gentlemen of Verona; Nashe, Christ's Tears over Jerusalem.

1593–7   Period of poor harvests, associated with dearth and famine, high prices and plague.

1594   Spenser marries Elizabeth Boyle. Nashe, *The Unfortunate Traveller*; Shakespeare, *The Rape of Lucrece, The Taming of the Shrew* and *Titus Andronicus.*

1595   Raleigh's first voyage to Guyana. Execution of Robert Southwell. Shakespeare, *Love's Labour's Lost, A Midsummer Night's Dream, Richard II* and *Romeo and Juliet*; Sidney, *Defence of Poetry*; Spenser, *Amoretti, Epithalamion, Colin Clout's Come Home Againe.*

1596   Sir John Davies, *Orchestra*; Shakespeare, *King John* and *The Merchant of Venice*; Spenser, *Faerie Queene*, I–VI, *Prothalamion, Fowre Hymns*

1597   New Poor Law. Bacon, *Essays*; Dowland, *First Book of Songs*; Shakespeare, *Henry IV* parts 1 and 2.

1598   Edict of Nantes ends Wars of Religion in France, with partial toleration guaranteed to protestants. Tyrone's rebellion in Ireland; Spenser flees to London. Jonson, *Every Man In His Humour*; Marston, *The Metamorphosis of Pygmalion's Image, with Certain Satires* and *Scourge of Villainie* (also verse satires by Guilpin and Hall); Shakespeare, *Much Ado About Nothing.*

1599   Episcopal action against satire and erotic verse. Globe Theatre opened. Death of Spenser. Dekker, *Shoemaker's Holiday* and *Old Fortunatus*; Jonson, *Every Man Out of His Humour*; Marston, *Histriomastix* and *Antonio and Mellida*; Shakespeare, *As You Like It, Henry V, Julius Caesar.*

1600   Mountjoy sent to Ireland. Death of Hooker and Nashe. *England's Helicon*; Dowland, *Second Book of Songs*; Marston, *Antonio's Revenge*; Shakespeare, *Merry Wives of Windsor* and *Twelfth Night.*

1601   Rebellion and execution of Earl of Essex. Donne marries secretly, is imprisoned, and loses his position. Jonson, *Cynthia's Revels*; Morley, *Triumphs of Oriana*; Shakespeare, *Hamlet.*

1602   Middleton, *The Family of Love*; Shakespeare, *All's Well That Ends Well* and *Troilus and Cressida*; Campion, *Art of English Poesie.*

1603   Death of Elizabeth; accession of James I. Mountjoy completes conquest of Ireland. Raleigh found guilty of high treason and imprisoned in Tower. Dekker, *The Wonderful Year*; Dowland,

Third Book of Songs; Jonson, *Sejanus*; Heywood, *A Woman Killed with Kindness*; Montaigne, *Essays* (trans. Florio).

1604   Peace with Spain. Hampton Court Conference fails to satisfy puritan demands, but James subsequently pursues a moderate policy in ecclesiastical appointments. Chapman, *Bussy D'Ambois*; Marston, *The Dutch Courtezan* and *The Malcontent*; Shakespeare, *Measure for Measure* and *Othello*.

1605   Gunpowder Plot. Bacon, *Advancement of Learning*; Jonson, *The Masque of Blackness*; Shakespeare, *King Lear*.

1606   Anon., *The Revenger's Tragedy* and *A Yorkshire Tragedy*; Jonson, *Volpone* and *Hymenaei*; Middleton, *A Mad World, My Masters* and *Michaelmas Term*; Shakespeare, *Macbeth*.

1607   Beaumont and Fletcher, *The Knight of the Burning Pestle*; Shakespeare, *Antony and Cleopatra* and *Timon of Athens*.

1608   Birth of Milton. Fletcher, *The Faithful Shepherdess*; Shakespeare, *Coriolanus* and *Pericles*.

1609   Twelve-year truce between Spain and United Provinces. Jonson, *Masque of Queens* and *Epicoene*; Shakespeare, *Sonnets* and *Cymbeline*; Tourneur, *The Atheist's Tragedy*.

1610   Parliament and King fail to agree on Salisbury's plan for financial reform, or 'Great Contract'. Beaumont and Fletcher, *The Maid's Tragedy*; Campion, *Two Bookes of Ayres*; Donne, *Pseudo-Martyr*; Jonson, *The Alchemist* and *Prince Henry's Barriers*; Shakespeare, *The Winter's Tale*.

1611   Authorized Version of the Bible. Donne, *First Anniversary* (*Anatomy of the World*); Jonson, *Catiline his Conspiracy* and *Oberon the Fairy Prince*; Middleton, *A Chaste Maid in Cheapside*; Shakespeare, *The Tempest*.

1612   Death of Prince Henry. Campion, *Third and Fourth Booke of Ayres*; Donne, *Second Anniversary*; Heywood, *Apology for Actors*; Webster, *The White Devil*.

1613   Princess Elizabeth marries Frederick, Elector Palatine. Countess of Essex obtains divorce and marries James's favourite, Somerset. Murder of Sir Thomas Overbury in the Tower. Globe Theatre burned. Anon., *Two Noble Kinsmen*; Shakespeare, *Henry VIII*.

1614   Jonson, *Bartholomew Fair*; Raleigh, *History of the World*; Webster, *The Duchess of Malfi*.

1615   Overbury murder scandal and trial of lesser figures. Donne ordained. Jonson, *The Golden Age Restored*.

1616   Trial and conviction of Earl and Countess of Somerset. Advancement of George Villiers, later Duke of Buckingham. Death of Shakespeare and of Beaumont. Jonson, *The Devil is an Ass*; *Works* published in folio.

1617   Raleigh sails on last voyage to Guyana. Jonson, *Lovers Made Men* and *The Vision of Delight*.

1618   Bohemian Revolt begins Thirty Years War. Execution of Raleigh. Bacon becomes Lord Chancellor. Jonson visits Scotland (1618–19). Jonson, *Pleasure Reconciled to Virtue*.

1619   Synod of Dort; apparent success for strict Calvinists against Arminians in United Provinces. Gill, *Logonomia Anglica*.

1620   Battle of the White Mountain; Elector Frederick (son-in-law of James) loses both Bohemia and the Palatinate. Voyage of *Mayflower*; New England officially named. Serious trade depression over whole decade causes much unemployment and misery, mainly among clothworkers. Death of Campion. Bacon, *Novum Organum*.

1621   Parliament meets to debate international crisis. Bacon impeached for taking bribes. Donne becomes Dean of St Paul's. Burton, *Anatomy of Melancholy*; Jonson, *The Gypsies Metamorphosed*; Massinger, *A New Way to Pay Old Debts*; Middleton, *Women Beware Women*.

1622   King James negotiates with Spain for marriage between Prince Charles and Infanta, with return of Palatinate to Frederick. Middleton, *The Changeling*; Peacham, *Compleat Gentleman*.

1623   Abortive expedition to Madrid by Charles and Buckingham; marriage negotiations with Spain abandoned. Shakespeare First Folio.

1624   New Parliament meets; Charles and Buckingham lead clamour for war with Spain. Donne, *Devotions upon Emergent Occasions*; Jonson, *Neptune's Triumph for the Return of Albion*; Middleton, *A Game at Chess*.

1625   Death of James I; accession of Charles I, who marries Henrietta Maria, sister of Louis XIII of France. War with Spain.

1626   Death of Bacon. Jonson, *The Staple of News*.

1627   Expedition sent to help French protestant rebels at La Rochelle. Death of Middleton.

1628   Assassination of Buckingham. Surrender of La Rochelle to Louis XIII and Cardinal Richelieu. Parliament passes Petition of Right. Laud becomes Bishop of London. Fulke Greville murdered. Earle, *Microcosmographie*.

1629	Parliament dissolved; Sir John Eliot and other leaders imprisoned. Personal rule of Charles I begins. Peace with France. Jonson, *The New Inn*; Ford, *The Broken Heart*.
1630	Peace with Spain.
1631	Death of Donne.
1632	Ford, *'Tis Pity She's a Whore*.
1633	Laud becomes Archbishop of Canterbury. Death of Herbert. Donne, *Poems*; Herbert, *The Temple*.
1634	Milton, *Comus*.
1637	Trial of John Hampden for non-payment of Ship Money. Death of Jonson.
1639	War with Scots rebels (First Bishops' War).
1640	Short Parliament. Scots defeat royal forces. Long Parliament meets.
1642	Civil War begins.

Suggestions for Further Reading

The following list records the main sources on which I have drawn, alongside those which seem likely to prove useful to students of the period. Because this book is concerned to provide background knowledge, many of those listed are historical rather than critical works. The place of publication is London unless otherwise stated.

As general literary histories of the period, the two relevant volumes of the Oxford History of English Literature have not been superseded: C. S. Lewis's consistently brilliant *English Literature in the Sixteenth Century* (Oxford 1954), and Douglas Bush's *English Literature in the Earlier Seventeenth Century* (Oxford 1945, revised 1962). Neither includes drama, arguably the age's crowning glory. The Revels History of Drama aims to fill the resulting gap; Volume III covers the period 1576–1613 (by J. Leeds Barroll, Alexander Leggatt, Richard Hosley and Alvin Kernan, 1975); Volume IV runs from 1613–60 (by Philip Edwards, G. E. Bentley, Kathleen MacLuskie and Lois Potter, 1981). For more detailed information on particular authors and their works, Volume I of the *New Cambridge Bibliography of English Literature*, edited by George Watson (Cambridge 1969) may be consulted.

Shakespearian quotations in the text are taken from *The Riverside Shakespeare*, ed. G. Blakemore Evans (Boston 1974); for Marlowe, *The Plays of Christopher Marlowe*, ed. Roma Gill (Oxford 1971) has been used; for Montaigne, *The Complete Essays of Montaigne*, translated by D. M. Frame (Stanford 1958); for Jonson's masques, *The Complete Masques*, ed. Stephen Orgel (1969). Line references to other plays are to standard single volume editions, normally the Revels editions, or where these are lacking, the Regents Renaissance Drama series. The sources of the epigraphs from Sir Thomas Browne are as follows: Introduction, from the dedicatory letter to *Hydriotaphia*; chapter 1, from *Religio Medici*, part one, section 13; chapter 2, from *Christian Morals*; chapter 3, from *Religio Medici*, part two, section 7; chapter 4, from *Pseudodoxia Epidemica*, Book I, chapter 6; chapter 5, from *Hydriotaphia*, chapter 5; chapter 6, from *Religio Medici*, part one, section 41.

Introduction

Outline accounts of some of the ground covered here are provided by

Peter Burke, *The Renaissance* (Problems and Perspectives in History, 1964) and Isabel Rivers, *Classical and Christian Ideas in English Renaissance Poetry* (1979). Stevie Davies has edited an anthology of *Renaissance Views of Man* (Manchester 1978), while the rejection of scholasticism and other related and important subjects are illuminatingly discussed by Basil Willey in *The Seventeenth-Century Background* (1934).

Chapter 1

The quotation from Keith Thomas on page 13 is from *Religion and the Decline of Magic* (1971), whose prologue on 'The Environment' paints a vivid picture of living conditions in early modern times. E. M. W. Tillyard's *The Elizabethan World Picture* (1943) and C. S. Lewis's more circumspect *The Discarded Image* (1964) set out to describe the traditional cosmology, as, more ambitiously, does Arthur O. Lovejoy's *The Great Chain of Being* (Cambridge, Mass. 1936). On the lyric, see Hallett Smith, *Elizabethan Poetry* (Cambridge, Mass. 1966), and Rosamund Tuve, *Elizabethan and Metaphysical Imagery* (1947). Christopher Butler has written a useful general account of numerology, *Number Symbolism* (1970); detailed approaches to Spenser's poetry along these lines are offered by A. Kent Hieatt in *Short Time's Endless Moment* (New York 1960) and Alastair Fowler in *Spenser and the Numbers of Time* (1964). Advances in scientific knowledge are charted by M. Boas Hall in *The Scientific Renaissance* (1962). Harry Levin has discussed *The Myth of the Golden Age in the Renaissance* (New York 1972), where the quotations from Peter Martyr on page 28 will be found. On pastoral, Frank Kermode gives brief but pointed accounts in his anthology *English Pastoral Poetry from the Beginnings to Marvell* (1952), and in his introduction to Shakespeare's *The Tempest* (New Arden edition 1958). Chapters V and VI of Helen Cooper's *Pastoral, Medieval into Renaissance* (Ipswich 1977) are also valuable. Helena Shire's admirable *A Preface to Spenser* (1978) discusses the importance of Ireland for the poet, while there is a general account of *The Elizabethans and the Irish* by D. B. Quinn (Ithaca 1966).

Chapter 2

Spenser's Anabaptist giant is discussed by Christopher Hill in 'The Many-headed Monster', reprinted in his *Change and Continuity in Seventeenth-Century England* (1974). Contemporary views on how society should be structured are examined by J. W. Allen in *A History of Political Thought in the Sixteenth Century* (1928, revised 1957), by Christopher Morris in *Political Thought in England, Tyndale to Hooker* (Oxford 1953) and, with unsurpassed intelligence and lucidity, by Quentin Skinner in *The Foundations of Modern Political Thought* (2 vols., Cambridge 1978). Keith Thomas's interesting paper on 'Age and Authority in Early Modern England' is printed in the *Proceedings of the British Academy* vol. 26 (1976).

Much important information is provided by Lawrence Stone's *The Family, Sex and Marriage in England, 1500–1800* (1977), some of it challenged or modified elsewhere, for example by Keith Wrightson in *English Society 1580–1680* (1982). The difficult area between demographic and social history is explored by J. D. Chambers, *Population, Economy and Society in Pre-Industrial England* (Oxford 1972) and in some of the essays in C. Webster (ed.), *Health, Medicine and Mortality in the Sixteenth Century* (Cambridge 1979). E. A. Wrigley and R. S. Schofield have now provided a definitive account of *The Population History of England, 1541–1871* (1981).

J. Hurstfield and A. G. R. Smith are joint editors of a delightful anthology, *Elizabethan People* (1972), from which the lines by Thomas Bastard quoted on page 54 are taken. Carl Bridenbaugh's *Vexed and Troubled Englishmen 1590–1642* (1968, revised Oxford 1976) and the first half of Robert Ashton's *The English Civil War 1603–1649* are concerned with society and its views generally, while in writing about enclosure and Poor Law reform I have drawn extensively on Penry Williams's full, detailed and very readable account of *The Tudor Regime* (Oxford 1979). The growth of towns is described by Peter Clark and Paul Slack in *English Towns in Transition 1500–1700* (Oxford 1976); and the associated problems of the displaced poor are tackled by John Pound in *Poverty and Vagrancy in Tudor England* (1971) and by Paul Slack in an article on 'Vagrants and Vagrancy in England, 1598–1664' in *The Economic History Review*, 2nd series, vol. xxvii, no. 3, August 1974. Cony-catching pamphlets are collected by A. V. Judges in *The Elizabethan Underworld* (1930), J. A. McPeek in *The Black Book of Knaves and Unthrifts* (1969), and most recently by G. Salgado in *Cony-catchers and Bawdy Baskets* (Harmondsworth 1972). The pioneering study of Jacobean comedy as a social phenomenon was that of L. C. Knights, *Drama and Society in the Age of Jonson* (1937), now overtaken by Alexander Leggatt, *Citizen Comedy in the Age of Shakespeare* (Toronto 1973) and Brian Gibbons, *Jacobean City Comedy* (1968, revised 1980).

Chapter 3

A. G. Dickens's *The English Reformation* (1964) sets out clearly and in sequence the main events concerned, and William Malden's reaction (see page 67) is taken from there. Keith Thomas's *Religion and the Decline of Magic* (1971) explores the difficult but central question of secularization in society, and is the source of the old man's words cited on page 70 and the details of Hooper's visitation on the same page. Penry Williams's question (page 73) is posed in *The Tudor Regime*, which briefly discusses regional variations in religious attitudes, as, more extensively and in much greater detail, does Margaret Spufford's *Contrasting Communities* (Cambridge 1974), also referred to on page 73. Ultra-protestantism (if that is what we should call it) is the subject of Christopher Hill's *Society and Puritanism in*

Pre-Revolutionary England (1964), and, on a much narrower time scale, of Patrick Collinson's *The Elizabethan Puritan Movement* (1967). Nicholas Tyacke writes on 'Puritanism, Arminianism and Counter-Revolution' in an article published in Conrad Russell's collection *The Origins of the English Civil War* (1973); the editor's introduction to the volume is also useful. Passages from Bradford's 'History of Plymouth Plantation' (see page 82) are reprinted in *The Puritans*, vol. I, ed. Perry Miller and Thomas H. Johnson (New York 1938); Perry Miller's *The New England Mind: the Seventeenth Century* (1939, reprinted Cambridge, Mass. 1963) also gives an account of protestant attitudes. William Haller has written a study of *Foxe's Book of Martyrs and the Elect Nation* (1963) but on Foxe see also Katharine R. Firth, *The Apocalyptic Tradition in Reformation Britain 1530–1645* (Oxford 1979). Frank Kermode considers Spenser as a celebrant of protestant empire and apocalypse in *Renaissance Essays* (1971).

The outstanding historian of Catholicism is John Bossy who has provided an account of *The English Catholic Community 1570–1850* (1975), as well as a more detailed article on 'The Character of Elizabethan Catholicism', reprinted in *Crisis in Europe*, ed. Trevor Aston (1965). Louis L. Martz's *The Poetry of Meditation* (1954) concentrates on sixteenth- and seventeenth-century religious verse influenced by meditative exercises, while a generous selection of sermons are reprinted by John Chandos in a collection entitled *In God's Name: Examples of Preaching in England 1534–1662* (1971). Baines's deposition against Marlowe (pages 92–3) is cited in an appendix to J. B. Steane's *Christopher Marlowe* (Cambridge 1964).

Chapter 4

Quotations on pages 95–6 are from Lawrence Stone's article 'The Educational Revolution in England, 1560–1640' from *Past and Present* 28 (1964), and from David Cressy's *Literacy and the Social Order* (Cambridge 1980), which is also cited on page 108. A number of short passages in this chapter are quoted from Hurstfield and Smith's *Elizabethan People*, including those from Harrison (p. 97), Hobbes (p. 103), and Mulcaster (p. 106). Passages from Weston and Bunyan (p. 102) are cited from *Contrasting Communities* by Margaret Spufford, who also discusses popular reading matter and its implicit attitudes in *Small Books and Pleasant Histories* (1981), though this is mainly concerned with the seventeenth century. R. R. Bolgar has traced out *The Classical Heritage and its Beneficiaries* (Cambridge 1954, reprinted 1973), and G. K. Hunter outlined the course of English humanism in the first chapter of his book on *John Lyly* (1962). The contribution of Erasmus is admirably assessed by Margaret Mann Phillips in *Erasmus and the Northern Renaissance* (1949).

Elizabethan Erotic Narratives are discussed by William Keach (New Brunswick 1977), while satire is examined by John Peter in *Complaint and*

214 *Suggestions for Further Reading*

Satire in Early English Literature (Oxford 1956) and Alvin Kernan in *The Cankered Muse* (New Haven 1959); *Tudor Verse Satire* is anthologized by K. W. Gransden (1970).

There are several useful introductory essays on education. M. H. Curtis writes on 'Education and Apprenticeship' in *Shakespeare in his Own Age*, ed. Allardyce Nicoll (Cambridge 1976). In *The Age of Milton*, ed. C. A. Patrides and R. B. Waddington (Manchester 1980), Patrides contributes an essay on 'The Experience of Otherness: Theology as a Means of Life', and Kenneth Charlton writes on 'The Educational Background'. The latter has provided a general account of *Education in Renaissance England* (1965), which may be supplemented by Joan Simon's carefully documented *Education and Society in Tudor England* (Cambridge 1966). On rhetoric, see George A. Kennedy's *Classical Rhetoric and its Christian and Secular Tradition from Ancient to Modern Times* (1980), or Brian Vickers, *Classical Rhetoric in English Poetry* (1970). The universities are the subject of M. H. Curtis's *Oxford and Cambridge in Transition, 1558–1642* (Oxford 1959), and Curtis is the author of a stimulating but widely refuted article on 'The Alienated Intellectuals of Early Stuart England', reprinted in *Crisis in Europe*, ed. Trevor Aston (1965).

Chapter 5

The quotation on page 119 is from Lawrence Stone's *The Crisis of the Aristocracy, 1558–1641* (Oxford 1965), which combines clarity of argument with exceptionally vivid detail. This chapter depends on it at many points, and the words of Sir Henry Lee (page 137), of Raleigh and Mrs Turner on the scaffold (p. 143), and of the over-solicited James (p. 150) are all quoted there. There is a stimulating discussion of 'Place and Patronage in Elizabethan Politics' by W. T. MacCaffrey in *Elizabethan Government and Society: Essays presented to Sir John Neale*, ed. S. T. Bindoff, J. Hurstfield and C. H. Williams (1961). The standard account of literature addressed to the governing classes is Ruth Kelso's *The Doctrine of the English Gentleman in the Sixteenth Century* (Gloucester, Mass. 1929, reprinted 1964). E. Cassirer has written on *The Platonic Renaissance in England* (trans. J. P. Pettegrove, 1953), and the best introduction to the difficult Hermetic writings and beliefs is the first half of Frances Yates's *Giordano Bruno and the Hermetic Tradition* (1964). D. P. Walker has written on the tradition of *The Ancient Theology* (1972), referred to on page 128, and includes a chapter on Sidney's debate on atheism, while the best general account of the latter as a man of his age is John Buxton, *Sir Philip Sidney and the English Renaissance* (1954).

On Elizabeth and her self-images, the earliest and fullest account is E. C. Wilson, *England's Eliza* (Cambridge, Mass. 1939), which should be supplemented by Frances Yates, *Astraea* (1975), and Roy Strong, *The Cult of*

Elizabeth (1977), cited on page 133. The problems facing professional writers are the subject of Phoebe Sheavyn's *The Literary Profession in the Elizabethan Age* (1909, revised J. W. Saunders, Manchester 1967), and E. H. Miller's *The Professional Writer in Elizabethan England* (Cambridge, Mass. 1959), both of which give some consideration to the question of literary patronage, touched on by John Danby in *Elizabethan and Jacobean Poets* (1952, revised 1964), and central to Eleanor Rosenberg's *Leicester, Patron of Letters* (1955). Two useful articles on this topic are David Nichol Smith on 'Authors and Patrons' in volume II of *Shakespeare's England*, ed. Sir W. Raleigh (1916), and Patricia Thomson on 'The Literature of Patronage 1580–1630', in *Essays in Criticism* II (1952). In a more specialized study, Dick Taylor Jr. considers 'The Third Earl of Pembroke as a patron of poetry' in *Tulane Studies in English* (1955).

On songs, Hallett Smith has a chapter in *Elizabethan Poetry*, and Wilfrid Mellers provides an introduction to 'Words and Music in Elizabethan England' in *The Age of Shakespeare*, vol. 2 of the Pelican Guide to English Literature, ed. Boris Ford (Harmondsworth 1955). Bruce Pattison's *Music and Poetry of the English Renaissance* (1948) is also recommended. D. Attridge in *Well-Weighed Syllables* (1974) describes the movement in favour of composing English verse in classical metres. The acknowledged authority on the Jacobean masque is Stephen Orgel, whose brilliant and suggestive *The Illusion of Power* (1975) should not be missed, and is cited on page 126. It may be supplemented by his narrower and more detailed study of *The Jonsonian Masque* (New York 1967, revised 1981). A carefully annotated anthology of examples of the form can be found in *A Book of Masques*, ed. T. J. B. Spencer *et al.* (Cambridge 1967). The best account of Middleton's *Game at Chess* is to be found in Margot Heinemann's *Puritanism and Theatre* (Cambridge 1980), which is primarily concerned with Middleton, and 'puritan' attitudes to court as reflected in Jacobean drama.

Chapter 6

A useful introduction to *The Shakespearean Stage, 1574–1642* is provided by Andrew Gurr (1970, revised Cambridge 1980). This may be supplemented by M. C. Bradbrook's *The Rise of the Common Player* (1962) and Alfred Harbage's account of *Shakespeare's Audience* (1941). Some interesting documents are reprinted in A. M. Nagler's *A Source Book in Theatrical History* (New York 1952, revised 1959), and several important essays are collected by G. E. Bentley in *The Seventeenth-Century Stage* (1968). A great authority on this subject himself, Bentley has helpfully explained *The Profession of Dramatist in Shakespeare's Time, 1590–1642* (Princeton 1971). Jonas Barish has provided a lively and detailed account of *The Anti-Theatrical Prejudice* (1981).

From the embarrassment of riches provided by critics of the drama, it is necessary, if invidious, to single out a few for special mention. The Stratford-upon-Avon Studies, under the general editorship of John Russell Brown and Brian Harris, provide a first volume on *Jacobean Theatre*, with a lively piece by Arthur Brown on Citizen Comedy, a ninth volume on *Elizabethan Theatre* including T. W. Craik on Tudor interludes, Jonas Barish on *The Spanish Tragedy*, and Nicholas Brooke on Marlowe (cited on page 187), while the sixteenth volume on *Medieval Drama* (ed. Neville Denny) includes Paula Neuss on *Mankind*. The third volume of the Sphere History of Literature, *English Drama to 1710*, ed. Christopher Ricks (1971), contains a number of stimulating essays, and Ricks's own contribution on 'The tragedies of Webster, Tourneur and Middleton' is quoted on pp. 180–1. On the coterie drama, see Alfred Harbage's *Shakespeare and the Rival Traditions* (1952) (although its overall thesis is now questioned) and Michael Shapiro's *Children of the Revels* (New York 1977).

One of the fullest and most rewarding accounts of the dramatic forms available to the Elizabethans is Madeleine Doran's *Endeavours of Art* (1954), which focuses predominantly on classical and European influences. The importance of native traditions is emphasized by S. L. Bethell in *Shakespeare and the Popular Dramatic Tradition* (1944, reprinted New York 1970), by A. P. Rossiter in *English Drama from Early Times to the Elizabethans* (1950) and more recently by Emrys Jones in *The Origins of Shakespeare* (Oxford 1977). The essays of Puttenham and Webbe are reprinted by G. Gregory Smith in *Elizabethan Critical Essays* (2 vols., Oxford 1904). On Jacobean tragedy and its social implications, see Robert Ornstein, *The Moral Vision of Jacobean Tragedy* (Madison and Milwaukee 1965), and J. W. Lever, *The Tragedy of State* (1971). Joel B. Altman has explored the dialectical tendencies of the drama in *The Tudor Play of Mind* (1978).

Conclusion

The argument here was mainly inspired by a re-reading of Mary Douglas's *Natural Symbols* (1970). Anne Righter's view cited on pp. 196–7 is from *Shakespeare and the Idea of the Play* (1962). Peter Burke's study of *Popular Culture in Early Modern Europe* is referred to on p. 198, and less directly on p. 164.

Index

224 *Index*

schools (*cont.*)
grammar schools, 96–7, 107–13,
115–16, 118; petty schools, 109–10;
the school day, 113
scientific revolution, the, 21–3, 25–6
Scotland, 29, 34, 39, 73; Church of
Scotland, 80, *see also* Calvin
Seneca, 98; *Hippolytus*, 141, 184;
Thyestes, 141
sermons, 14, 16, 46, 66, 70, 79, 89–90,
112, 137, 142, 167–9
servants, 14, 29–31, 40, 49–50, 57, 64,
102, 122; gentleman servants, 49;
living-in servants, 45, 49; serving
men categorized by Awdeley, 57
Shakespeare, John, 96, 116; Judith (his
grand-daughter), 96
Shakespeare, William, 2, 7, 9, 12–13,
42, 44, 55, 59, 74, 96–7, 116, 118,
136, 138, 150, 158, 160–3, 165–7,
177–93 *passim*, 199–201; first folio,
166–7, 170; histories, 9, 124; Roman
plays, 98–9, 199; tragedies, 2, 182;
All's Well that Ends Well, 43; *Antony
and Cleopatra*, 58, 122, 180–1; *As
You Like It*, 33–4, 47, 157; *Comedy
of Errors*, 186; *Coriolanus*, 54–5, 184;
Hamlet, 5, 112, 144, 157–9, 162–3,
166–7, 171, 173, 175–6, 196, 201; *1
Henry IV*, 157; *2 Henry IV*, 115;
Henry V, 24, 112, 175, 191; *Henry
VI* trilogy, 123; *1 Henry VI*, 186; *3
Henry VI*, 33; *Henry VIII*, 8, 150;
Julius Caesar, 11, 162; *King Lear*,
40–1, 48, 57, 108, 122–3, 136,
157–8, 160, 175, 178, 184, 199–200;
Love's Labour's Lost, 34, 110–11;
Macbeth, 40, 47, 150, 173, 183, 192,
196; *Measure for Measure*, 43, 59, 91,
178, 179; *The Merchant of Venice*, 18;
The Merry Wives of Windsor, 110,
188–9; *A Midsummer Night's Dream*,
11, 134, 150, 177, 188; *Much Ado
About Nothing*, 47, 49, 59, 125, 177;
Othello, 43, 48–9, 58, 175, 180, 183,
201; *Pericles*, 175; *The Rape of
Lucrece*, 104; *Richard II*, 112, 160,
169; *Richard III*, 175, 183, 193;
Romeo and Juliet, 45, 47, 50, 91, 186;
Sonnets, 17, 67, 172, 200; *The*

Taming of the Shrew, 175; *The
Tempest*, 30, 129, 179; *Timon of
Athens*, 40, 122, 158; *Titus
Andronicus*, 98, 104, 182, 184, 186;
Troilus and Cressida, 13, 184, 196;
Twelfth Night, 49, 177, 181, 184;
Two Gentlemen of Verona, 188; *Venus
and Adonis*, 104; *The Winter's Tale*,
48, 57, 145, 174, 184, 186
Sidney, Sir Philip, 1–2, 9, 31–2, 34–5,
74, 93, 108, 121, 128–32, 136, 139,
148–51, 153, 173, 197, 200–1;
Arcadia, 9, 31, 34–5, 125, 130–3,
148–9, 197; *Astrophil and Stella*, 7,
127, 130, 132, 197, 200; *Certain
Sonnets*, 148; 'Dispraise of a Courtly
Life', 142; *Defence of Poetry*, 1, 18,
129–30, 162, 172, 189–90; *The Lady
of May*, 135; metrical translations of
the psalms, 87
Sir Thomas More, 160
Skelton, John, 141–2
Socrates, 99–100, 127–8
Somerset, Robert Carr, Earl of, 121,
143–4
Southwell, Robert, 67, 87
Spain, 10, 82, 84–5, 174; invasion
expected from, 9, 83; Spanish
marriage proposed, 10, 154, 156
Spenser, Edmund, vi, 1–2, 7, 9, 11, 19,
30–3, 36–8, 46, 67, 75, 80, 93, 100,
107, 113, 118, 128, 130, 132–3,
135–6, 139–41, 152, 199; *Amoretti*,
46; *Colin Clout's Come Home Againe*,
30, 135, 140–1; *Epithalamion*, 19, 46;
The Faerie Queene, 2, 9, 16–17, 30–3,
36–7, 44, 75–6, 82, 119, 125, 130,
132–3, 135, 139–40, 150, 199;
dedicatory letter to Raleigh, 130,
132–3, 135; *Mother Hubberd's Tale*,
139–40; *The Shepheardes Calendar*,
1–2, 9, 19 (envoy), 31, 80, 113, 135,
140; *A Vue of the Present State of
Ireland*, 30
Stanley, Sir William, 85
state, the, 8, 39, 119, 123, 197;
centralized power of, 5, 122; 'reasons
of state', 123
Stratford-upon-Avon, 34; grammar
school, 97

OXFORD

MORE OXFORD PAPERBACKS

Details of a selection of other books follow. A complete list of Oxford Paperbacks, including The World's Classics, Twentieth-Century Classics, OPUS, Past Masters, Oxford Authors, Oxford Shakespeare, and Oxford Paperback Reference, is available in the UK from the General Publicity Department, Oxford University Press (JN), Walton Street, Oxford OX2 6DP.

In the USA, complete lists are available from the Paperbacks Marketing Manager, Oxford University Press, 200 Madison Avenue, New York, NY 10016.

Oxford Paperbacks are available from all good bookshops. In case of difficulty, customers in the UK can order direct from Oxford University Press Bookshop, 116 High Street, Oxford, Freepost, OX1 4BR, enclosing full payment. Please add 10 per cent of published price for postage and packing.

OPUS

General Editors

Keith Thomas   Alan Ryan   Walter Bodmer

OPUS books provide concise, original, and authoritative introductions to a wide range of subjects in the humanities and sciences. They are written by experts for the general reader as well as for students.

Economics and Business Studies

The State and the Economic System
An Introduction to the History of Political Economy
Phyllis Deane

The Way People Work
Job Satisfaction and the Challenge of Change
Christine Howarth

Democracy at Work
Tom Schuller

History

The Industrial Revolution 1760–1830 2/e
T. S. Ashton

Rebellion or Revolution?
England 1640-1660
G. E. Aylmer

Early Modern France 1560–1715
Robin Briggs

Modern Spain
Raymond Carr

The Workshop of the World
British Economic History 1820–1880 2/e
J. D. Chambers

The Economy of England 1450–1750
Donald C. Coleman

The Impact of English Towns 1700–1800
P. J. Corfield

The Russian Revolution
Sheila Fitzpatrick

War in European History
Michael Howard

The Medieval Expansion of Europe
J. R. S. Phillips

The First World War
Keith Robbins

The French Revolution
J. M. Roberts

The Voice of the Past
Oral History 2/e
Paul Thompson

Town, City, and Nation
England 1850–1914
P. J. Waller

Law

Law and Modern Society
P. S. Atiyah

Introduction to English Law 9/e
William Geldart

The Lawful Rights of Mankind
An Introduction to the International
  Legal Code of Human Rights
Paul Sieghart

Literature

The Modern American Novel
Malcolm Bradbury

The English Language
R. W. Burchfield

Ancient Greek Literature
K. J. Dover

Shakespeare
A Writer's Progress
Philip Edwards

Linguistic Criticism
Roger Fowler

British Theatre since 1955
A Reassessment
Ronald Hayman

Modern English Literature
W. W. Robson

Structuralism and Since
From Lévi-Strauss to Derrida
John Sturrock

English Literature and its Background

This Stageplay World
English Literature and its Background
  1580–1625
Julia Briggs

Medieval Writers and their Work
Middle English Literature and its
  Background 1100–1500
J. A. Burrow

Romantics, Rebels and Reactionaries
English Literature and its Background
  1760–1830
Marilyn Butler

Philosophy

Aristotle the Philosopher
J. L. Ackrill

Metaphysics
The Logical Approach
José A. Benardete

Karl Marx
His Life and Environment 4/e
Isaiah Berlin

The Standing of Psychoanalysis
B. A. Farrell

The Character of Mind
Colin McGinn

Understanding Plato
David J. Melling

Moral Philosophy
D. D. Raphael

The Problems of Philosophy
Bertrand Russell

Aesthetics
An Introduction to the Philosophy of
Art
Anne Sheppard

Ethics since 1900 3/e
Mary Warnock

Existentialism
Mary Warnock

Philosophy and the Brain
J. Z. Young

A History of Western Philosophy

The Rationalists: Volume 4
John Cottingham

Classical Thought: Volume 1
Terence Irwin

Continental Philosophy since 1750:
Volume 7
The Rise and Fall of the Self
Robert C. Solomon

The Empiricists: Volume 5
R. S. Woolhouse

Politics and International Affairs

Devolution
Vernon Bogdanor

Marx's Social Theory
Terrell Carver

Philosophers and Pamphleteers
Political Theorists of the
Enlightenment
Maurice Cranston

International Relations in a Changing
World 4/e
Joseph Frankel

Contemporary International Theory and
the Behaviour of States
Joseph Frankel

The Life and Times of Liberal
Democracy
C. B. Macpherson

Socialisms
Theories and Practices
Anthony Wright

Religion

Christianity in the West 1400–1700
John Bossy

Judaism
Nicholas de Lange

An Introduction to the Philosophy of
Religion
Brian Davies

Islam
A Historical Survey 2/e
H. A. R. Gibb

Modern Theology
A Sense of Direction
James P. Mackey

Religion and the People of Western
Europe
Hugh McLeod

Roman Catholicism in England from the
Elizabethan Settlement to the Second
Vatican Council
Edward Norman

What is Theology?
Maurice Wiles

Hinduism 2/e
R. C. Zaehner

Science

What is Psychotherapy?
Sidney Bloch

The Philosophies of Science
An Introductory Survey 2/e
Rom Harré

A Historical Introduction to the
Philosophy of Science 2/e
John Losee

The Making of the Atomic Age
Alwyn McKay

The Primeval Universe
Jayant V. Narlikar

The Structure of the Universe
Jayant V. Narlikar

What is Ecology? 2/e
Denis F. Owen

Energy
A Guide Book
Janet Ramage

The Problems of Science

The Problems of Physics
A. J. Leggett

The Problems of Biology
John Maynard Smith

The Problems of Chemistry
W. G. Richards

The Problems of Evolution
Mark Ridley

The Problems of Mathematics
Ian Stewart

Social Sciences

Thinking about Peace and War
Martin Ceadel

*Science and Technology in World
    Development*
Robin Clarke

Changes in British Society 3/e
A. H. Halsey

*Urban Planning in Rich and Poor
    Countries*
Hugh Stretton

Crime and Criminology
A Critical Introduction
Nigel Walker

Policing Liberal Society
Steve Uglow